The Long Distance Walkers' Handbook

The Long Distance Walkers' Handbook

The LDWA Directory of Long Distance Paths

Sixth Edition

Researched and edited by
Brian Smith

Additional research and assistance by
Malcolm Olbison
Keith Warman
Ann Sayer'
Peter Robins

A & C Black • London

Published by A & C Black (Publishers) Ltd
35 Bedford Row, London WC1R 4JH

Sixth edition 1998
Fifth edition 1994
Fourth edition 1990
Third edition 1986
Second edition 1982
First edition 1980

First and second editions published by
Greenaway, Surrey

ISBN 0 7136 4835 X

A CIP catalogue record for this book
is available from the British Library.

Acknowledgements
Cover photograph by Ashley Cooper, courtesy of Collections
Maps by ML Design.

Printed and bound in Great Britain by Bell and Bain Ltd., Glasgow

CONTENTS

INTRODUCTION

The Long Distance Walkers' Association (LDWA) was established in 1972 with the aim of furthering the interests of those who enjoy long distance walking.

Although attempts are made to define a long distance walk, it is, in reality, a matter of capability for the individual. Within the ethos of the Association a long distance walk is considered to be 20 miles or more but which might be completed as a day long or multi-day walk. Additionally, the route should be mainly off road and in a rural area. In pursuing the aim of the LDWA and, in turn, promoting the activity of long distance walking, the Association has, since 1980, in one guise or another, been involved in the publication of this directory of routes. The first and second editions were compiled by our now Vice President Barbara Blatchford, in her own right with subsequent editions published under the direct auspices of the LDWA. This latest edition has been completely researched, revised and updated. Some routes from earlier editions have been omitted for reasons beyond the control of the LDWA, but in excess of 100 new routes are listed.

Other material changes from the last edition include the removal of a separate Anytime Challenge Walks section, all routes are now included in the one alphabetical sequence, and some information has been compacted in order to provide a more comprehensive base for particular routes.

Details of formally named routes only are included with no reference made to those used primarily for road walking; by runners; or for competition purposes. There are many routes of less than 20 miles distance listed but in each case, they will have some special significance such as readily linking with another. Additionally, routes are listed only where a relevant route description publication in whatever form is readily available or the availability is known to be imminent.

This book is not intended to be a guide for the listed routes but a source of reference as to what information can be obtained for them.

ROUTE ENTRY CONTENT

The details provided for each route includes the regional area - shown by county(ies); the distance in miles/kilometres; a brief description of the route; the start/finish points with grid references; the appropriate Ordnance Survey Landranger map reference number(s); whether or not the route is waymarked; an indication as to whether or not a user group exists; the type and source of route publication(s) and other relevant information such as specific accommodation guide details and badge/certificate availability.

A reference number is shown alongside each route entry. This number is of benefit insofar as the use of the map section of this book is concerned and in which routes are identified.

Most of the waymarked routes, and others of particular signifi- cance, are actually marked on the maps with the route entry reference number clearly shown. For other routes, the reference numbers are listed on the maps to which they are relevant. This caters for easy reference; the planning of extended walks using more than the one route and the identification of routes to particu- lar areas.

The entry of the few routes not marked or referred to in the map section is so endorsed.

REGIONAL AREA

In identifying the area of the route, the previously simple method of listing the county/counties is used. Because local authority changes and the creation of Unitary Authorities have had some impact it is now not so simple a matter.

There have been a number of changes and some of the long established county names have been removed from mapping. Gen- erally, the changes affecting Wales, Scotland and Northern Ireland have been accommodated but because those in England might well have led to some confusion, the former county names, such as Avon and Cleveland, have been retained.

DISTANCES

For some routes various distances are quoted in different publica- tions. For the purposes of this book, the generally accepted dis- tance is used. For reference, a Route Distance Index is included and in which all routes of 10 miles or more are shown.

MAPS

The Landranger Map Series numbers continue to be used, these being at present the only static reference available. The Ordnance Survey (OS) is currently involved in extending the Explorer Series, at the expense of the Pathfinder which, with the Outdoor Leisure mapping, provides a more informative and walker friendly refer- ence. The OS aim to phase in the Explorer Series on a south to north basis with England and Wales fully covered by 2001.

An updated index of map availability is produced annually by the OS and a copy can be obtained from the OS direct or from many other outlets.

The map reference part of the entry is marked ON OS MAPS or OS MAPS. Based on OS provided information, the former indicates that these routes are either currently included on Landranger maps or it is intended to include them on the next edition of the particular map(s). Similarly, the exact line of routes are currently included, or will be included, on the larger scale mapping.

It is expected that a colour map/chart of routes, covering the whole of the UK and based on the content of this handbook, will be published by Harvey Maps in the summer of 1998. It is being produced jointly by the LDWA/Harvey Maps and will be available through the Association and booksellers (ISBN 1851373020).
Contact address:
Ordnance Survey, Romsey Road, Southampton SO16 4GU (0345 330011).

WAYMARKING

Not all routes are specifically waymarked and of those that are, the standard will vary from route to route. Some, the National Trails are good examples, can instill confidence in the user to the extent where the carrying of a guidebook is almost superfluous. There are many others however, where the opposite will apply.

On the unwaymarked routes, there will be occasions when they are marked periodically with the standard right of way signs but others where navigational skills are most appropriate.

USER GROUPS

The successful ongoing promotion of a route is often brought about by the involvement of a user group such as the South West Way or Pennine Way Association. In addition to the promotion of the route, they are often able to supply more in-depth information than is otherwise available. Their existence is endorsed in each of the relevant entries. By supporting these groups, there can be a sense of belonging as well as the added incentive of assisting them in maintaining/improving existing standards in path promotion and services offered.

PUBLICATIONS

The actual type of publication available varies enormously. On the one hand, it may take the form of a coffee-table type presentation and, on the other, typewritten sheets. The publication description provided under each entry is considered the most appropriate for what is on offer.

Whilst correct at the time of going to press, the very nature of publishing means that some publications will be quickly out of print and that the costs shown for those priced publications could change.

It is advisable therefore, to determine current availability and costs. The source addresses are shown in the List of Addresses Index but for the commercially published books, more often than not, these will be available from good book shops, specialist book dealers and even international outlets.

In cases where Council Authorities are shown as the source, it may well be that the relevant publication is available at local tourist information centres.

For those routes where more than one guide book publication is available, any temptation to provide grading has been resisted. It is a matter of personal choice and only the Aurum/Ordnance Survey books have been endorsed to indicate that these are the designated official guides for the National Trails in England and Wales. The choice of publication is often dependent on the needs of the user. Some provide just the basic route detail whilst others list accommodation options, transport and other services - some updated on an annual basis.

Contact addresses for books/maps:
Cordee Ltd. 3a, De Montfort Street, Leicester LE1 7HD (0116 254 3579).
Northern Map Distributors, 101, Broadfield Road, Sheffield S8 0XH (0800 834290).
Stanfords, 12/14, Long Acre, London WC2E 9LP (0171 836 1321).

ACCOMMODATION

Accommodation publication information is included under a number of routes. In addition to these listed sources, there are, of course, many others which can be of assistance in achieving overnight stays/planning multi-day walks.

The value of tourist information centres should not be underestimated. The telephone numbers of all British T.I.C.'s are included in the publication *British Map* published by the BTA at £1.20(+£0.35 p+p).

The annually updated *Rambler's Yearbook and Accommodation Guide*, the 1998 cost - £4.99, the ISBN:0900613947 published by the Ramblers' Association provides details of accommodation including camping barn, bunkhouse, hostel and outdoor centre details with entries endorsed when they have specific relevance to a particular long distance route. The Yearbook is distributed free to members of the Ramblers' Association but is also available from bookshops.

The various Youth Hostel Associations maintain youth hostels and camping barns, and in some cases provide a booking service.

The Backpackers Press publish two guides by Sam Dalley, *The Independent Hostel Guide*, ISBN:0952338157, costing £3.95 and *Accommodation for Groups*, ISBN:0952338165, £2.95.

Contact addresses:
British Tourist Authority, Thames Tower, Black's Road, Hammersmith, London W6 9EL (0181 846 316517).
Ramblers' Association, 1-5, Wandsworth Road, London SW8 2XX (0171 339 8500).
Youth Hostels Association, Trevelyan House, 8, St Stephen's Hill, St Albans, Hertfordshire AL1 2DY
(01727 855215).
Youth Hostels Association - Northern Ireland, 22, Donegal Road, Belfast BT12 5JN (01232 324733).
Youth Hostels Association - Scotland, 7, Glebe Street, Stirling FK8 2JA (01786 451181).
Backpackers Press, 2, Rockview Cottages, Matlock Bath, Derbyshire DE4 3PG (01629 580427).

BADGES / CERTIFICATES

Many walkers welcome having a memento of their walking adventures. For this reason, reference is included to the availability of badges and certificates. In addition to those listed in the route entries, badges for in excess of 60 other routes are available from P & R Pennants Ltd.
Contact address:
P & R Pennants Ltd, 13D, Queensway, Stem Lane Industrial Estate, New Milton, Hampshire BH25 5NN (01425 611911).

OTHER WALKING OPPORTUNITIES

All members of the LDWA receive, three times each year, a copy of the Association journal, aptly named *Strider*. Included in each edition are details of non-competitive challenge walks, mainly day length walks but occasionally up to 48 hours, throughout the UK. These offer opportunities to take part in an organised event and for many, mementoes are on offer. The 38 or so LDWA Groups also offer a wide range of social walks.

The availability of canal towpaths and former railway lines provide extensive walking opportunities. Whilst just the few routes are included in this book, more information is available from British Waterways (Canal Towpaths) and *Vinter's Gazetteer 1997-98*, published by Crosswave Publishing at £2.00, lists all known former railway lines.

Those multi-use routes under development through SUSTRANS input will have an impact on walking opportunity.
Contact addresses:
British Waterways, Customer Services, Willow Grange, Church Road, Watford, Hertfordshire WD1 3QA (01923 226422).
Crosswave Publishing, 1, Victoria Road, Chichester, West Sussex PO19 4HY (01243 783270).

SCOTLAND

The mapping section of this handbook clearly highlights the relatively few in number established/supported routes in Scotland which hardly mirrors the walking opportunities to be found. Certainly the wilderness areas are an attraction in themselves but, and especially in view of the lack of rights of way shown generally on mapping, those planning walks there are recommended to make use of the publication, *Scottish Hill Tracks*, ISBN:0950281158, costing £10.95, published by the Scottish Rights of Way Society and The Scottish Mountaineering Trust. Listed are 330 cross country walks across hills and moors, through glens and passes in all areas from the Cheviot Hills to the Highlands. A marked map section complements the content.
Contact address:
Scottish Rights of Way Society, John Cotton Business Centre, 10, Sunnyside, Edinburgh EH7 5RA (0131 652 2937).

IRELAND

This directory includes reference to the two long distance routes in Northern Ireland but it is mainly in Eire that walking opportunities are being developed. There are well in excess of 20 long distance routes fully backed up with route guides and waymarking.

Details are available from the Irish Tourist Board and the Association for Adventure Sports and for relevant publications, East-West Mapping and other sources.

Contact addresses:

Irish Tourist Board, 150, New Bond Street, London W1Y 0AQ (0171 493 3201)

Association for Adventure Sports, House of Sport, Longmile Road, Dublin 12 (00353 1 450 9845).

EastWest Mapping, Ballyredmund, Clonegal, Enniscorthy, Co Wexford (00353 54 77835).

MAINLAND EUROPE

In each edition of *Strider*, news of walking opportunities in Europe and elsewhere is included. In addition, information is available through the Association concerning the established European routes.

INTERNET

For those with access to the Worldwide Web, there is an increasing amount of online information on walking. Because of the rapidly changing nature of this information, no details are given here, but the LDWA maintains a website giving information on long distance paths, both in Britain and in Europe, which includes links to other relevant sites set up by organisations such as local authorities.

Start at - http://www.bibloset.demon.co.uk/LDWA/GBLDP.htm

INFORMATION UPDATE

Ever increasing outdoor activity results in many new routes being devised and the receipt of such information is always welcomed as is detail of changes to listed information. The LDWA is a focal point for the many publishers of associated and relevant publications which, together with ongoing research, caters for the maintenance of a comprehensive record of current information.

Members of the LDWA are kept aware of ongoing changes through the circulation of *Strider*. Within each edition, reference is included to all manner of long distance path news which lends itself to a relatively low cost but efficient way of keeping abreast of walking opportunities. As at January, 1998, the cost of membership was £7/year.

DISCLAIMER

Inclusion of a route in this book is not intended in any way to provide an indication of the quality of it in terms of scenery attraction or usability. Care has been taken to include only details of routes where rights of way, access areas or permission exists, but as with all other aspects of the information detailed, reliance has had to be placed on the information providers. In this respect, therefore, heed has to be taken of any specific advice offered in the various publications.

Whilst there are inherent risks in any outdoor exercise, it would be remiss to ignore any specific safety advice offered in the various publications. Such advice is not necessarily included in this handbook.

The content of this book represents well in excess of 2000 enquiries and whilst every effort has been made to ensure correctness of detail, it may well be that errors/omissions have escaped notice. Neither the LDWA nor the publishers can be held responsible for any inconvenience caused thereby.

ACKNOWLEDGEMENTS

In producing this directory, all efforts have been conducted on a voluntary basis. Whilst some possible providers of information have failed or refused to cooperate, the vast majority have done so. Appreciation is offered to those who responded promptly and to all who provided relevant information.

It is also more than deserved to make mention of those who have assisted in the compilation of this book. Keith Warman researched those routes previously entitled Anytime Challenge Walks; Malcolm Olbison assisted in other research and diligently and patiently processed all results; Peter Robins, the editor of the fifth edition willingly offered guidance/advice on many aspects; and last, but certainly not least, Ann Sayer who as with the previous edition checked and plotted routes for inclusion in the mapping section.

Brian Smith
Long Distance Paths Information/LDWA Membership Enquiries
10 Temple Park Close
Leeds LS15 0JJ

ABBREVIATIONS

AONB	Area of Outstanding Natural Beauty
LDWA	Long Distance Walkers Association
RA	Ramblers' Association
RSPB	Royal Society for the Protection of Birds
SSSI	Site of Special Scientific Interest
TBA	To be announced

DETAILS OF ROUTES

1066 Country Walk   1

E Sussex	50 km / 31 miles

A route through Battle taking in topics of historical interest, the walk connects the Saxon Shore Way (at Rye), with the South Downs Way (at Alfriston). A link to Hastings is incorporated into the Walk.

Start	Rye, E Sussex	TQ918205
Finish	Alfriston, E Sussex	TQ521030
On OS maps	189, 199	
Waymark	Red & white named logo	

Publication(s)
Leaflet: *1066 Country Walk* (Rother District Council). 1997\A4/3\ Free(+9"x4" SAE).

Abberley Amble   2

Worc	32 km / 20 miles

A route of mixed terrain through woods and valleys it passes a number of points of local interest including Glasshampton Monastery, the Burf (a cider house) and Grubbers Alley.

Start and finish	Bewdley, Worc	SO788754
OS maps	138	

Publication(s)
Looseleaf: *Abberley Amble* (Eric Perks). A4\Free(+Large SAE). Badge and certificate (£2.00/SAE/£0.75/SAE) available from Eric Perks.

Abbeys Amble   3

N Yorks	167 km / 104 miles

A walk linking three Yorkshire Abbeys (Fountains, Bolton and Jervaulx) and three Yorkshire castles (Ripley, Bolton and Middleham), which uses stretches of some already established routes viz Harrogate Ringway, Dales Way, Yoredale Way and Ripon Rowel.

Start and finish	Ripon, N Yorks	SE315710
OS maps	98, 99, 104	

Publication(s)
Booklet: *Abbeys Amble* (John Eckersley). 1997\A5\55pp\£2.00.
Certificate (£1.00 incl p&p) available from John Eckersley.

Abbott's Hike 4

Cumbria, N Yorks, W Yorks	172 km / 107 miles

The Hike, named after its originator, links 25 miles of the Dales Way, 14 miles of the Three Peaks Walk and three miles of the Pennine Way to provide a route from Yorkshire to the Lake District.

Start	Ilkley, W Yorks	SE117476
Finish	Pooley Bridge, Cumbria	NY470247
OS maps	90, 91, 97, 98, 104	

Publication(s)
Paperback: *Abbott's Hike* by Peter Abbott (Peter Abbott). 1980\210 x 149\64pp\£2.00.

Ainsty Bounds Walk 5

N Yorks	71 km / 44 miles

A walk through the area of Ainsty which is bounded by the Rivers Wharf, Nidd and Ouse. As far as is possible the route is along river banks passing through Boston Spa, Wetherby, Moor Monkton, the outskirts of York and Bolton Percy. Proceeds from the sales of the publication are donated to the local Wheatfield Hospice.

Start and finish	Tadcaster, N Yorks	SE488434
OS maps	105	

Publication(s)
Looseleaf: *Ainsty Bounds Walk* (Simon Townson). A4\3pp\£1.50 (incl p+p).

Airedale Way 6

N Yorks, W Yorks	80 km / 50 miles

The Way provides a natural route from Leeds to the heart of the Yorkshire Dales, by following as far as possible paths by the River Aire and, in spite of passing through such small industrial towns as Shipley, Bingley and Keighley, is very largely rural. There are links with the Bradford-Dales Way at Shipley and the Pennine Way at Gargrave and Malham.

Start	Leeds, W Yorks	SE298333
Finish	Malham Tarn, N Yorks	SD894661
OS maps	98, 103, 104	

Publication(s)
Paperback: *The Airedale Way* by Douglas Cossar (RA West Riding Area). ISBN:0900613955. 1996\A5\80pp\£4.50 (+80p).
Badge (£1.50) available from RA West Riding Area.

Allerdale Ramble   7

Cumbria	87 km / 54 miles

From central Lakeland the route heads northwards along the western side of Borrowdale and Derwent Water to Keswick. Here there is a choice of route, either across the foothills of Skiddaw or over its summit, before heading along the Derwent valley to Cockermouth. The Ramble then crosses the agricultural land of mid-Allerdale to reach the coast at Maryport, where it turns along the flat coastline providing extensive views across the Solway Firth.

Start	Seathwaite, Cumbria	NY235119
Finish	Grune Point, Cumbria	NY145571
On OS maps	85, 89, 90	
Waymark	Named posts	

Publication(s)
Paperback: *The Cumbria Way and the Allerdale Ramble* by Jim Watson (Cicerone Press). ISBN:1852842423. 1997\144pp\£6.99.

Almscliff Amble   8

N Yorks, W Yorks	48 km / 30 miles

A route visiting Otley Chevin, Bramhope, Harewood House, Almscliff Crag and Farnley. A 20-miles alternative route is available.

Start and finish	Otley, W Yorks	SE217457
OS maps	104	

Publication(s)
Looseleaf: *Almscliff Amble* (L. Mallinson). Free(+9" x 4" SAE).
Badge and certificate (£1.50/SAE) available from L. Mallinson.

Altrincham Circular   9

Cheshire, Gtr Man	27 km / 17 miles

A route around the town of Altrincham, passing along the district boundary to Davenport Green, through Halebarns to the Bollin and Ashley Heath, Bow Green and Little Bollington, returning via Dunham and Oldfield Brow.

Start and finish	W Timperley, Gtr Man	SJ771901
OS maps	109	

Publication(s)
Paperback: *The Altrincham Circular* by Altrincham WEA (Willow Publishing). ISBN:0946361282. 1989\A5\56pp\£3.75(+80p).

Angles Way 10

Norfolk, Suffolk	126 km / 78 miles

The Way was devised by the RA, and together with the Peddars Way, Norfolk Coast Path and Weavers Way, forms the 220-mile Around Norfolk Walk. From Great Yarmouth the route goes by Bredon Water, along the River Waveney to its source, and by the Little Ouse through heathland and marsh to Knettishall Heath. See Mid Suffolk Footpath.

Start	Great Yarmouth, Norfolk	TG522081
Finish	Knettishall Heath, Suffolk	TL944807
On OS maps	134, 144, 156	
Waymark	Named discs	

Publication(s)
Paperback: *Langton's Guide to the Weavers Way and Angles Way* by Andrew Durham (Langton's Guides). ISBN:1899242015. 1995\210 x 130\144pp\£6.95.
Paperback: *The Angles Way - Walking in an Historic Landscape* by Kate Skipper and Tom Williamson (Suffolk County Council).132pp\£5.00.
Paperback: *Angles Way* (RA Norfolk Area). 1995\210 x 143\20pp\£1.80(+35p).
Leaflet: *The Angles Way - The Broads to Brecks Path* (Norfolk County Council). 1997\A5\Free(+SAE).

Anglesey Coast Path 11

Anglesey	195 km / 121 miles

First created by the Ynys Mon (Anglesey) Group of the RA, this circuit around the island uses existing rights of way, linked by roads which form about a quarter of the route, to follow the coastline as closely as possible. It passes attractive bays, fine cliff scenery, marshes and sands.

Start and finish	Menai Bridge, Anglesey	SH556716
OS maps	114	

Publication(s)
Paperback: *Walking the Anglesey Coast* by Jan Harris (Walking Routes). ISBN:095181480X. 1994\118pp\£4.95.

Paperback: *Walking the Anglesey Coast / Cerdded Arfordir Mon* by Jan Harris (Walking Routes). ISBN:0951814818. 1994\122pp\ £5.95.
Paperback: *Walking the Isle of Anglesey Coastline* by John Merrill (Happy Walking International Ltd). ISBN:1874754136. 1993\ 60pp\£4.50.
Badge and certificate (£3.00/post free) available from Happy Walking International Ltd.

Anglezarke Amble 12

Lancs	34 km / 21 miles

Devised by the West Lancs group of the LDWA, this route is over Rivington Pike, Winter Hill and passes several reservoirs across moor and farmland.

Start and finish	Rivington Hall Barn, Lancs	SD633144
OS maps	109	

Publication(s)
Looseleaf: *Anglezarke Amble* (Robert Waller). Free(+SAE).
Badge and certificate (£1.50/A4 SAE) available from Robert Waller.

Anglezarke Anguish 13

Lancs	32 km / 20 miles

The walk is in the West Pennine Moors Country Park, taking in Leverhulme Park and the seven-arched Romanesque style bridge. It passes Pidgeon Tower, Rivington Pike and three reservoirs, over rough moorland to the village of White Coppice. There is an alternative 10-mile route.

Start and finish	Rivington Hall Barn, Lancs	SD633144
OS maps	109	

Publication(s)
Looseleaf: *Anglezarke Anguish Walk* (Norman Thomas). Free (+SAE).
Badge and certificate (£1.50/SAE) available from Norman Thomas.

Apostles Walk 14

Lancs, W Yorks	129 km / 80 miles

A walk from the outskirts of Bradford to the southern Yorkshire Dales along parts of the Dales Way, Pennine Way and the towpath of the Leeds - Liverpool Canal visiting such as Ilkley, Grassington, Malham and Skipton.

Start and finish	Wilsden, W Yorks	SE094362
OS maps	98, 103, 104	

Publication(s)
Looseleaf: *Apostles Walk* (A T Ashworth). 1pp \ Free(+9" x 4" SAE).
Badge (£1.00/SAE) available from A T Ashworth.

Around the Carneddau   15

Aberconwy	64 km / 40 miles

A circuit around the edge of the Carneddau visiting the lakes of
Llyn Crafnant, Llyn Cowlyd, Melynnllyn and Llyn Dulyn. It descends to the Aber Falls via the Roman Road over Bwlch y Ddeu-
faen, traverses Moel Wnion to Gerlon and Ogwen then skirts Llyn
Ogwen.

Start and finish	Capel Curig, Aberconwy	SH721583
OS maps	115	

Publication(s)
Looseleaf: *Around the Carneddau* (Dave Irons). 1994 \ £1.00(incl
p+p).

Around the Lakes   16

Cumbria	233 km / 145 miles

Based on the Bob Graham Round, a circular route primarily for
fell-runners, this route also includes Kentmere the Far Eastern
and Coniston Fells, and provides a circular taking in all the peaks
of the Lake District, involving 50,000ft of ascent.

Start and finish	Grasmere, Cumbria	NY339072
OS maps	89, 90, 96, 97	

Publication(s)
Paperback: *Walking Round the Lakes* by John and Anne Nuttall
(Cicerone Press). ISBN:1852840994. 116 x 176 \ 240pp \ £6.99.

Arun Way   17

W Sussex	35 km / 22 miles

A route along the Lower Arun Valley, through a varied landscape
of beach, remote villages, riverside meadows and the South Downs,
inhabited at various times by Romans, Saxons and Normans. The
Way links with the Wey-South Path at Amberley.

Start	Littlehampton, W Sussex	TQ024022
Finish	Pulborough, W Sussex	TQ042187

OS maps	197

Publication(s)
Paperback: *Along the Arun* by John Adamson (Alexius Press).
ISBN:0951988611. 1994\A5\114pp\£7.95(incl p&p).

Avon Valley Path 18

Dorset, Hants, Wilts	55 km / 34 miles

The Path follows the lower reaches of one of England's best-known chalk rivers, through a valley much of which is designated as an SSSI and of great botanical interest, besides being known for its salmon. Though much of the Path does not follow the riverbank, it aims to keep as close to it as possible through Downton, Fordingbridge and Ringwood.

Start	Salisbury, Wilts	SU143297
Finish	Christchurch, Dorset	SZ160925
On OS maps	184, 195	
Waymark	Green and beige with bridge	

Publication(s)
Paperback: *The Avon Valley Path* (RA New Forest Group).
ISBN:086146088X. 1994\A5\61pp\£4.00(incl p+p).
Leaflet: *Avon Valley Path* (Hampshire County Council). A4/3\Free (+SAE).

Aylesbury Ring 19

Bucks, Herts	50 km / 31 miles

Originally created by the Aylesbury and District group of the RA, the route is never more than 5 miles from the centre of Aylesbury encompassing some of the remoter areas of the Vale and passing through Great Kimble, Dinton, Waddesdon, Hardwick, Rowsham, Hulcott and Aston Clinton. Much of the western section is coincident with the North Bucks Way. See Thame Valley Walk.

Start and finish	Wendover, Bucks	SP869078
On OS maps	165	
Waymark	Aylesbury duck	

Publication(s)
Paperback: *Vale of Aylesbury Walker* by Peter Gulland and Diana Gulland (RA Buckinghamshire). ISBN:090061367X. A5\140pp\ £3.00.
Leaflet: *The Aylesbury Ring* (Buckinghamshire County Council). 1993\A4/3\Free(+SAE).

Back o' Skidda 20

Cumbria	45 km / 28 miles

A high-level circuit, with over 7,600ft of ascent, across the relatively unfrequented mountains of the northern Lake District, including the summits of High Pike, Calva, Skiddaw, Blencathra and Bannerdale Crags.

Start and finish	Mosedale, Cumbria	NX357323
OS maps	90	

Publication(s)
Looseleaf: *Back o'Skidda* (Joyce Sidebottom). Free(+9" x 4" SAE). Badge and certificate (£2.50/9" x 7" SAE) available from Joyce Sidebottom.

Barnsley Boundary Walk 21

S Yorks, W Yorks	119 km / 74 miles

Created by Barnsley Borough Council in association with the publishing arm of the Barnsley Chronicle, the Walk aims to provide a view of the varied countryside, industrial heritage and other points of interest in the Borough. Included are Langsett Reservoir, the former salt road to Dunford Bridge, several reservoirs and the Country Parks at Cannon and Bretton Halls.

Start and finish	Flouch Inn, S Yorks	SE197016
On OS maps	110, 111	
Waymark	Named posts	

Publication(s)
Booklet: *Barnsley Boundary Walk* (Wharncliffe Publishing Ltd). ISBN:1871647177. 1993\A5\48pp\£3.95.

Basingstoke Canal Walk 22

Hants, Surrey	60 km / 37 miles

A route through the Surrey and Hampshire countryside along the tree-lined towpath of the recently restored 200 years old canal and through woodland, heathland, wetland and pasture.

Start	Byfleet, Surrey	TQ070630
Finish	Basingstoke, Hants	SU640527
OS maps	186	

Publication(s)
Booklet: *Guide to the Basingstoke Canal* (Surrey and Hampshire Canal Society). 1996\A5\28pp\£3.95(incl p+p).

Stripmap: *Basingstoke Canal Walk* (GEOprojects). ISBN: 0863510205. 426 x 1000\£3.00.

Beacon Way   23

W Midlands	27 km / 17 miles

This green route from Handsworth, via the outskirts of West Bromwich and Walsall, through the heart of the West Midlands conurbation to the Staffordshire border takes in the Beacon Regional Park, lakes, nature reserves, woods, and the banks of canals. Plans are under way to link the northern end with the Heart of England Way.

Start	Sandwell Park, W Midlands	SP018913
Finish	Chasewater, W Midlands	SK040070
On OS maps	139	
Waymark	Named posts and standard arrows	

Publication(s)
Leaflet: *Beacon Regional Way* (Walsall Metropolitan Borough Council). 1989\A4/3\Free.

Beating the Bounds   24

Essex	26 km / 16 miles

A walk around the parish boundary of Great Waltham, visiting several locations of historical note including the Causeway and the Black Chapel. There is a link with the Essex Way near to Great Waltham.

Start and finish	Great Waltham, Essex	TL696135
OS maps	167	

Publication(s)
Leaflet: *Beating the Bounds* (Ways through Essex). 1996\A3/6\ Free(+9"x4" SAE).

Beeches Way   25

Bucks, Gtr London	25 km / 16 miles

This route connecting the river Thames at Cookham with the Grand Union Canal at West Drayton passes through several ancient woodlands now designated as SSSIs, including part of Burnham Beeches and the village of Stoke Poges.

Start	Cookham, Bucks	SU898858
Finish	West Drayton, Gtr London	TQ061801
On OS maps	175, 176	

Waymark	Named standard discs and posts with beechnut logo

Publication(s)
Leaflet: *The Beeches Way* (Buckinghamshire County Council).
A4/3 \ Free(+SAE).

Bell Walk Major   26

Derbys, S Yorks	58 km / 36 miles

The Bell Walk devised by the Dronfield Parish Church Bellringers
links the churches of Dronfield, Old Whittington, Norton, Dore,
Hathersage, Totley and Holmesfield, all of which have bells. The
route is through woodland, past a little industry, by historical sites,
in parkland, over moorland, through villages, by riverside, into
valleys and within easy reach of 50 pubs.

Start and finish	Dronfield, Derbys	SK353784
OS maps	110, 119	

Publication(s)
Looseleaf: *Bell Walk Major* (Vic Cox). Free(+A5 SAE).
Badge and certificate (£2.00/-/A5 SAE) available from Vic Cox.

Belmont 30   27

Lincs	48 km / 30 miles

A route taking in some of Lincolnshire's finest Wolds views and
passing through many small hamlets and villages.

Start and finish	Tetford, Lincs	TF334746
OS maps	122	

Publication(s)
Looseleaf: *Belmont 30* (Mike Surr). £0.20 (+9" x 4" SAE).
Badge (£1.50/SAE) available from Mike Surr.

Belvoir Witches Challenge Walk   28

Leic	40 km / 25 miles

A walk around the Vale of Belvoir where 17th century witches were
in residence. The route takes in part of the Grantham Canal,
Denton Reservoir and Belvoir Castle.

Start and finish	Bottesford. Leic	SK806392
OS maps	130	

Publication(s)
Booklet: *The Belvoir Witches Challenge Walk* by John Merrill
(Happy Walking International Ltd). ISBN:1874754489. A5 \ £3.00.
Badge and certificate (£3.00/incl p+p) available from Happy Walking International Ltd.

Bilsdale Circuit 29

N Yorks	48 km / 30 miles

A strenuous circuit with over 4,000ft of ascent, mainly along tracks
and the high moors within sight of the Bilsdale TV mast. The route
takes in Roppa Edge, Urra Moor where it is coincident with the
Lyke Wake Walk and Cleveland Way, and West Moor.

Start and finish	Newgate Bank Top, N Yorks	SE564890
OS maps	93, 100	

Publication(s)
Looseleaf: *Bilsdale Circuit* (Michael Guest). Free(+9" x 4" SAE).
Badge and certificate (£0.80/£0.20/SAE) available from Michael
Guest (cheques to Cleveland LDWA).

Black and White Village Trail 30

Heref & Worc	99 km / 61 miles

Originally conceived by David Gorvett as a route for car-drivers,
the Trail provides a similar route for walkers through the villages
between Leominster and Kington, an area characterised by the
large number of timbered and half-timbered buildings. The landscape is generally undulating farmland, and provides good views
of the surrounding hill ranges.

Start and finish	Leominster Station, Heref & Worc	SO502589
OS maps	148, 149	

Publication(s)
Paperback: *The Black and White Village Trail* by David Gorvett
and Les Lumsdon (Scarthin Books). ISBN:0907758479. 1991 \ A5 \
64pp \ £5.50.

Black Mountains Traverse Challenge 31

Heref, Powys	37 km / 23 miles

An undulating route across the Black Mountain ridge taking in the
highest peaks and lowest valley points.

Start	Llangorse Church, Powys	SO135276
Finish	Craswall, Heref	SO278361

OS maps   161

Publication(s)
Looseleaf: *The Black Mountains Traverse Challenge* (Richard Hill).
Free(+9" x 6" SAE).
Certificate (£3.00/10" x 8" SAE) available from Richard Hill.

Blackmore Vale Path   32

Dorset, Somerset	114 km / 71 miles

A route using ancient tracks, it takes in Dorchester and Yeovil,
many villages within the Blackmore Vale, Sherborne Abbey, Sturminster Newton, Okeford Hill Ridgeway and the Cerne Giant.

Start and finish	Blandford Forum, Dorset	ST886064
OS maps	183, 194	

Publication(s)
Booklet: *The Blackmore Vale Path* by Edward R Griffiths (Green
Fields Books). ISBN:0951937634. 1995\A5\150pp\£4.95(+80p).

Blackwater Valley Footpath   33

Berks, Hants, Surrey	30 km / 19 miles

This route along the Surrey/Berks/Hampshire border via Sandhurst, Farnborough and Aldershot is planned to link eventually to
the North Downs Way at Farnham, and via the Loddon Valley to
the Thames between Reading and Henley.

Start	Farnham, Surrey	SU844468
Finish	Swallowfield, Berks	SU727648
OS maps	175	
Waymark	Named posts and arrows with coot and reed logo	

Publication(s)
Booklet: *Discover the Blackwater Valley Footpath* (Blackwater
Valley Team). 1996\A5\32pp\£2.00(incl. p+p).
Looseleaf: *Discover the Blackwater Valley* (Blackwater Valley
Team). A4\4pp\Free.

Blue Man Walk   34

N Yorks	26 km / 16 miles

A walk developed and fully waymarked by the Forestry Commission through the upland coniferous forests on the east side of the
North York Moors.

Start	Reasty Bank Top, N Yorks	SE965944

Finish	Allerston, N Yorks	SE876830
OS maps	101	
Waymark	Blue man	

Publication(s)
Looseleaf: *Blue Man Walk Route* (Dalby Forest Visitor Centre).
A4 \ 1pp \ Free(+SAE).
Badge (£0.75) available from Dalby Forest Visitor Centre.

Bollin Valley Way 35

Cheshire, Gtr Man	36 km / 22 miles

The River Bollin rises in the Pennine Foothills and flows through Macclesfield, Prestbury, Wilmslow, Hale and Bowdon, eventually running into the Manchester Ship Canal (i.e. the Mersey) at Bollin Point. The Way is a spiral route giving access to a wider footpath network

Start	Macclesfield, Cheshire	SD915746
Finish	Partington, Gtr Man	SJ706912
On OS maps	109, 118	
Waymark	Named discs with river logo	

Publication(s)
Folder: *The Bollin Valley Way* (Bollin Valley Project). 1997 \ A4/3 \ 5pp \ Free(+SAE).

Bonnie Prince Charlie Walk 36

Derbys	28 km / 17 miles

Devised to celebrate the RA Diamond Jubilee, the walk follows the general route taken by Prince Charles Edward Stuart on his march from Ashbourne to Derby in 1745, through woods and farmland. Links with the Centenary Way (Derbyshire) at Ashbourne.

Start	Ashbourne, Derbys	SK180467
Finish	Derby, Derbys	SK353363
OS maps	128	
Waymark	Named logo - in east to west direction	

Publication(s)
Leaflet: *Bonnie Prince Charlie Walk* (John Pritchard-Jones). 1995 \ A5/4 \ Free(+9" x 4" SAE).

Boudica's Way 37

Norfolk	61 km / 38 miles

Named after the legendary warrior Queen of the Iceni, the route incorporates a strong historical theme. Presently the Way is developed only as far as Tyrell's Wood, the second part is due to be completed in 1999 and when it will then connect with the Angles Way.

Start	Railway Station, Norwich, Norfolk	TG230080
Finish	Diss, Norfolk	TM128797
OS maps	134, 156	
Waymark	Yellow & green discs/sword in centre	

Publication(s)
Folder: *Boudica's Way* (South Norfolk Council). 1997\A5\20pp\ £3.50(incl p+p).

Bourne Blunder 38

Lincs	32 km / 20 miles

A route to the south of Grantham taking in a sculpture trail, the Grimsthorpe Castle Estate, an 11th century castle mound, a chestnut avenue and lakes at Hollywell Hall.

Start and finish	Bourne Woods Car Park, Lincs	TF077202
OS maps	130	

Publication(s)
Looseleaf: *The Bourne Blunder* (Martyn Bishop). Free(+SAE). Badge and certificate(£1.50/SAE) available from Martyn Bishop.

Bowland Round 39

Lancs, N Yorks	128 km / 79 miles

A walk around some of the 312 square miles of Bowland, a designated AONB, yet still a relatively peaceful backwater. Can also be completed as a series of day walks.

Start and finish	Lancaster, Lancs	SD476619
OS maps	97, 98, 102, 103	

Publication(s)
Paperback: *The Bowland Round* by Stan Jones (Camelot Books). A5\193pp\£7.95.

Bowland-Dales Traverse 40

| Lancs, N Yorks | 153 km / 95 miles |

An upland route across the Forest of Bowland and the Yorkshire Dales, contrasting Bowland's heather-clad gritstone hills with the limestone terraces of the Dales. Besides visiting the villages of Slaidburn, Malham, Kettlewell, Aysgarth and Reeth, the route passes Attermire Scar, Malham Cove, Kilnsey Crag and Buckden Pike, the latter being the highest point at 2302ft.

Start	Garstang, Lancs	SD492450
Finish	Richmond, N Yorks	NZ171009
OS maps	92, 98, 99, 102, 103	

Publication(s)
Paperback: *The Bowland-Dales Traverse* by John Gillham (Grey Stone Books). ISBN:0951599623. 1991\105 x 150\64pp\£2.95.

Bradford Ring 41

| W Yorks | 51 km / 32 miles |

Fourteen walks (each with a return route), forming a chain encircling Bradford, make up the main ring walk and its alternatives, and provide very flexible walking routes. From Cottingley the walk heads along the Aire valley to Shipley and Apperley, where it loops to Pudsey, Birkenshaw, Scholes, Shelf and Thornton.

| Start and finish | Cottingley Bridge, W Yorks | SE112380 |
| OS maps | 104 | |

Publication(s)
Booklet: *Bradford Ringwalks* by Arthur Gemmell and Paul Sheldon (Stile Publications). ISBN:0906886449. 1989\200 x 120\128pp\£1.50(+SAE).

Bromley Circular Walks 42

| Gtr London | 69 km / 43 miles |

A series of inter-linking circular walks and trails based on *Nash* (4.5 miles), *Leaves Green* (6.5 miles), *Farnborough* (4.5 miles), *Cudham* (7.5 miles), *Berrys Green* (7.5 miles), *Green Street Green* (7 miles) and *Chelsfield* (5.5 miles) and which connect with the North Downs Way at Biggin.

Start and finish	Various
OS maps	177, 187, 188
Waymark	Named posts

Publication(s)
Folder: *Bromley Circular Walks & Trails* by Bromley Countryside
Rangers (Local Studies Section). 1996\A5\7pp\£2.00(+36p).

Bronte Round 43

W Yorks	37 km / 23 miles

The circuit crosses open moorland to Haworth, passing Top
Withins before returning to Hebden Bridge via riverside and farm
paths. It links places associated with the Bronte Family.

Start and finish	Hebden Bridge, W Yorks	SD992272
OS maps	103, 104	

Publication(s)
Booklet: *Bronte Round / Pendle and Ribble Round* by Derek Mag-
nall (Derek Magnall). 1994\A5\36pp\£1.85.
Badge and certificate (£1.50/-/SAE) available from Derek Magnall.

Bronte Way 44

Lancs, W Yorks	64 km / 40 miles

The Way provides a cross-Pennine route linking various places
associated with the lives and works of the Bronte sisters. It takes
in the Thursden Valley to Wycoller Hall (Ferndean Manor in the
novel Jane Eyre), the moors to Top Withins (Wuthering Heights),
Haworth Parsonage, where the Brontes lived and now a Bronte
Museum, the Brontes' birthplace at Thornton, along the hills west
of Bradford to the Spen Valley (Shirley country) before finishing at
Oakwell Hall (Fieldhead in the novel Shirley). The Worth Way (11
miles circular) can be linked with the Bronte Way at Haworth.

Start	Gawthorpe Hall, Lancs	SD805340
Finish	Oakwell Hall, W Yorks	SE217271
On OS maps	103, 104	
Waymark	Named posts	

Publication(s)
Paperback: *The Bronte Way* by Marje Wilson (RA West Riding).
ISBN:1901184056. 1997\A5\64pp\£4.50(+80p).
Folder: *The Bronte Way* (Lancashire County Council). 1997\A5\
£3.50(+80p).
Leaflet: *The Worth Way* (Haworth Tourist Information Centre).
A3/4\£0.30(+SAE).
Badge - The Worth Way (£1.20/SAE) available from Haworth
Tourist Information Centre.

Bunyan Trail   45

Beds, Herts	121 km / 75 miles

The Trail was created by the Bedfordshire Group to celebrate the RA Diamond Jubilee and is dedicated to the memory of John Bunyan, the Puritan Evangelist and author of the book Pilgrim's Progress. The route passes through a number of attractive villages and scenic countryside, taking in many places of historic interest connected with Bunyan. There are links with the Greensand Ridge Walk and the Icknield Way.

Start and finish	Sundon Hills Country Park, Beds	TL047286
OS maps	153, 166	
Waymark	Circular disc with name and silhouette of head	

Publication(s)
Leaflet: *The John Bunyan Trail - Section One* (G.J. Edwards). A3/6 \ £0.60(+31p SAE).
Leaflet: *The John Bunyan Trail - Section Two* (G.J. Edwards). A3/6 \ £0.60(+31p SAE).

Burley Bridge Hike   46

W Yorks	34 km / 21 miles

A route over Ilkley Moor passing the Cow and Calf Rocks, Riddlesden, Crossflatts and Burley Woodhead. Proceeds of sales towards the costs of a bridge provision over the River Wharfe at Burley.

Start and finish	Burley-in-Wharfedale, W Yorks	SE164458
OS maps	104	

Publication(s)
Looseleaf: *Burley Bridge Hike* (John Sparshatt). A4/2pp/Free (+SAE).
Badge and certificate (£2.00/9" x 6" SAE) available from John Sparshatt.

Cairngorm Passes   47

Aberdeenshire	Various km

These passes through the Cairngorms comprise, *Bealach Dearg* (Braemar - Tomintoul) 22 miles; *Glen Feshie* (Braemar - Kincraig) 32 miles; *Lairig an Laoich* (Braemar - Nethy Bridge) 32 miles; *Lairig Ghru* (Braemar - Aviemore) 28 miles. In poor or winter conditions, they should only be attempted by well equipped/experienced hill walkers.

Start	Braemar, Aberdeenshire	NJ152915

Finish	Various	Various
OS maps	34, 36	

Publication(s)
Leaflet: *The Cairngorm Passes* (Scottish Rights of Way Society).
1995\105 x 142\£1.00(+SAE).

Caistor Challenge 48

Lincs	40 km / 25 miles

A circular route providing scenic views of the Lincolnshire Wolds
and taking in eight villages/churches. See also Caistor Challenge
Alternative.

Start and finish	Caistor, Lincs	TA117013
OS maps	113	

Publication(s)
Looseleaf: *Caistor Challenge* (Mike Surr). £0.20(+9" x 4" SAE).
Badge and certificate (£1.40/£0.10/SAE) available from Mike Surr.

Caistor Challenge Alternative 49

Lincs	42 km / 26 miles

As the name implies, an alternative route to the Caistor Challenge.
Coincident with that between Nettleton and Tealby, this route then
runs east and returns via Rothwell.

Start and finish	Caistor, Lincs	TA117013
OS maps	113	

Publication(s)
Looseleaf: *Caistor Challenge Alternative* (Mike Surr). £0.20(+9" x
4" SAE).
Badge and certificate (£1.40/£0.10/SAE) available from Mike Surr.

Cal-Der-Went Walk 50

Derbys, S Yorks, W Yorks	48 km / 30 miles

A route taking in Bretton Park, High Hoyland and Penistone
crossing the watersheds and valleys of the Calder, Dearne, Don
and Derwent.

Start	Horbury Bridge, W Yorks	SE281179
Finish	Ladybower Reservoir, Derbys	SK195865
OS maps	110	

Publication(s)
Booklet: *The Cal-Der-Went Walk* by Geofrey Carr (Happy Walking International). £3.75.
Looseleaf: *The Cal-Der-Went Walk- walk/badge/certificate information* (Geoffrey Carr). Free(+SAE).

Calderdale Way 51

W Yorks	80 km / 50 miles

The Way, a circuit around Calderdale, was pioneered by local civic trusts. The main and link routes to the valley bottom are designed so that they can be completed in short stages. The walk encircles Halifax, Hebden Bridge and Todmorden, following old packhorse ways across the open gritstone hillsides, passing through hillside villages and old mill towns on the banks of the River Calder.

Start and finish	Greetland, W Yorks	SE097214
On OS maps	103, 104, 110	
Waymark	Letters CW/trefoil	

Publication(s)
Paperback: *The Calderdale Way Guide* by the Calderdale Way Association (Hebden Bridge Tourist Information Centre). A5\ 72pp\£4.99(+80p).
Badge (£0.60/£0.26 p&p) available from Hebden Bridge Tourist Information Centre.

Cambrian & Lleyn Coast Path 52

Caernarfon, Cardigan	414 km / 257 miles

A route along the coastline of West Wales, which can be linked to the Pembrokeshire Coast Path at Cardigan and by use of a described link path between Caernarfon and Bangor, with the North Wales Coast Path. The Lon Eifion route (12 miles) provides a link from Bryncir into Caernarfon, that route and others being described in the *Gwynedd Recreational Routes* publication. The Eifionydd and Lleyn Footpath Network publications include details of paths on the Peninsula which could be incorporated into longer circular walks besides providing historical information.

Start	Cardigan	SN178461
Finish	Caernarfon	SH476627
OS maps	115, 123, 124, 135, 145, 146	

Publication(s)
Paperback: *Walking the Cambrian Coast* by Jan Harris (Walking Routes). ISBN:0951814842. 1996\A5\84pp\£4.95(incl p+p).
Paperback: *Walking the Lleyn Coast* by Jan Harris (Walking Routes). ISBN:0951814826. 1995\A5\72pp\£4.95(incl p+p).

Paperback: *The Lleyn Peninsula Coastal Path* by John Cantrell (Cicerone Press). ISBN:1852842520. 1997\176 x 115\160pp\ £6.99(+75p).
Folder: *Eifionydd Footpath Network* (Gwynedd County Council). A4/3\6 leaflets\£2.50.
Folder: *Lleyn Footpath Network* (Gwynedd County Council). A4/3\8 leaflets\£2.50.
Leaflet: *Gwynedd Recreational Routes (Lon Eifion)* (Gwynedd County Council). 1997\A4/3.\Free(+SAE).

Cambrian Way   53

Aberconwy, Caernarfon, Cardiff, Monmouth, Powys	441 km / 274 miles

Described as the Mountain Connoisseur's Walk, this route through upland Wales involves 61,540ft of ascent and requires much stamina to complete. It is a tough, high-level route which should not be underestimated. From the south coast, it follows a meandering northerly route over the Black Mountains, Brecon Beacons, Carmarthen Fan, Plynlimon, Cadair Idris, the Rhinogs, the Snowdon massif and the Carneddau to reach the north coast. Tony Drake pioneered the route, and his guide includes a comprehensive accommodation and services list (with periodic update insert). He is willing to give advice and information on the route, and provide and update the accommodation list as necessary, 50p + SAE, (2 Beech Lodge, 67 The Park, Cheltenham, Glos GL50 2RX (01242 232131). Navigational skills are of paramount importance

Start	Cardiff	ST180765
Finish	Conwy, Aberconwy	SH783775
OS maps	115, 124, 135, 147, 160, 161, 171	

Publication(s)
Paperback: *Cambrian Way: the Mountain Connoisseur's Walk* by A J Drake (Ramblers' Association). ISBN:0950958034. 1995\210 x 128\96pp\£4.50(+70p).

Camel Trail   54

Cornwall	30 km / 19 miles

Two sections of disused railway line from Padstow via Wadebridge and Boscarne Junction to Bodmin (11 miles), and from Boscarne Junction to Poley's Bridge on the edge of Bodmin Moor (7 miles). The Padstow to Wadebridge section is along the Camel estuary, the rest through densely wooded landscapes.

Start	Padstow, Cornwall	SW920754
Finish	Poley's Bridge, Cornwall	SX082742
On OS maps	200	

Publication(s)
Leaflet: *The Camel Trail* (Camel Trail Ranger). 1993\A4/3\Free (+SAE).

Cape Wrath Trail 55

Highland	330 km / 205 miles

Initially following the Great Glen, the route turns north to cross Glen Garry, Glen Loyne and Glenshiel before crossing the wilderness to Strathcarron, continuing north through Torridon, Dundonnell (ferry) and Ullapool, where the coast is followed to Cullnacraig. The Coigach and Assynt Hills are traversed followed by the high moorland to Achfary and then via Foinaven, Rhiconich, Kinlochbervie and Sandwood Bay to the finish.

Start	Banavie, Highland	NN112769
Finish	Cape Wrath, Highland	NC269747
OS maps	9, 15, 19, 25, 33, 34, 41	

Publication(s)
Paperback: *The Cape Wrath Trail* by David Paterson (Peak Publishing Ltd). ISBN:0952190826. 1996\260 x 225\128pp\£13.95.

Capital Walk - Cardiff 56

Caerphilly, Cardiff, Newport, Vale of Glamorgan	59 km / 37 miles

A route around Cardiff taking in Dinas Powys, St Fagan's, Taff's Well, Ruperra Castle and Castleton linking with the Taff-Ely Ridgeway Walk and Taff Trail at Taff's Well, and the Rhymney Valley Ridgeway Walk near Caerphilly.

Start	Swanbridge, Vale of Glamorgan	ST174676
Finish	Peterstone-Wentlooge, Newport	ST292810
OS maps	171	

Publication(s)
Booklet: *More Capital Walks* (RA Cardiff). 1997\A5\40pp\Free (+38p SAE).

Carneddau Challenge Walk 57

Caernarfon, Aberconwy	32 km / 20 miles

A route from sea level near Bangor to the summit of Carnedd Llewelyn with 4750ft of ascent.

Start and finish	Aber-Ogwen, Caernarfon	SH613721
OS maps	115	

Publication(s)
Booklet: *The Carneddau Challenge Walk* by Tony Hill (Happy Walking International Ltd). ISBN:1874754462. A5\£3.00.
Badge and certificate (£3.00/incl p+p) available from Happy Walking International Ltd.

Carpet Baggers 50 — 58

Shrops, Staffs, Worcs	80 km / 50 miles

This route passes through Bewdley, along the Severn Valley, through Seckley Wood, Alverley, and other villages, to Abbot's Hill and along the Staffordshire Way. A climb over Kinver Edge is followed by a return to the Severn.

Start and finish	Stourport-on-Severn, Worcs	SO815736
OS maps	138, 139	

Publication(s)
Looseleaf: *Carpet Baggers 50* (Eric Perks). Free(+9" x 6" SAE).
Badge and certificate (£2.00/£0.75/9" x 6" SAE) available from Eric Perks.

Castleman Trailway — 59

Dorset	26 km / 16 miles

For much of the route the Trailway is along the former Southampton and Dorchester Railway. It can be linked with the Stour Valley Way (Dorset) at Wimbourne Minster. It is hoped to link the route in due course with Ringwood.

Start	Upton Park, Dorset	SY993930
Finish	Ashley Twinning, Dorset	SU137050
On OS maps	195	
Waymark	Green locomotive on yellow footprint	

Publication(s)
Leaflet: *The Castleman Trailway* (Avon Heath Country Park). 1994\A5\Free.

Cat Walk — 60

Cumbria, Lancs	64 km / 40 miles

So named after the villages of Carnforth, Arnside and Tebay, the route takes in the coastal area of Silverdale and Arnside, continues via Heversham Head, Kendal and the Borrowdale and Lune Valleys.

Start	Carnforth Station, Lancs	SD497707

Finish	Tebay, Cumbria	SD617044
OS maps	90, 91, 97	

Publication(s)
Looseleaf: *Cat Walk* (Frank Hodson). Free(+2 x 20p stamps).
Badge and Certificate (£1.00/SAE/£0.50/SAE) available from
Frank Hodson.

Cavendish 27 Circuit 61

N Yorks	43 km / 27 miles

A route encircling the Barden Fell, it follows the river Wharfe to
Bolton Bridge, and then takes in the villages of Draughton, Eastby,
Embsay, Hasby, Rylstone, Cracoe, Thorpe, Burnsall and Howgill
before climbing up to Simon's Seat.

Start and finish	Bolton Abbey Hall, N Yorks	SE071540
OS maps	98, 103, 104	

Publication(s)
Looseleaf: *Cavendish 27 Circuit* (L Turner). 1pp\£0.20(+9" x 4"
SAE).
Badge and certificate (£1.00/£0.50/9" x 4" SAE) available from L
Turner.

Centenary Circle 62

Essex	37 km / 23 miles

A route around Chelmsford passing via Sandon, Galleywood, Writ-
tle, Broomfield and the River Chelmer.

Start and finish	Sandford Mill, Essex	TL740060
On OS maps	167	
Waymark	Profiles of Queens Victoria and Elizabeth II in garland	

Publication(s)
Folder: *Country Ways* (Chelmsford Borough Council). A5\11pp\
£3.00.

Centenary Way (Derbyshire) 63

Derbys	38 km / 24 miles

A walk devised by the Derbyshire Footpaths Preservation Society
to commemorate their centenary, visiting the lesser known but
attractive villages of South Derbyshire. The Way links with the
Bonnie Prince Charlie Walk at Ashbourne.

Start	Ilkeston, Derbys	SK460418

Finish	Ashbourne, Derbys	SK180470
OS maps	119, 129	

Publication(s)
Booklet: *Centenary Way - Ilkeston to Ashbourne* (Derbyshire Footpaths Preservation Society). 1994\A5\24pp\£2.00(+£0.25 SAE).

Centenary Way (North Yorkshire)   64

N Yorks	133 km / 83 miles

A route devised to celebrate the 100th anniversary of Yorkshire County Council. It runs across the Howardian Hills and Yorkshire Wolds via Castle Howard and Wharram Percy, linking York and the Foss Walk with the Wolds and Cleveland Ways. It combines riverside walks in deep valleys with forest tracks.

Start	York, N Yorks	SE603522
Finish	Filey Brigg, N Yorks	TA126817
On OS maps	100, 101, 105	
Waymark	Letters CW on standard waymarks	

Publication(s)
Booklet: *The Centenary Way from Filey Brigg to York Minster* (North Yorkshire County Council). 1989\A5\36pp\£1.00.

Centenary Way (Warwickshire)   65

Warks	158 km / 98 miles

The Way was devised to celebrate one hundred years of Warwickshire County Council. It passes the Tame Valley, Atherstone Ridge, the George Eliot country around Nuneaton, before passing to the east of Coventry to Kenilworth, Warwick and Leamington Spa. From here it heads to the Burton Dassett Hills, Edge Hill, Shipston-on-Stour and Ilmington Downs.

Start	Kingsbury, Warks	SP204959
Finish	Meon Hill, Warks	SP176454
OS maps	139, 140, 151	
Waymark	Bear and ragged staff	

Publication(s)
Paperback: *The Centenary Way* by Geoff Allen and John Roberts (Walkways/Quercus). ISBN:0947708332. 1996\210 x 145\120pp\£6.45.
Folder: *Centenary Way* (Warwickshire County Council). 1989\A4/3\11pp\£4.00.

Central Scottish Way 66

Borders, East Dunbarton, Edin, Glasgow, Midlothian, N Lanark, Northumb, W Lothian	251 km / 156 miles

This route commences from the start of the West Highland Way and taking in some of the Glasgow Walkways/Cycleways reaches initially the Union Canal and subsequently the Forth & Clyde Canal to Edinburgh using the towpaths wherever possible. It then strikes south meeting with the Southern Upland Way at Lauder and the Pennine Way via Dere Street at Black Hills. The Glasgow Walkways which include the Clyde Walkway cater for many other links being achieved.

Start	Milngavie, East Dunbarton	NS555745
Finish	Byrness, Northumb	NT028763
OS maps	64, 65, 66, 72, 73, 74, 80	

Publication(s)
Hardback: *Walking the Central Scottish Way* by Erl B Wilkie (Mainstream Publishing Co Ltd). ISBN:1851587470. 1996\220 x 130\176pp\£9.99.
Paperback: *Exploring the Edinburgh to Glasgow Canals* by Hamish Brown (Stationery Office). ISBN:0114957355. 1997\135 x 220\106pp\£8.99.
Paperback: *Glasgow's Pathways* by Erl B Wilkie (Mainstream Publishing Co Ltd). ISBN:1851585222. 1993\215 x 125\158\ £6.99.
Leaflets: *Fit For Life - Glasgow Walkways (x 4 - North West, North East, South East, South West)* (Glasgow City Council). 1996\A4/3\ Free(+SAE).
Leaflet: *Pedestrian and Cycle Routes in Strathclyde* (Glasgow City Council). 1995\A4/3\Free(+SAE).

Cestrian Link Walk 67

Cheshire, Denbigh, Derbys, Flints	182 km / 113 miles

Designed to link the Pennine Way with Offa's Dyke Path, the Link leaves the Peak District via Castleton and the Goyt valley and takes a meandering route across the Cheshire lowlands avoiding the northern industrial areas, passing through many Cheshire villages, including Gawsworth, Church Minshull, Beeston and Aldford. From Mold it follows a route along the lower Clwydian hills.

Start	Edale, Derbys	SK125858
Finish	Prestatyn, Denbigh	SJ081838
OS maps	116, 117, 118, 119	

Publication(s)
Hardback: *A Cestrian Link Walk* by John N Davenport (Westmorland Gazette). ISBN:0902272454. 1983\116 x 177\108pp\ £2.50(+40p).

Chaddesley Chase   68

Worcs	35 km / 22 miles

A route taking in Chaddesley, Santery Hill, Pepper Wood and Hillpool Mill making use of open fields and following streams and country lanes.

Start and finish	Chaddesley Corbett, Worcs	SO892736
OS maps	138, 139	

Publication(s)
Looseleaf: *Chaddesley Chase* (Eric Perks). Free(+9" x 6" SAE).
Badge and certificate (£2.00/£0.75/9" x 6" SAE) available from Eric Perks.

Chalkland Way   69

E Yorks	61 km / 40 miles

A tour around the most northerly chalk outcrop in Britain - the Yorkshire Wolds, noted for green, dry valleys. A route taking in the villages of Great Givendale, Bugthorpe, Thixendale, Fimber, Wetwang and Huggate.

Start and finish	Pocklington, E Yorks	SE802488
OS maps	100, 101, 106	

Publication(s)
Looseleaf: *The Chalkland Way* (Ray Wallis). 1994\Free(+SAE).
Badge (£1.00/SAE) available from Ray Wallis.

Charnwood Forest Challenge Walk   70

Leics	40 km / 25 miles

A walk around the hill country to the north-east of Leicester passing Newtown Lifford, Ulverscroft Priory, Bardon Hill, Mount St Bernard Abbey, Beacon Hill and Woodhouse Eaves.

Start and finish	Bradgate Park, Leics	SK543114
OS maps	129	

Publication(s)
Paperback: *Charnwood Forest Challenge Walk* by John Merrill (Happy Walking International Ltd). ISBN:0907496644. 1992\132 x 210\32pp\£3.00.
Badge and certificate (£3.00/post free) available from Happy Walking International Ltd.

Charnwood Round 71

| Leics | 53 km / 33 miles |

A walk round the ancient Charnwood Forest which lies on high ground to the north-west of Leicester. Peaceful countryside, once quarried by Romans, settled by monks, criss-crossed with paths and full of interesting relics of the past. Links with the Leicestershire Round.

| Start and finish | Newtown Linford, Leics | SK521098 |
| OS maps | 129, 140 | |

Publication(s)
Leaflet: *The Charnwood Round* by Heather MacDermid (Cordee Ltd). ISBN:1871890128. A4\10\£2.95.

Cheltenham Circular Footpath 72

| Glos | 40 km / 25 miles |

A route around Cheltenham with views of the Cotswold escarpment and the Severn Vale.

Start and finish	Cheltenham, Glos	SO237955
OS maps	162, 163	
Waymark	Walk name under a green tree	

Publication(s)
Booklet: *Cheltenham Circular Footpath* by Cheltenham Borough Council and others (Reardon Publishing). ISBN:187387717X. 1996\210 x 150\40pp\£3.50(+50p).

Cheshire Ring Canal Walk 73

| Cheshire, Gtr Man, Staffs | 156 km / 97 miles |

A route following the towpaths along six historic canals of various ages and character, this Walk offers the solitude of quiet countryside, the hustle and bustle of city streets and views of the Cheshire Plain and Peak District hills.

| Start and finish | Marple, Gtr Man | SJ962884 |
| On OS maps | 108, 109, 117, 118 | |

Waymark	Metal plaque with bridge and barge

Publication(s)
Paperback: *The Cheshire Ring* by John N. Merrill (Happy Walking International Ltd). ISBN:0907496636. 80pp \ £4.95.
Folder: *Cheshire Ring Canal Walk* (Cheshire County Council). 100 x 210 \ 11pp \ £8.00(+£1.25).
Badge and certificate (£1.00/£0.50/SAE) available from Frank Hodson.

Cheshire Ways 74

Cheshire	Various km

These Ways comprise the *Baker Way* (8 miles) Brines Brow - Christleton; *Delamere Way* (22 miles) Stockton Heath - Frodsham; *Eddisbury Way* (18 miles) Frodsham - Burwardsley; *Longster Trail* (11 miles) Helsby - Pipers Ash. They provide links with the Sandstone Trail at Frodsham.

Start and finish	Various
OS maps	109, 117, 118
Waymark	Named discs

Publication(s)
Booklet: *Waymarked Walks in Central Cheshire - Baker Way (Brines Brow - Christleton)* (Mid-Cheshire Footpath Society). 100 x 223 \ 16pp \ £0.90 (+A5 SAE).
Booklet: *Waymarked Walks in Central Cheshire - Baker Way (Christleton - Brines Brow)* (Mid-Cheshire Footpath Society). Details TBA 1998.
Booklet: *Waymarked Walks in Central Cheshire - Delamere Way (Stockton Heath - Frodsham)* (Mid-Cheshire Footpath Society). 100 x 223 \ 16pp \ £0.90 (+A5 SAE).
Booklet: *Waymarked Walks in Central Cheshire - Delamere Way (Frodsham - Stockton Heath)* (Mid-Cheshire Footpath Society). 100 x 223 \ 16pp \ £0.90 (+A5 SAE).
Booklet: *Waymarked Walks in Central Cheshire - Eddisbury Way (Frodsham - Burwardsley)* (Mid-Cheshire Footpath Society). 100 x 223 \ 16pp \ £0.90 (+A5 SAE).
Booklet: *Waymarked Walks in Central Cheshire - Eddisbury Way (Burwardsley - Frodsham)* (Mid-Cheshire Footpath Society). Details TBA 1998.
Booklet: *Waymarked Walks in Central Cheshire - Longster Trail (Helsby - Pipers Ash)* (Mid-Cheshire Footpath Society). 100 x 223 \ 8pp \ £0.90 (+A5 SAE).
Booklet: *Waymarked Walks in Central Cheshire - Longster Trail (Pipers Ash - Helsby)* (Mid Cheshire Footpath Society). 100 x 223 \ 8pp \ £0.90 (+A5 SAE).
Booklet: *Longer Trails in Vale Royal* - reference included to Delamere Way; Eddisbury Way; Longster Trail: (Vale Royal Borough Council). 1993 \ A5 \ 76pp \ £1.95.

Chess Valley Walk and Chiltern Link   75

Bucks, Herts	29 km / 18 miles

These are two routes linking at Chesham and connecting Rickmansworth with The Ridgeway at Concord Wood. From the confluence of the Rivers Chess and Colne, the walk follows the River Chess to its source at Chesham where it then takes to the ancient trade route to Wendover through the Chiltern countryside.

Start	Rickmansworth, Herts	TQ057946
Finish	Wendover, Bucks	SP869078
On OS maps	165, 166	
Waymark	Fish/water and named posts	

Publication(s)
Leaflet: *Chess Valley Walk* (Buckinghamshire County Council). 1996\A4/3\Free(+SAE).
Leaflet: *The Chiltern Link* (Buckinghamshire County Council). A4/3\Free(+SAE).

Chesterfield Round   76

Derbys	80 km / 50 miles

A route devised to celebrate the Ramblers' Association Golden Jubilee and is, as the name suggests, a walk through the countryside around the town.

Start and finish	Troway, Derbys	SK412792
OS maps	119	

Publication(s)
Folder: *Chesterfield Round Walk* (RA Chesterfield & NE Derbyshire). A5\3pp\£1.00(+SAE).

Cheviot Hills 2,000ft Summits   77

Northumb	40 km / 25 miles

This upland walk over rough terrain and involving 5,000ft of ascent links the Cheviot, Windy Gyle, Bloodybush Edge, Cushat Law, Comb Fell and Hedgehope, each over 2000ft. Good navigation skills are required. An alternative route from Wooler, adding 10 miles is described.

Start and finish	Hawsen Burn, Northumb	NT954225
OS maps	75, 80	

Publication(s)
Looseleaf: *Cheviot Hills 2,000ft Summits Walk* (LDWA Northumbria Group). Free(+SAE).
Certificate (£0.10/C5 SAE) available from LDWA Northumbria Group.

Chilterns Hundred 78

Berks, Bucks, Herts, Oxon	161 km / 100 miles

A circuitous tour of the Chilterns, taking in some of the most picturesque villages and scenery, numerous historic churches and inns. It passes the Chiltern Society's Open Air Museum at Chorley Wood and the Quakers' Meeting House at Jordans to reach the River Thames at Cookham and Marlow. It then continues to Stonor, Watlington, Princes Risborough, Wendover, Tring and Great Missenden.

Start and finish	Amersham, Bucks	SU964982
OS maps	165, 166, 175, 176	

Publication(s)
Paperback: *Chilterns Hundred* by Jimmy Parsons (Chiltern Society). 1988\210 x 149\32pp\£1.80.

Chorley Botany Bay Round 79

Lancs	34 km / 21 miles

A route to the east of Chorley visiting Spitlers Edge, Heapey Moor and Copthurst.

Start and finish	St Peters Parish Club, Chorley, Lancs	SD592184
OS maps	102, 103, 108, 109	

Publication(s)
Looseleaf: *Chorley Botany Bay Round* (F. Jolly). Free(+SAE).
Badge and certificate (£2.00/£0.50/SAE) available from F. Jolly.

Churnet Valley Challenge Walk 80

Staffs	39 km / 24 miles

Set in the Churnet Valley, the route takes in several villages, a section of the Caldon Canal and part of the Staffordshire Way. There is 2600ft of ascent.

Start and finish	Froghall, Staffs	SK027476
OS maps	119	

Publication(s)
Looseleaf: *Churnet Valley Challenge Walk* (Alan S Edwards).
Free(+SAE).
Certificate (£0.30/Large SAE) available from Alan S Edwards.

Cistercian Way 81

Cumbria	53 km / 33 miles

A route along the paths, tracks and byways of the low limestone
hills that fringe the northern shores of Morecambe Bay via woodlands to Hampsfell and Cartmel Priory to Cark and Holker Hall.
The route then continues over the sands of the Leven Estuary, but
this is dangerous and should only be attempted with the recognised
Sand Pilot. Otherwise the train should be caught to Ulverston
where the Way continues by Dalton to Furness Abbey and the
coast.

Start	Grange-over-Sands, Cumbria	SD412781
Finish	Roa Island, Cumbria	SD232648
On OS maps	96	
Waymark	Monk	

Publication(s)
Leaflet: *Cistercian Way* (South Lakeland District Council). A4/3 \
Free.

Clarendon Way 82

Hants, Wilts	39 km / 24 miles

Named after Clarendon Park on the eastern edge of Salisbury, the
Way links that city on the River Avon with Winchester on the River
Itchen. Crossing the River Test at Kings Somborne, the scenery
ranges from the water meadows of the valleys with their charming
villages through woodland to chalk downs with their fine views.

Start	Salisbury, Wilts	SU143297
Finish	Winchester, Hants	SU483293
On OS maps	184, 185	
Waymark	Bishop's mitre	

Publication(s)
Leaflet: *Test & Clarendon Way* (Hampshire County Council). A4/3 \
Free.

Cleveland Way 83

Cleveland, N Yorks	177 km / 110 miles

The Way climbs to the North York Moors at Sutton Bank, where there is a short extension to the Kilburn White Horse, and then heads north along the western edge of the high heather moors to Osmotherley from where it follows tracks along the northern escarpment to Greenhow Moor. It turns over Kildale Moor, Roseberry Topping and Guisborough Moor to leave the North York Moors National Park and to reach the coast at Saltburn-by-the-Sea then following a varied and undulating coastal path southwards along clifftops, sands and passing several harbours and resorts.

This roughly horse-shoe shaped trail has led to the development of suggested routes linking the start and finish including the way-marked Tabular Hills Link Walk (48 miles). Relevant publications etc. are listed.

Start	Helmsley, N Yorks	SE611839
Finish	Filey Brigg, N Yorks	TA126817
On OS maps	93, 94, 99, 100, 101	
Waymark	National Trail Acorn	

Publication(s)
Softback: *Cleveland Way* (Official Guide) by Ian Sampson (Aurum Press). ISBN:1854100211. 1989\210 x 130\144pp\£9.99.
Paperback: *Walking the Cleveland Way and the Missing Link* by Malcolm Boyes (Cicerone Press). ISBN:1852840145. 1989\116 x 176\144pp\£5.99.
Softback: *Cleveland Way Companion* by Paul Hannon (Hillside Publications). ISBN:1870141172. 1992\175 x 115\96pp\£5.99.
Paperback: *The Cleveland Way* by John Merrill (Happy Walking International Ltd). ISBN:0907496709. 80pp\£4.95.
Paperback: *Cleveland Way plus the Tabular Hills Link* by Martin Collins (Dalesman Publishing Ltd). ISBN:1855681137. 1997\165 x 100\128pp\£6.99.
Booklet: *The Link Through the Tabular Hills Walk* (North York Moors National Park). ISBN:0907480446. 1993\120 x 170\44pp\ £3.95.
Stripmap: *The Cleveland Way* (Footprint). £2.95.
Booklet: *Cleveland Way Accommodation and Information Guide* (North York Moors National Park). Annual\A4/3\24pp\Free(+A5 SAE).
Leaflet: *Cleveland Way* (Countryside Commission Postal Sales). 1996\A4/3\Free.
Badges - woven/metal (£0.75/SAE/£1.50/SAE) available from North York Moors National Park).
Badge and certificate (£3.00/post free) available from Happy Walking International Ltd.
Missing Link badge and certificate (£1.35/£0.30+SAE) available from Missing Link Recorder.

Clitheroe 60K 84

Lancs	60 km / 37 miles

A walk devised to commemorate the RA Diamond Jubilee. From the Ribble Valley the route takes in Longridge Fell, the Hoddle Valley, Newton, then skirting Grindleton Fell to Sawley and Downham, finally traversing Pendle Hill. The route includes almost 5000ft of ascent and links with the Pendle Way (on Pendle Hill) and Ribble Way (at Sawley Bridge).

Start and finish	Clitheroe, Lancs	SD742419
OS maps	103	

Publication(s)
Leaflet: *Clitheroe 60k route card* by Eddie Ross (Ribble Valley Borough Council). 1995\A5\2pp\Free(+SAE).
Certificate (Free+SAE) available from Ribble Valley Borough Council.

Clopton Way 85

Cambs	17 km / 11 miles

The walk offers commanding views over much of south-west Cambridgeshire, as it follows the top of an escarpment through the deserted medieval village of Clopton. It connects the Wimpole Way with the Greensand Ridge Walk.

Start	Wimpole Hall, Cambs	TL343511
Finish	Gamlingay, Cambs	TL226533
On OS maps	154	
Waymark	Clopton Way posts and discs	

Publication(s)
Leaflet: *Clopton Way* (Cambridgeshire County Council). 1990\A4/3\£0.40(+50p).

Cloud 7 Circuit 86

Cheshire, Staffs	53 km / 33 miles

Named after the seven Cloud hills, this strenuous route with 5400ft of ascent covers the area between Leek, Buxton, Macclesfield and Congleton. There is an option for a 28 miles route.

Start and finish	Rushton Spencer, Staffs	SJ939624
OS maps	118, 119	

Publication(s)
Leaflet: *Cloud 7 Circuit* (Derek Nash). 1989\A4\Free(+SAE).

Badge and certificate (£1.45/£0.50/SAE) available from Derek Nash.

Coast to Coast   87

Cumbria, N Yorks	306 km / 190 miles

The classic route by Alfred Wainwright was intended in part to encourage others to devise their own routes in connecting the Irish and North Seas. This particular route also links three National Parks taking a high level traverse wherever possible. From the west, the coastal plain is crossed to, and through, the Lake District to Shap, followed by the crossing of the Westmorland limestone plateau to Kirkby Stephen, a climb to the Pennine watershed and then through Keld, Reeth and Richmond to the low level Vale of Mowbray before again achieving height across the North York Moors. To prevent any additional and unnecessary erosion, three seasonal alternatives have been created on the main route where the path enters the Yorkshire Dales National Park from Cumbria (free map leaflet available). In keeping with AW's intentions, details of other Coast to Coast route publications are listed.

Start	St Bees, Cumbria	NX959119
Finish	Robin Hood's Bay, N Yorks	NZ953048
OS maps	89, 90, 91, 92, 93, 94, 98, 99, 100	

Publication(s)
Hardback: *Coast to Coast Walk* by A Wainwright (Michael Joseph). ISBN:0718140729. 1994\175 x 117\£9.99.
Hardback: *Wainwright's Coast to Coast Walk* by A Wainwright (Michael Joseph). ISBN:0718140982. 250 x 215\208pp\£20.00.
Paperback: *Wainwright's Coast to Coast Walk* by A Wainwright (Michael Joseph). ISBN:0718140931. 250 x 215\208pp\£13.99.
Stripmap: *Coast to Coast Walk: St Bees Head to Keld* (Ordnance Survey). ISBN:0319260461. 1994\£4.99.
Stripmap: *Coast to Coast Walk: Keld to Robin Hood's Bay* (Ordnance Survey). ISBN:031926047X. 1994\£4.99.
Stripmap: *Coast to Coast: Part 1: St Bees Head to Swaledale - map & guide* (Footprint). ISBN:1871149118. 1994\£3.50.
Stripmap: *Coast to Coast: Part 2: Swaledale to Robin Hood's Bay - map & guide* (Footprint). ISBN:1871149126. 1994\£3.50.
Booklet: *Coast to Coast Accommodation Guide* (Mrs Doreen Whitehead). Annual\100 x 150\56pp\£2.50(incl p+p).
Booklet: *Coast to Coast Walk Accommodation Guide* by Ewen Bennett (North York Moors Adventure Centre). (Bi-annual)\A6\36pp\£3.00.
Leaflet: *Accommodation Booking Service* (YHA Northern Region). 1997\Free(+SAE).
Leaflet: *Coast to Coast Walk - route of the season* (Yorkshire Dales National Park). 1996\211 x 150\1pp\Free(+SAE).
Leaflet: *The Coast to Coast Walk* (Richmondshire District Council). 1996\A5/2\Free(+SAE).

OTHER ROUTE PUBLICATIONS:
Softback: *The Northern Coast to Coast*: St Bees to Robin Hood's Bay (178 miles) by Terry Marsh (Cicerone Press). ISBN:1852841265. 1993\116 x 176\280pp\£7.99.
Paperback: *Coast to Coast Walk*: St Bees to Robin Hood's Bay (190 miles) by Paul Hannon (Hillside Publications). ISBN:1870141555. 1997\175 x 115\152pp\£7.99.
Booklet: *A One Week Coast to Coast Trek Irish to North Sea*: Arnside to Saltburn-by-the-Sea (120 miles). by Dick French (Richard French). 1994\105 x 150\24pp\£3.00(+9" x 4" SAE).
Paperback: *Lakeland to Lindisfarne*: Ravenglass to Holy Island (190 miles) by John Gillham (Crowood Press). ISBN:1852239751. £7.99.
Paperback: *The Alternative Coast to Coast*: Walney Island to Holy Island (192 miles) by Derek Brook & Phil Hinchcliffe (Cicerone Press). ISBN:1852842024. 272pp\£9.99.
Paperback: *On Foot From Coast to Coast - the North of England Way*: Ravenglass to Scarborough (206 miles) by David Maughan (Penguin Books Ltd). ISBN:0718141512. 1997\192pp\£9.99.
Paperback: *The Ravenber*: Ravenglass to Berwick-upon-Tweed (210 miles) by Ron Scholes (Pentland Press Ltd). ISBN:1858213894. 1997\121 x 176\302pp\£7.50.
Paperback: *Blackpool to Bridlington - The Aerospace Way*: (148 miles) by Harry Cadman and Anthony Johnson (British Aerospace Ltd). ISBN:0952966107. 1997\A5\108pp\£5.95 (cheques made payable to RNLI).
Booklets: *A Morecambe to Whitby Walk*: (131 miles) by Stan Jones (Camelot Books). 1997\A5\Series of 4 books\£2.95 each or £9.99 full set.

Coast to Coast - Scotland   88

Various	Various km

No set route is provided, which is in keeping with the spirit of the annual TGO Challenge, an event which allows for participants to plan their own routes within broad limits. The book by Ronald Turnbull suggests various alternatives.
Not included in map section.

Start	Optional
Finish	Optional
OS maps	Various

Publication(s)
Paperback: *Across Scotland on Foot* by Ronald Turnbull (Grey Stone Books). ISBN:095159964X. 205 x 130\160pp\£5.95(incl p+p).

Coast to Coast - Southern England   89

Various	Various km

Not necessarily inspired by AW but certainly offering alternative coast to coast routes, the two publications provide details of connecting the Bristol and English Channels by mainly taking advantage of established long distance paths. The first listed publication covers 242 miles to finish at Lydd-on-Sea, the second 283 miles at Dover.
Not included in map section.

Start	Weston-super-Mare, Somerset	ST316615
Finish	See text	
OS maps	Book 1: 173, 174, 182, 183, 185, 189, 197, 198, 199.	
	Book 2: 179, 182, 183, 184, 185, 186, 187, 188, 189	

Publication(s)
Booklet: *Channel to Channel* by Ian & Kay Sayer (Kimberley Publishing). 1996\A5\96pp\£3.95.
Paperback: *The Southern Coast-to-Coast Walk* by Ray Quinlan (Cicerone Press). ISBN:1852841176. 1993\116 x 176\200pp\ £6.99.

Coast to Coast - Wales   90

Aberconwy, Caernarfon, Carmarthen, Powys, Swansea	357 km / 222 miles

The walk climbs to and crosses the peaks of the Carneddau and the Glyders before dropping down through the Llanberis Pass then up and over Snowdon, the Moelwyns, the Rhinogs, Cadair Idris and the Tarrens before descending into the Dyfi valley and Machynlleth. The route, by then becoming more wild and remote, passes Bwlch Hyddgen, Plynlimon, Rheidol, and enters the Elan valley. The Carmarthen Fan and the Black Mountain are crossed, continuing over the Lliw Hills, passing to the west of Swansea, on to the Gower and the coast path. See also Cambrian Way.

Start	Llanfairfechan, Aberconwy	SH680750
Finish	Parkmill, Swansea	SS545892
OS maps	115, 124, 135, 136, 147, 159, 160	

Publication(s)
Hardback: *Snowdonia to the Gower* by J Gillham (Diadem/Baton Wickes). 225 x 272\100pp\£16.95 (with paperback route text - £17.95).
Paperback: *A Welsh Coast to Coast Walk - Snowdonia to Gower* by John Gillham (Cicerone Press). ISBN:1852842180. 1996\115 x 174\152pp\£7.99.

Coed Morgannwg Way 91

Merthyr Td, Neath, Rhondda	58 km / 36 miles

The Way, most of which is on Forestry Commission land, meets the Taff Trail at the finish. It crosses part of the Coed Morgannwg, a complex of four upland forests visiting the Dare Valley and Craig y Llyn, climbing to several more viewpoints, to reach Afan Argoed Country Park. From here the route follows less elevated paths past a number of archaeological remains from prehistoric to industrial times. Near to Bodvic Stone the Way links with the Ogwr Ridgeway Walk. See St Illtyd's Walk.

Start	Gethin Woodland Park, Merthyr Td	SO057032
Finish	Margam, Neath	SS814860
On OS maps	170	
Waymark	White footprint on brown background	

Publication(s)
Booklet: *Coed Morgannwg Way* (Neath & Port Talbot County Borough Council). 1995\A5\10pp\£1.00.

Colne Valley - Way & Trail 92

Herts, Gtr London, Surrey	27 km / 17 miles

The Colne Valley Way (10 miles) links the Thames Path at the start with the Grand Union Canal at Cowley Lock near Uxbridge and where it connects with the Colne Valley Trail (7 miles). The earlier part of the route generally avoids the urban development and the Trail mainly runs parallel to the towpath of the Grand Union Canal. At Rickmansworth, use can be made of the Ebury Way (3 miles) to gain access to the Ver-Colne Valley Walk.

Start	Staines, Surrey	TQ025717
Finish	Rickmansworth, Herts	TQ054944
On OS maps	176	
Waymark	Named posts	

Publication(s)
Leaflet: *Colne Valley Way* (Groundwork Thames Valley). 1993\ Free(+SAE).
Leaflet: *Colne Valley Trail* (Groundwork Thames Valley). 1996\ A4/3\Free(+SAE).
Leaflet: *Explore the Ebury Way* (Three Rivers District Council). 1996\A4/3\Free(+SAE).

Community Forest Path 93

Avon   71 km / 44 miles

A route around Bristol using footpaths, tracks and some sections of rural lanes providing a variety of landscapes with views of the Mendip Hills, Severn Estuary and the Severn road bridges. It takes in Ashton Court, Blaise Castle and the Clifton Suspension Bridge. It is coincident with part of the Two Rivers Way and links with the Avon Walkway at Keynsham.

Start and finish	Keynsham, Avon	ST659690
OS maps	172	

Publication(s)
Leaflet: *Community Forest Path* (Forest of Avon). 1998\cost to be announced.

Compo's Way 94

S Yorks, W Yorks   61 km / 38 miles

A route over moors and through country associated with the television series - Last of the Summer Wine.

Start	Hunter's Bar, Sheffield, S Yorks	SK333857
Finish	Sid's Cafe, Holmfirth, W Yorks	SE145083
OS maps	110	

Publication(s)
Paperback: *Compo's Way* by Alan Hiley (Happy Walking International Ltd). ISBN:187475473X. A5\£3.00.
Badge and certificate (£3.00) available from Happy Walking International Ltd.

Cotswold Ring 95

Glos, Heref & Worc   89 km / 55 miles

A route from the spa town of Cheltenham taking in many villages such as Bourton-on-the-Water, Stow-on-the-Wold and Moreton-in-Marsh. Links with the Cotswold Way, Heart of England Way, Windrush Way and Wardens Way.

Start and finish	Cheltenham, Glos	SO237955
OS maps	150, 151, 163	

Publication(s)
Booklet: *The Cotswold Ring* by Christopher Knowles (Reardon Publishing). ISBN:1873877161. 1996\210 x 150\40pp\£2.95 (+50p).

Cotswold Way 96

Avon, Glos, Heref & Worc	166 km / 103 miles

The route is currently the subject of a proposal for upgrading to National Trail status, which would include some improvements to the current line. The Way meanders along the western edge of the Cotswold Hills, mainly following the top of this limestone escarpment, from where there are extensive views over the Severn Vale to the Malverns and the distant hills of the Mendips and the Welsh border, but descending from time to time to visit attractive villages nestling under the shelter of the edge. It crosses stone-walled farming countryside, passing villages and country houses built from the local limestone, and many sites of archaeological interest. See Limestone Link Path/Warden's Way/Windrush Way.

Start	Chipping Campden, Glos	SP152392
Finish	Bath, Avon	ST751647
On OS maps	150, 151, 162, 163, 172	
Waymark	White spot	

Publication(s)
Paperback: *The Cotswold Way* by Anthony Burton (Aurum Press). ISBN:1854103172. 1995\£10.99.
Paperback: *Complete Guide to the Cotswold Way* by Mark Richards (Penguin Books Ltd). ISBN:0140469168. £6.99.
Softback: *Guide to the Cotswold Way* by Richard Sale (Constable and Co Ltd). ISBN:0094691304. 1988\171 x 114\£8.99.
Paperback: *The Cotswold Way* by Kev Reynolds (Cicerone Press). ISBN:1852830498. 116 x 176\168pp\£6.99.
Paperback: *The Cotswold Way* by Mark Richards (Reardon Publishing). ISBN:1873877102. 1995\A5\64pp\£3.95(+50p).
Paperback: *The Magic of the Cotswold Way* by Mollie Harris (Sutton Publishing Ltd). ISBN:0750911891. £8.99.
Booklet: *Cotswold Way Handbook & Accommodation List* Edited by Mavis Rear (RA Gloucestershire Area). ISBN:1901184072. Annual\130 x 225\32pp\£1.50(+50p).
Badge (£1.30/40p) available from RA Gloucestershire Area.

Cotswolds Walk 97

Glos, Heref & Worc, Warks	133 km / 83 miles

Linking many of the north Cotswold villages and other places of interest, this walk, beginning at Shakespeare's birthplace, goes south to Mickleton then on to Chipping Campden. The walk continues to Broadway, Stanton, Blockley, Batsford Arboretum, Stow-on-the-Wold, Upper and Lower Slaughter and Bourton-on-the-Water where it turns to Wood Stanway, Sudeley Castle and Winchcombe.

Start	Stratford-upon-Avon, Warks	SP204549

Finish	Cheltenham, Glos	SO947222
OS maps	150, 151, 163	

Publication(s)
Paperback: *Footpath Touring: Cotswolds* by Ken Ward (Footpath Touring). 221 x 114 \ 64pp \ £3.50.

Cown Edge Way   98

Derbys, Gtr Man	30 km / 19 miles

This generally U-shaped route on the eastern edge of Greater Manchester rises to Cown Edge Rocks via Strines and Mellor, returning via Charlesworth and Werneth Low. There is a mixture of terrain from urban to moorland.

Start	Hazel Grove, Gtr Man	SJ927875
Finish	Gee Cross, Gtr Man	SJ945930
On OS maps	109, 110	
Waymark	Named posts and amber discs and arrows	

Publication(s)
Booklet: *The Cown Edge Way* (RA Manchester Area). 1985 \ A5 \ 29pp \ £1.00.

Cranborne Chase Path   99

Dorset, Wilts	122 km / 76 miles

A route taking in Salisbury Cathedral and Shaftesbury Abbey. A long stretch of Roman road and an old drove road are included giving fine high-level views whilst passing ancient barrows, manor houses and many small villages.

Start and finish	Wimborne Minster, Dorset	SZ009999
OS maps	183, 184, 195	

Publication(s)
Paperback: *Cranborne Chase Path* by Edward Griffiths (Green Fields Books). ISBN:951937626. A5 \ 168pp \ £4.95(+80p).

Cromer to the M11   100

Cambs, Essex, Norfolk, Suffolk	265 km / 165 miles

Using established trails and ancient trackways, this walk follows closely the lines of communication used since prehistoric times to traverse this region of East Anglia. Passing along the Norfolk Heritage Coast, south to Breckland and on into the chalk hills of Cambridgeshire and north Essex, the walk has the M11 motorway as its modern, symbolic end, close to Saffron Walden. In addition to the Peddars Way and Norfolk Coast Path, links are made with the Nar Valley Way and Icknield Way.

Start	Cromer, Norfolk	TG219425
Finish	Audley End, Essex	TL509372
OS maps	132, 133, 144, 154, 155	

Publication(s)
Paperback: *Treading Gently from Cromer to the M11 -Cromer to Wells-next-the-Sea* by C Andrews & D Dear (Pathway Publishing). ISBN:952662817. 1996\A5\32pp\£2.25.
Paperback: *Treading Gently from Cromer to the M11 -Wells-next-the-Sea to Hunstanton* by C Andrews & D Dear (Pathway Publishing). ISBN:952662825. 1996\A5\28pp\£2.25.
Paperback: *Treading Gently from Cromer to the M11 -Hunstanton to Thetford* by C Andrews & D Dear (Pathway Publishing). ISBN:952662833. 1996\A5\32pp\£2.25.
Paperback: *Treading Gently from Cromer to the M11 -Thetford to M11* by C Andrews & D Dear (Pathway Publishing). ISBN:952662841. 1997\A5\28pp\£2.25.

Crooked Spire Walk 101

Shrops, Worcs	35 km / 22 miles

A route from Wyre Forest passing through Buckridge, Bayton, Cleobury Mortimer (the scene for the crooked spire) and Shakenhurst.

Start and finish	Bewdley, Worcs	SO752740
OS maps	138	

Publication(s)
Looseleaf: *Crooked Spire Walk* (Eric Perks). Free (+9" x 6" SAE). Certificates (£1.00/SAE) available from Eric Perks.

Cross Bucks Way 102

Beds, Bucks	38 km / 24 miles

A route mainly through agricultural land linking the Oxfordshire Way, at Stratton Audley, with the North Bucks Way, at Addington, and the Swan's Way at Swanbourne.

Start	Stratton Audley, Bucks	SP609260
Finish	Linslade, Beds	SP912262
On OS maps	164, 165	
Waymark	Named standard waymarks	

Publication(s)
Leaflet: *Cross Bucks Way* (Buckinghamshire County Council).
A4/3 \ Free(+SAE).

Crowthorn Crawl   103

Lancs	43 km / 27 miles

A walk in the West Pennine Moors skirting the reservoir country
north of Bolton taking in Darwen Tower, Snig Hole, Irwell Vale and
Stubbins Wood.

Start and finish	Clough Head Information Centre, Lancs	SD752232
OS maps	103, 109	

Publication(s)
Looseleaf: *Crowthorn Crawl* (Margaret Griffiths). Free(+9" x 4"
SAE).
Badge (£1.50/SAE) available from Margaret Griffiths.

Cuckoo Walk   104

Gtr Man, W Yorks	29 km / 18 miles

A strenuous and at times boggy upland circuit via Wessenden
Reservoir, Black Hill and White Moss and is partly coincident with
the Pennine Way and several of the walks in this area.

Start and finish	Marsden, W Yorks	SE049116
OS maps	110	

Publication(s)
Looseleaf: *The Cuckoo Walk* (D E Wilkins). Free(+6" x 4" SAE).
Badge and certificate (£0.90/£0.10/ 6" x 4" SAE) available from D
E Wilkins.

Cuckoo Way   105

Derbys, Notts, S Yorks	74 km / 46 miles

A walk along the 220yrs old Chesterfield Canal, known locally as
the Cuckoo Dyke. It ceased to be used commercially in the 1950s.
Efforts are being made to restore the canal, but in some places the
path is overgrown and occasionally difficult to find on the ground.
The path passes through or close to Staveley, Worksop and Ret-
ford.

Start	Chesterfield, Derbys	SK338717
Finish	West Stockwith Lock, Notts	SK786946
OS maps	112, 119, 120	
Waymark	Canal company plaque	

Publication(s)
Paperback: *A Walkers' and Boaters' Guide to the Chesterfield Canal and Cuckoo Way* by Christine Richardson and John Lower (Hallamshire Press). ISBN:1874718253. 1994\£5.95.

Cumberland Way 106

Cumbria	129 km / 80 miles

The Way takes a meandering route from the Irish Sea across the historic county of Cumberland and the Lake District National Park to reach the former Westmorland boundary and the old market town of Appleby. It avoids the mountain summits and follows old tracks and footpaths, providing a safe route across the open fells, over passes and along lakesides. The Way visits Strands, Wast Water, Black Sail Pass, Buttermere, Keswick, Castlerigg stone circle, Aira Force, Brougham Castle and Cliburn.

Start	Ravenglass, Cumbria	SD083963
Finish	Appleby-in-Westmorland, Cumbria	NY683203
OS maps	89, 90, 91, 96	

Publication(s)
Softback: *Cumberland Way* by Paul Hannon (Hillside Publications). ISBN:1870141113. 1990\175 x 115\88pp\£5.99.

Cumbria Coastal Way 107

Cumbria, Lancs, Dumfries & Gall	305 km / 189 miles

The route follows the Cumbrian coast from the Lancashire boundary to the Scottish border. There are links with the Lancashire Coastal Way, the Coast to Coast route at St Bees, and the proposed Hadrian's Wall Path National Trail at Bowness on Solway.

Start	Silverdale, Lancs	SD461749
Finish	Gretna, Dumfries & Gall	NY315670
On OS maps	85, 89, 96, 97	
Waymark	Named posts (Milnthorpe - Carlisle)	

Publication(s)
Paperback: *The Cumbria Coastal Way: A Walker's Guide* by Ian and Krysia Brodie (Ellenbank Press). ISBN:187355110X. 1994\116 x 175\224pp\£7.99.
Leaflet: *Cumbria Coastal Way* (Cumbria County Council). 1993\A5\Free.
Leaflet: *The Cumbria Coastal Way - Morecambe Bay estuaries* (South Lakeland District Council). A4/3\12pp\Free(+9"x4" SAE).
Leaflet: *West Cumbria Coastal Heritage Trail* (West Cumbria Tourist Initiative). A4/3\Free(+9"x4" SAE).

Cumbria Way 108

Cumbria	112 km / 70 miles

The Way provides a relatively low-level crossing of the Lake District National Park, following tracks and paths along valleys and over passes in the midst of splendid and varied scenery. It passes Coniston Water, Tarn Hows and Dungeon Ghyll and crosses the Stake Pass to Borrowdale, Derwent Water and Keswick. The Way continues to Caldbeck either via Dash Falls or over High Pike, and then follows the Caldew valley to Carlisle.

Start	Ulverston, Cumbria	SD284785
Finish	Carlisle, Cumbria	NY400554
On OS maps	85, 89, 90, 96, 97	
Waymark	Named posts	

Publication(s)
Paperback: *The Cumbria Way* by John Trevelyan (Dalesman Publishing Ltd). ISBN:1855680009. 1994\130 x 200\56pp\£4.95.
Paperback: *The Cumbria Way and the Allerdale Ramble* by Jim Watson (Cicerone Press). ISBN:1852842423. 1997\144pp\£6.99.
Paperback: *Guide to the Cumbria Way* by Phillip Dubock (Miway Publishing). ISBN:0952915014. 1995\200 x 135\72pp\ £3.75(+50p).
Booklet: *Cumbria Way Accommodation Guide* by Phillip Dubock (Miway Publishing). 1996\150 x 105\8pp\£0.60 post free. (Miway Publishing).
Leaflet: *Accommodation Booking Service* (YHA Northern Region). 1997\Free(+SAE).

d'Arcy Dalton Way 109

Oxon, Warks, Wilts	104 km / 65 miles

The Way, devised to mark the RA Golden Jubilee, is named after the late Col WP d'Arcy Dalton who worked for over half a century to preserve rights of way in Oxfordshire. The Way takes a meandering route, first crossing ironstone hills to Epwell and Hook Norton, and then following footpaths and tracks across the limestone uplands of the eastern Cotswolds via Great and Little Rollright, Churchill, Fifield, Great Barrington and Holwell. The river Thames is crossed at Radcot Bridge and the Way continues across the flatter farmland of the Vale of the White Horse, finally climbing to the crest of the chalk ridge of the Oxfordshire Downs, along which the Ridgeway Path runs.

Start	Wormleighton, Warks	SP448518
Finish	Wayland's Smithy, Wilts	SU281853
OS maps	151, 163, 164, 174	
Waymark	Named signs	

Publication(s)
Paperback: *d'Arcy Dalton Way* (Oxfordshire County Council).
1987\210 x 148\60pp\£2.00(+40p).

Daffodil Dawdle   110

Cambs	42 km / 26 miles

A route linking villages to the south-west of Cambridge.

Start and finish	Mill Lane, Cambridge, Cambs	TL447581
OS maps	154	

Publication(s)
Looseleaf: *Daffodil Dawdle* (Bobbie Sauerzapf). Free(+SAE).
Badge and certificate (£1.50/A4 SAE) available from Bobbie Sauerzapf.

Dales Traverse   111

N Yorks	40 km / 25 miles

Based in Upper Wharfedale, the route takes in Kettlwell, Cam Head, Buckden Pike, Litton and Mastiles Lane. Proceeds from sales of badges are donated to a local hospice.

Start and finish	Kilnsey, N Yorks	SD974679
OS maps	98	

Publication(s)
Looseleaf: *Dales Traverse* (Simon Townson). Free(+10" x 7" SAE).
Badge and certificate (£2.00/10" x 7" SAE) available from Simon Townson.

Dales Walk   112

Cumbria, N Yorks	112 km / 70 miles

The walk follows the River Ure upstream to Aysgarth and Hawes, before traversing the dramatic Mallerstang Valley to Kirkby Stephen. The second part of the walk passes Nine Standards Rigg to Keld, continuing east along the River Swale to finish at Richmond. The Walk links with the Pennine Way at Hawes and Keld, and is coincident in parts with both the Coast to Coast Walk and the Yoredale Way.

Start	Leyburn, N Yorks	SE112905
Finish	Richmond, N Yorks	NZ172011
OS maps	91, 92, 98, 99	

Publication(s)
Hardback: *A Dales Walk* by Bob Allen (Michael Joseph).
ISBN:0718141350. 1997\270 x 205\192pp\£16.99.

Dales Way   113

Cumbria, N Yorks, W Yorks	130 km / 81 miles

The Way mainly follows attractive dales through the Yorkshire and Howgill Fells and the south-eastern part of the Lake District. From Ilkley it heads along Wharfedale passing Bolton Abbey, The Strid, Grassington and Buckden before crossing Cam Fell and the Pennine Way to descend to Dentdale. From here, the River Dee is followed to Sedbergh, then the Lune to the Crook of Lune. The Way crosses farmland to reach Burneside and the River Kent, which is traced for several miles before the path branches off to the finish. There are three link routes to the Way: from Leeds (Leeds-Dales Way) and Shipley/Bradford (Shipley-Dales Way), each described in the Stile Publication and Harrogate (Harrogate-Dales Way) - publication listed.

Start	Ilkley, W Yorks	SE117476
Finish	Bowness-on-Windermere, Cumbria	SD402968
On OS maps	96, 97, 98, 104	
Waymark	Named signposts	
User group	Dales Way Association	

Publication(s)
Paperback: *The Dales Way* by Anthony Burton (Aurum Press). ISBN:1854103148. 1995\£9.99.
Paperback: *Dales Way* by Colin Speakman (Dalesman Publishing Ltd). ISBN:1855680726. 1994\200 x 130\72pp\£5.95.
Paperback: *Dales Way Companion* by Paul Hannon (Hillside Publications). ISBN:1870141539. 1997\175 x 115\88pp\£5.99.
Paperback: *The Dales Way* by Terry Marsh (Cicerone Press). ISBN:1852841028. 1992\116 x 176\136pp\£5.99.
Paperback: *The Dales Way Walk - Seven Glorious Days* by Alistair Wallace (Jema Publications). ISBN:1871468531. 1997\A5\96pp\ £5.99.
Booklet: *Dales Way Route Guide* by Arthur Gemmell and Colin Speakman (Stile Publications). ISBN:0906886724. 1996\197 x 120\44pp\£4.00.
Paperback: *The Dales Way - T'Other Way Up* by Ron Shaw (Dunderdale Press). ISBN:0953120902. 1997\180 x 115\84pp\£5.99.
Booklet: *Dales Way Handbook* (Dales Way Association). Annual\ A5\20pp\£1.20.
Stripmap: *The Dales Way* (Footprint).£2.95.
Looseleaf: *Harrogate-Dales Way* (RA Harrogate Group). A4\10pp\£0.50(+SAE).
Badge and certificate (£1.50/ - /£1.50/ -) available from Dales Way Association.

Dambusters Challenge Walk 114

Derbys	32 km / 20 miles

A high level route around Howden, Derwent and Ladybower reservoirs, visiting Win Hill, Alport Castles, Back Tor and Dovestone Tor. There is opportunity for a less arduous 15 miles route.

Start and finish	Ladybower car park, Derbys	SK203680
OS maps	110	

Publication(s)
Booklet: *The Dambusters Challenge Walk* (J Pepperdine). A5 \
15pp \ £2.00(+A5 SAE).
Certificate (£3.00/SAE) available from J Pepperdine.

Danum Trail 115

S Yorks	113 km / 70 miles

Devised to celebrate the RA Diamond Jubilee, this walk explores the open countryside in the outer reaches of Doncaster Metropolitan Borough. A combination of woodlands, nature reserves, country parks, farmland and limestone escarpments with views of the North York Moors and Wolds, there is much of historical interest, Saxon, Roman - even prehistoric.

Start and finish	Dome Leisure Park, Doncaster, S Yorks	SE598017
OS maps	111	
Waymark	Roman centurian	

Publication(s)
Paperback: *The Danum Trail* by David C Ward (RA Doncaster). ISBN:0900613920. 1995 \ 210 x 145 \ 80pp \ £2.95(+70p).
Badge (£2.50/50p) available from Doncaster Tourist Information Centre.

Darent Valley Path 116

Kent	31 km / 19 miles

The River Darent flows from its source in the Greensand hills south of Westerham to join the Thames, north of Dartford. The walk, through a varied landscape: riverside fringed with ancient willows, hop gardens and cornfields, secretive woodlands, downland carpeted with wildflowers and expanses of marshland, has the added attractions of Roman remains, majestic viaducts, historic houses, old mills and picturesque villages with beautiful churches. There is an alternative start point from Chipstead (TQ500561).

Start	Sevenoaks, Kent	TQ522554
Finish	Confluence of Rivers Darent and Thames	TQ542779
On OS maps	177, 188	
Waymark	Stylised tree and river	

Publication(s)
Booklet: *Darent Valley Path* by Lorna Jenner and Elia Lawton (Kent County Council). ISBN:1873010532. 1997\210 x 210\92pp\ £4.95.

Dark Peak Boundary Walk 117

Derbys	131 km / 81 miles

A mainly high-level circuit of the three great moorland masses of Kinder Scout, Bleaklow and Black Hill, the Walk passes Glossop, Marsden, Hathersage and Bradwell, and traverses gritstone edges, moorland, wooded cloughs and stone villages passing numerous reservoirs.

Start and finish	Hayfield, Derbys	SK037869
OS maps	110	

Publication(s)
Looseleaf: *Dark Peak Boundary Walk* (Dave Irons). 1994\A4\ 14pp\£2.00(incl p+p).

Dark Peak Challenge Walk 118

Derbys	38 km / 24 miles

This is a demanding high-level walk taking in Stanage Edge, Derwent Edge, Back Tor, Derwent Reservoir, Win Hill and Bamford. There is 3,300ft of ascent.

Start and finish	Hathersage, Derbys	SK232815
OS maps	119	

Publication(s)
Paperback: *John Merrill's Dark Peak Challenge Walk* by John Merrill (Happy Walking International Ltd). ISBN: 0907496660. 134 x 210\32pp\£3.00.
Badge and certificate (£3.00/post free) available from Happy Walking International Ltd.

Dart Valley Trail 119

Devon	27 km / 17 miles

A route linking Totnes with the South Devon Coast Path comprising east and west banks walks along the River Dart between

Dartmouth and Greenway and a west bank route to Totnes. Ferries at Dartmouth, Dittisham and Totnes cater for the completion of a circular route with a difference.

Start	Dartmouth, Devon	SX879514
Finish	Totnes, Devon	SX806603
OS maps	202	
Waymark	Stylised river and castles	

Publication(s)
Leaflet: *Dart Valley Trail* (Devon County Council). A4/3\3 leaflets\£2.00.

Dartmoor Perambulation   120

Devon	80 km / 50 miles

The Perambulation marks the boundary of the ancient forest of the moor and is one of the oldest and longest walks on Dartmoor. From Cosdon Beacon, the route heads south through Thirlstone, King's Oven, Dartmeet and Ryder's Hill. At Eastern White Barrow the Perambulation reaches its most southerly point. The return journey north passes Nun's Cross, Great Mis Tor and Yes Tor.

Start and finish	Cosdon Beacon, Devon	SX633939
OS maps	191, 202	

Publication(s)
Looseleaf: *Dartmoor's Ancient Boundary Walk* (Ian & Caroline Kirkpatrick). Free(+SAE).
Badge and certificate (£2.00/SAE/£0.30/A4 SAE) available from Ian & Caroline Kirkpatrick.

Denby Way   121

S Yorks, W Yorks	80 km / 50 miles

The Way is situated in the area to the west of the M1, bounded by the River Calder to the north and the River Don to the south. The Way takes in Denby Dale, famous for the giant pie, Penistone, Silkstone, Bretton Park and Emley Moor.

Start and finish	Denby Dale, W Yorks	SE228084
OS maps	110	

Publication(s)
Folder: *Walking in Pie Country* (Yorkshire Footpath Trust). ISBN:1898978026. 1995\210 x 147\26pp\£3.45.

Derby Canal Ring 122

Derbys, Notts	45 km / 28 miles

A walk taking in the Derby, Erewash and Trent & Mersey canals.

Start and finish	Railway Station, Derby	SK362356
OS maps	128	

Publication(s)
Booklet: *Walking the Derby Canal Ring* by John Merrill (Happy Walking International Ltd). ISBN:1874754284. A5\£3.25.
Badge and certificate (£3.00/incl p+p) available from Happy Walking International Ltd.

Derbyshire Twenty Dales Challenge 123

Derbys	60 km / 37 miles

A figure of eight route visiting many well and lesser known dales in the Peak District. There is 4757ft of ascent.

Start and finish	Bakewell, Derbys	SK220687
OS maps	110, 119	

Publication(s)
Booklet: *Derbyshire Twenty Dales Challenge* (J. Pepperdine). 20pp\£2.00.
Certificate (£3.00/incl p+p) available from J. Pepperdine.

Doncastrian Way 124

S Yorks	53 km / 33 miles

A walk around the old County Borough of Doncaster following a route from the urban fringes to open fields, river banks and green lanes towards the settlements of Barnby Dun and Dunsville returning through Sprotbrough and along the River Don.

Start and finish	Doncaster, S Yorks	SE566041
OS maps	111	
Waymark	Named signposts	

Publication(s)
Leaflet: *Doncastrian Way* (W. Hopkin) A5\Free(+SAE).
Badge and certificate (£1.25/A5 SAE) available from W. Hopkin.

Donnington Way 125

| Glos | 99 km / 61 miles |

Based on the real ale brewery of Donnington in Stow-on-the-Wold, the Way's theme is the brewery's 15 pubs and the brewery. It visits the villages of Bourton-on-the-Water, Naunton, Guiting Power, Broadway, Chipping Campden and Moreton-in-Marsh.

Start and finish	Stow-on-the-Wold, Glos	SP192258
OS maps	163	
Waymark	Beer mug	

Publication(s)
Paperback: *The Donnington Way* by Colin Handy (Reardon Publishing). ISBN:1874192006. 1991\A5\44pp\£2.95(+50p).

Dorset Jubilee Trail 126

| Dorset | 145 km / 90 miles |

A trail created to celebrate the RA Diamond Jubilee crossing Dorset, through quiet villages, passing old churches, historic sites and stately homes, offering extensive views of the rolling downs and secret valleys. Links are made with the South West Coast Path, Wessex Ridgeway, Monarch's Way, Macmillan Way and Hardy Way.

Start	Forde Abbey, Dorset	ST362052
Finish	Bokerley Dyke, Dorset	SU050187
On OS maps	183, 184, 193, 194, 195	
Waymark	Combined tree/arrow and name on green background	

Publication(s)
Paperback: *Dorset Jubilee Trail* (RA Dorset). ISBN:1901184048. A5\64pp\£4.00(+£1.00).
Leaflet: *Dorset Jubilee Trail* (Dorset County Council). 1995\A4/3\ Free(+SAE).
Looseleaf: *Dorset Jubilee Trail* (RA Dorset). 1995\A4\£0.50(+large SAE).
Badge (£2.50 + 9" x 6" SAE) available from Richard Jones.

Douglas Way 127

| Gtr Man, Lancs | 58 km / 36 miles |

The Way follows the River Douglas from its source to its confluence with the River Ribble near Hesketh Bank, south of Preston. It descends from the open moorland of Winter Hill to salt marshes, via farmland and urban areas around Wigan where there are many sites of interest to industrial archaeologists.

Start	Winter Hill, Gtr Man	SD661145
Finish	Longton, Lancs	SD458255
OS maps	108, 109	

Publication(s)
Softback: *The Douglas Valley Way* by Gladys Sellers (Cicerone Press). ISBN:1852840730. 1991\116 x 176\64pp\£4.99.
Paperback: *The Douglas Way* by Lawrence Hubbard (RA Bolton Group). 1987\150 x 208\36pp\£3.15.

Downs Link 128

Surrey, W Sussex	59 km / 37 miles

A bridleway link between the two Downs National Trails. From St Martha's Hill on the North Downs Way the Link is over wooded heath and farmland to meet and follow the trackbed of the former Horsham and Guildford direct railway through Cranleigh and the former Shoreham to Itchingfield Junction line through Partridge Green and Bramber, crossing farmland to meet the South Downs Way, and then on to Shoreham-by-Sea.

Start	St Martha's Hill, Surrey	TQ032483
Finish	Shoreham-by-Sea, W Sussex	TQ208060
On OS maps	186, 187, 198	
Waymark	Green/white disc with bridge	

Publication(s)
Paperback: *The South Downs Way and Downs Link* by Kev Reynolds (Cicerone Press). ISBN:1852840234. 116 x 176\136pp\£5.99.
Folder: *Downs Link* (West Sussex County Council). 1996\210 x 147\12pp\£2.00(+SAE).

Ducal Nottinghamshire 129

Derbys, Notts	51 km / 32 miles

Two circular 18-mile bridleways which can be linked together to form this figure-of-eight route through the rolling countryside to the south of Clumber Park, and reaching as far west as Cresswell Crags.

Start and finish	Bothamsall, Notts	SK675734
OS maps	120	
Waymark	Signposts and standard (blue) waymarks	

Publication(s)
Leaflet: *Ducal Nottinghamshire Eastern Circuit* (Nottinghamshire County Council). 1993\A5\Free(+35p).

Leaflet: *Ducal Nottinghamshire Western Circuit* (Nottinghamshire County Council). 1993\A5\Free(+35p).

Duddon Horseshoe   130

Cumbria	32 km / 20 miles

A hard mountain walk for experienced walkers which follows an undulating route around the Duddon Valley to cross both Hard-knott Pass and Wrynose Pass, two of the highest road passes in the Lakeland area.

Start and finish	Seathwaite, Cumbria	NY227950
OS maps	96	

Publication(s)
Looseleaf: *Duddon Horseshoe* (Brian Richmond). Free(+9" x 4" SAE).
Badge and certificate (£0.85/£0.15/SAE) available from Brian Richmond.

Duddon Triangle Walk   131

Cumbria	32 km / 20 miles

A tough mountain walk encircling Duddon Valley and taking in Whitfell and Harter Fell.

Start and finish	Ulpha Bridge, Cumbria	NY196930
OS maps	96	

Publication(s)
Looseleaf: *Duddon Triangle Walk* (Brian Richmond). Free (+9" x 4" SAE).
Badge and certificate (£1.00/SAE) available from Brian Richmond.

Dunford Round   132

S Yorks	37 km / 23 miles

One of a series of walks, this route crosses Thurlstone Moors and visits Dunford Bridge.

Start and finish	Flouch Inn, S Yorks	SE197016
OS maps	110	

Publication(s)
Booklet: *Dunford Parish Footpaths* (Allen Pestell). 1997\£1.00(+9" x 6" SAE).

Durham Railway Paths   133

Durham	92 km / 57 miles

A network of former railway lines which have been reclaimed for use by walkers, horseriders and cyclists. The network comprises the *Derwent Valley Walk* (11 miles), *Lanchester Valley* (12 miles), *Waskerley Way* (7 miles), *Deerness Valley* (8 miles), *Brandon-Bishop Auckland* (9 miles), *Tees Rail Way* (6 miles) and *Auckland Way* (4 miles). With the exception of the latter two, they can be linked to provide extended linear walks.

Start and finish	Various	Various
OS maps	87, 88, 92, 93	

Publication(s)
Folder: *Railway Paths in County Durham* (Durham County Council). 1997\A5\16pp\£2.25(+£0.50 p&p).

Durham Round   134

Durham	250 km / 155 miles

A route which basically follows the boundary of County Durham and takes in such as the City of Durham, Beamish, Cow Green Reservoir, the River Tees and the coastline.

Start and finish	Durham	NZ270426
OS maps	87, 88, 92, 93	

Publication(s)
Paperback: *The Durham Round* by Jill Delaney (Printability Publishing Ltd). ISBN:187223917X. 1997\A5\78pp\£5.95(+£1.00).

Dyfi Valley Way   135

Caernarfon, Cardigan, Powys	175 km / 109 miles

The Dyfi (English Dovey) valley is one of the most beautiful valleys in Wales. This route follows the north side of the Dyfi through Pennal and the Centre for Alternative Technology at Llwyngwern Quarry. Across the site of King Arthur's last battle at Camlan, the Way takes in the strenuous climb up to the summit of Aran Fawddwy, which at 2,971ft is the highest peak south of Snowdon. At Llanuwchllyn the route retraces its steps south of the Dyfi through Llanymawddwy and Machynlleth.

Start	Aberdyfi, Caernarfon	SN614959
Finish	Borth, Cardigan	SN609901
OS maps	124, 125, 135, 136	
Waymark	Letters DVW in shape of salmon	

Publication(s)
Paperback: *A Guide to the Dyfi Valley Way* by Laurence Main
(Western Mail & Echo). ISBN:1900477009. 1996\130 x 210\82pp\
£7.95(+£1.00).

East Devon Way 136

| Devon | 64 km / 40 miles |

A route that follows the estuary of the river Exe to Lympstone and
then turns east over the commons and rolling hills of the East
Devon AONB via Harpford, Sidbury, Farway and Colyton. It can
be combined with part of the South West Coast Path to form a
circular walk.

Start	Exmouth, Devon	SX999814
Finish	Uplyme, Devon	SY333933
On OS maps	192, 193	
Waymark	Foxglove (logo of AONB)	

Publication(s)
Booklet: *The East Devon Way* by Norman Barns (Devon County
Council). 1993\60pp\£5.50.

East Riding Heritage Way 137

| E Yorks, N Yorks | 136 km / 84 miles |

This is the overall name given to four linked walks devised by Glen
Hood, and now under the auspices of the East Yorkshire Group,
LDWA. The walks are:
Beverley Twenty - 20 miles from the Humber Bridge car park to
the Beverley Minster. Initially along the Humber Estuary and then
following a meandering north-easterly course (with variations
available), on field paths and tracks across flat to gently undulating farmland. Links also with Wolds Way and Trans-Pennine Trail.
Hutton Hike - 23 miles from Beverley Minster to Driffield, along
farmland and riverside paths, dykes, and a Yorkshire Water nature
reserve, passing through Arram, Cranswick and Hutton to Driffield.
Rudston Roam - 21 miles from Driffield to Bridlington following
river, beckside and field paths over level to gently undulating
farmland, visiting a number of villages with historical interest,
including Nafferton, Burton Agnes and the Rudston monolith.
Headland Walk - 20 miles from Bridlington to Filey along the
chalk cliffs of the Heritage coast to Flamborough Head and the
RSPB reserve at Bempton giving spectacular views, before the
final promenade along the sea shore at Filey, with an alternative
finish at the Brigg where it connects with the Cleveland and Wolds
Ways.

Start	Hessle (Point), E Yorks	TA026253
Finish	Filey Brigg, N Yorks	TA126817
OS maps	101, 106, 107	
Waymark	Standard waymarks with path initials	

Publication(s)
Looseleaf: *East Riding Heritage Way* by Glen Hood (Glen Hood). 1993\A4\9pp\Free(+SAE).
Badge and certificate for East Riding Heritage Way (£1.00/SAE/ £0.15/9"x6" SAE) available from Glen Hood.
Individual route badges - each (£0.60/SAE) available from Glen Hood.

East Thriding Treble Ten 138

E Yorks	48 km / 30 miles

A figure-of-eight route over the southern chalk wolds of East Yorkshire, it crosses farmland and mixed woodland, going through attractive dales and visiting Brantingham, South Cave and North Cave.

Start and finish	Welton, E Yorks	SE959272
OS maps	106	

Publication(s)
Looseleaf: *East Thriding Treble Ten* (Kim Peacock). Free(+9" x 4" SAE).
Badge (£1.00/9" x 4" SAE) available from Kim Peacock.

Ebbw Valley Walk 139

Caerphilly, Blaenau	26 km / 16 miles

The Walk goes through forests and woodlands, exploring the industrial history, farming techniques and local superstitions associated with the valley. The way-marked Raven Walk - a 12 miles circular, based on the Cwmcarn Forest Drive Visitor Centre, crosses the Ebbw Valley Walk to the west of the centre. The Sirhowy Valley Walk can be linked at Full Moon Visitor Centre.

Start	Full Moon Centre, Crosskeys, Caerphilly	ST223917
Finish	Festival Park, Ebbw Vale, Blaenau	SO169078
OS maps	161, 171	
Waymark	Blue & orange named circles with beech husk	

Publication(s)
Booklet: *The Ebbw Valley Walk* (Caerphilly County Borough Council). 1996\98 x 210\24pp\£1.25.
Booklet: *The Raven Walk* by Islwyn Access Network (Caerphilly County Borough Council). 1995\A5\10pp\£1.00.

Badge available for Raven Walk - free on completion, details in booklet.

Ebor Way 140

N Yorks, W Yorks	112 km / 70 miles

A relatively gentle walk, taking its name from Eboracum, Roman York. From Helmsley it heads southwards to Hovingham and crosses undulating farmland to Strensall, from where the river Foss is followed to York. The city is crossed on the path along its medieval walls and is left along the banks of the river Ouse. At Tadcaster the route turns west and continues along the Wharfe valley and the Ainsty bounds to Wetherby and Harewood. Here the Way climbs to the gritstone outcrops of the Chevin and Cow and Calf Rocks on the edge of Ilkley Moor before descending to Ilkley in Wharfedale.

Start	Helmsley, N Yorks	SE611839
Finish	Ilkley, W Yorks	SE117476
On OS maps	100, 104, 105	
Waymark	Ebor Way signposts	

Publication(s)
Folder: *The Ebor Way* by J K E Piggin (Yorkshire Footpath Trust). ISBN:1872881009. 1990\204 x 117\22pp\ £2.70.
Badge (£1.50+SAE) available from Yorkshire Footpath Trust.

Edale Skyline 141

Derbys	35 km / 22 miles

A route visiting Lose Hill, Mam Tor, Jacob's Ladder and Win Hill.

Start and finish	Hope, Derbys	SK168836
OS maps	110	

Publication(s)
Looseleaf: *Edale Skyline* (William J Lowe). Free(+9" x 4" SAE).
Badge and certificate (£2.00/SAE) available from William J Lowe.

Eden Valley Walk 142

Kent, Surrey	24 km / 15 miles

This walk explores the variety of the Surrey and Kent countryside along the valleys of the River Eden and River Medway, passing through the High Weald AONB and taking in a rolling landscape of rides and valleys with a patchwork of small fields, hedges and broad-leaved woods. Upstream the route traces the River Eden as it meanders through a more level landscape. Historic houses, set in parkland, are passed en route, whilst downstream the route keeps company with the River Medway through Haysden Country Park.

Start	Cernes Farm, Haxted, Surrey	TQ425445
Finish	Tonbridge, Kent	TQ590465
On OS maps	187, 188	
Waymark	Tree, castle, river	

Publication(s)
Booklet: *Eden Valley Walk* edited by Caroline Wing (Kent County Council). ISBN:1873010060. 1991\210 x 210\28pp\£3.45.

Eden Way   143

Cumbria	126 km / 78 miles

The route follows the River Eden from the Solway Firth through quiet countryside to the source on Mallerstang Edge, south of Kirkby Stephen.

Start	Rockcliffe Marsh, Cumbria	NY333619
Finish	Black Fell Moss, Cumbria	SD807998
OS maps	85, 86, 90, 91, 98	

Publication(s)
Paperback: *Eden Way* by Charlie Emett (Cicerone Press). ISBN: 1852840404. 1990\176 x 116\192pp\£5.99.

Elham Valley Way   144

Kent	37 km / 23 miles

The Way explores the variety of countryside along and around the unspoilt Elham Valley in East Kent. It is mainly a valley walk through the Kent Downs occasionally affording striking panoramic views from the chalk hills.

Start	Hythe, Kent	TR165349
Finish	Canterbury, Kent	TR150578
On OS maps	179, 189	
Waymark	Stylised valley & church spire	

Publication(s)
Booklet: *Along and around the Elham Valley Way* by Brian Hart (Kent County Council). ISBN:1873010958. 1997\215 x 215\ 108pp\£4.95.

Epperstone Park to Southwell Minster   145

Notts	32 km / 20 miles

A route through the rolling countryside to the southwest of South-well, it passes through the villages of Halloughton and Morton.

Start and finish	Epperstone, Notts	SK648487
OS maps	120	
Waymark	Signposts and standard (blue) arrows	

Publication(s)
Leaflet: *Epperstone Park to Southwell Minster* (Nottinghamshire County Council). 1993\A5\Free(+35p).

Epping Forest Centenary Walk   146

Essex, Gtr London	24 km / 15 miles

The route was published to mark the centenary of the Epping Forest Act of 1878, which preserved this remnant of the Great Forest of Waltham from development. From Manor Park on the urban fringe, the Walk heads north through a narrow strip of forest to Leytonstone, Highams Park, and the outskirts of Chingford. From here the route becomes more undulating and tree-covered as it passes Connaught Water and High Beach Conservation Centre to reach Epping.

Start	Manor Park Station, Gtr London	TQ419858
Finish	Epping, Essex	TL465012
On OS maps	166, 167, 177	

Publication(s)
Booklet: *Epping Forest Centenary Walk: Manor Park - Epping* by Fred Matthews and Harry Bitten (Epping Forest Information Centre). ISBN:0852030215. 1992\A5\16pp\£1.00(+30p).

Esk Valley Walk   147

N Yorks	56 km / 35 miles

This route through the North York Moors National Park starts with a circular walk over Danby and Westerdale moors from Castleton to the source of the river at Esklets, and then follows the river valley through Glaisdale and Grosmont to the sea. There is a variety of countryside from open moorland to riverside pastures.

Start	Blakey, N Yorks	SE683989
Finish	Whitby, N Yorks	NZ900117
OS maps	94, 100	
Waymark	Leaping salmon emblem	

Publication(s)
Booklet: *Esk Valley Walk* (North York Moors National Park).
ISBN:090748039X. 1992\120 x 170\32pp\£2.95.
Booklet: *Regional Routes Accommodation Guide* (North York
Moors National Park). Annual\120 x 170\12pp\Free(+SAE).
Badge (£0.75/SAE) available from North York Moors National
Park.

Eskdale Way 148

Cleveland, N Yorks	134 km / 83 miles

A varied circuit of the fields, woodlands, moors and country lanes
of Eskdale, from the fishing port of Whitby along the northern side
of the valley via Glaisdale and Commondale and looping over the
Guisborough Moors before returning to the valley at Kildale. The
return route meanders along or near the south side of the dale,
looping south to visit Wheeldale and Goathland before returning
to Whitby.

Start and finish	Whitby, N Yorks	NZ900117
OS maps	94	

Publication(s)
Folder: *Eskdale Way* by Louis S Dale (Yorkshire Footpath Trust).
1998 - price TBA.

Essex Country to the Coast 149

Essex	45 km / 28 miles

A walk across the breadth of Essex, taking in many different
aspects of the Essex countryside, including farmland, riverside
paths, ancient woodlands and a river valley. Attractive buildings
along the walk are plentiful.

Start	Bures, Essex	TL906340
Finish	West Mersea, Essex	TM001128
OS maps	168	

Publication(s)
Booklet: *The Essex Country to the Coast Walk* by John Edwards
(John Edwards Footpath Guides). 1995\120 x 190\16pp\
£1.49(incl p+p).
Certificate (free/SAE) available from John Edwards Footpath
Guides.

Essex Way 150

| Essex | 130 km / 81 miles |

The Way heads across gently undulating agricultural land, passing through or near many attractive old villages including Willingale, Pleshey, Coggeshall, Dedham, which has connections with the painter John Constable, and Manningtree where it takes to the Stour Estuary. To celebrate the 21st year of the Essex Way, the Ridley Round (13 miles) was created. Taking in part of the Essex Way this walk visits such parishes as Great and Little Waltham. See Beating the Bounds/Stour Valley Path (East Anglia).

Start	Epping, Essex	TL465012
Finish	Harwich, Essex	TM259329
On OS maps	167, 168, 169	
Waymark	Named green discs and posts	

Publication(s)
Booklet: *The Essex Way - Guide & Accommodation List* (Ways through Essex). ISBN:1852810874. 1994\A5\32pp\£3.00.
Leaflet: *The Ridley Round* (Ways through Essex). 1993\A5\ Free(+SAE).

Exe Valley Way 151

| Devon | 72 km / 45 miles |

This route from the Exe Estuary to the steeply wooded valleys on Exmoor follows, for the most part, quiet country lanes and footpaths along the Exe Valley through Bickleigh, Tiverton and Bampton.

Start	Starcross, Devon	SX977817
Finish	Hawkridge, Devon	SS861307
On OS maps	181, 192	
Waymark	Named discs with stylised V symbol	

Publication(s)
Leaflet: *The Exe Valley Way* (Devon County Council). 210 x 98\ 24pp\£1.00.

Exmoor & Lorna Doone 152

| Devon, Somerset | 161 km / 100 miles |

A walk taking in some of the most attractive scenery of the National Park and the countryside in which the novel Lorna Doone is set, passing Dunkery Beacon (at 1,703ft, the highest point on Exmoor), then to Dulverton, Withypool via the famous Tarr Steps, Simonsbath and down through the Doone valley.

Start	Dunster, Somerset	SS992437
Finish	Lynmouth, Devon	SS724494
OS maps	180, 181	

Publication(s)
Paperback: *Footpath Touring: Exmoor and Lorna Doone* by Ken Ward (Footpath Touring). ISBN:0711701954. 1985\224 x 114\ 64pp\£3.50.

Famous Highland Drove Walk 153

Highland, Perth	290 km / 180 miles

A walk tracing one of the routes taken by the cattle drovers from Skye, through seven mountain ranges, along riversides, quiet glens and wild mountain passes, to the mart at Crieff, Perthshire.

Start	Glenbrittle, Highland	NG411211
Finish	Crieff, Perth	NN863218
OS maps	32, 33, 34, 41, 50, 51, 52, 57, 58	

Publication(s)
Paperback: *The Famous Highland Drove Walk* by Irving Butterfield (Grey Stone Books). ISBN:0951599658. 1996\A5\128pp\ £9.95.

Fen Rivers Way 154

Cambs	27 km / 17 miles

The route follows the well drained floodbanks of the rivers linking Cambridge with Ely. There are plans to extend the Way through Norfolk to King's Lynn, where it will then be possible to link with the Peter Scott Walk (10 miles) along the western edge of the Great River Ouse, to the Wash. See also Nene Way.

Start	Cambridge, Cambs	TL462572
Finish	Ely, Cambs	TL546800
OS maps	132, 143, 154	
Waymark	Name and eel logo	

Publication(s)
Folder: *The Fen Rivers Way* (Cambridge County Council. 1995\ A5\36pp\£2.50(incl p+p).
Leaflet: *The Peter Scott Walk* (Norfolk County Council). A4/3\ Free(+SAE).

Fife Coast Path 155

Edin, Fife	132 km / 82 miles

The Fife Coast Path keeps faithfully to the shore between the Forth
Road Bridge and St Andrews Bay, though, for convenience, this
route starts and finishes at railway stations. It includes numerous
castles, fishing villages, remarkable rock formations, caves and
long sandy beaches. The coast is a haven for bird life and flora.
Apart from an exposed chain walk at Kincraig Point, the walking
is easy, though times of high tide are best avoided in some places
as the walk uses the foreshore. The Kingdom of Fife Council are
in the process of developing relevant services for the route.

Start	Dalmeny Station, Edin	NT139779
Finish	Leuchars Station, Fife	NO449207
OS maps	59, 65, 66	

Publication(s)
Hardback: *The Fife Coast* by Hamish Brown (Mainstream Publish-
ing Co Ltd). ISBN:1851586083. 1994\155 x 232\226pp\£12.99.
Leaflets: *Fife Coastal Path* (Kingdom of Fife). Due for publication
Summer 1998.

Fife Walks 156

Fife	306 km / 190 miles

A series of ten interconnecting walks in Fifeshire, they being:
Kincardine to Ballingry (23 miles), *Colinswell to Wester Balgedie*
(23 miles), *Dunfermline to Kirkcaldy* (18 miles), *Balfarg to Ab-
ernethy* (14 miles), *East Wemyss to Kettlebridge* (9 miles), *Crail to
Gateside* (38 miles), *Boarhills to Leven* (22 miles), *Ceres to Luthrie*
(13 miles), *Dairsie to Gauldry* (11 miles) and *Tayport to Newburgh*
(20 miles). The publication includes details of several short walks
in the area.

Start and finish	Various	Various
OS maps	58, 59, 65, 66	

Publication(s)
Paperback: *Fife and Kinross-shire Walks* by Owen Silver (Owen
Silver). ISBN:095139830X. 1997\141 x 255\84pp\£3.00(+50p).

Flitch Way 157

Essex	24 km / 15 miles

A route along a former railway line through countryside taking in
wildlife, railway cuttings and Victorian railway stations.

Start	Start Hill, Bishops Stortford, Essex	TL525214
Finish	Braintree, Essex	TL759230
OS maps	167	

Publication(s)
Leaflet: *Flitch Way* (Essex Ranger Service). 118 x 210\12pp\ Free(+SAE).

Flower of Suffolk   158

Suffolk	42 km / 26 miles

A route using coastal and heathland paths. There is also a choice of shorter 10 and 17 miles circuits.

Start and finish	Walberswick, Suffolk	TM498746
OS maps	156	

Publication(s)
Looseleaf: *Flower of Suffolk* (Bobbie Sauerzapf). Free(+9" x 4" SAE).
Badge and certificate (£1.50/SAE) available from Bobbie Sauerzapf.

Forest of Bowland Challenge Walk   159

Lancs	42 km / 26 miles

A route in the southern area of the Forest of Bowland taking in three summits - Beacon Fell, Parlick and Fair Snape. Langden Beck links them together. There are no facilities on the route.

Start and finish	Beacon Fell, Lancs	SD565426
OS maps	103	

Publication(s)
Paperback: *Forest of Bowland Challenge Walk* by John Merrill (Happy Walking International Ltd). ISBN:1874754500. A5\£3.00.
Badge and certificate (£3.00) available from Happy Walking International Ltd.

Forest Way   160

Essex	40 km / 25 miles

The Way links two forests and several open spaces in south-west Essex. From the edge of Epping Forest it runs north over farmland, from where there are views over the Lea valley, and crosses Latton and Harlow Commons to Hatfield Heath, Woodside Green and Hatfield Forest.

Start	Loughton Station, Essex	TQ423956
Finish	Takeley Street, Essex	TL534213
On OS maps	167, 177	
Waymark	Bright green Forest Way signposts & plaques	

Publication(s)
Paperback: *The Forest Way* (Ways through Essex). ISBN:
1852810238. 1996\A5\14pp\£2.50.

Forest & Worth Ways (Sussex) 161

E Sussex, W Sussex	27 km / 17 miles

Two relatively short routes taking advantage of former railway
lines which are linked and together provide a walk following the
course of the Upper Medway Valley, through the High Weald AONB
to East Grinstead (Forest Way - 10miles) and then on to the Worth
Way (7miles) through Crawley Down.

Start	Groombridge, E Sussex	TQ530371
Finish	Three Bridges, W Sussex	TQ280375
On OS maps	187, 188	
Waymark	Named signs	

Publication(s)
Leaflet: *The Forest Way* (East Sussex County Council). A4/3\
Free(+SAE).
Leaflet: *The Worth Way* (West Sussex County Council). 1997\
A3/6\Free(+SAE).

Formartine and Buchan Way 162

Aberdeenshire	87 km / 54 miles

Former railway lines which have been developed for leisure use.
The main route links Fraserburgh with Dyce (Aberdeen) - 38 miles.
At Maud there is a spur - 16 miles, through Mintlaw to Peterhead.

Start	Parkhill, Dyce, Aberdeenshire	NJ884128
Finish	Fraserburgh, Aberdeenshire	NJ994667
On OS maps	30, 38	
Waymark	Initials F & BW	

Publication(s)
Leaflet: *The Formartine and Buchan Way* (Aberdeenshire County
Council). A4/3\Free(+SAE).

Foss Walk 163

N Yorks	45 km / 28 miles

The Walk follows footpaths along or near the river Foss, from its confluence with the Ouse in the historic city of York to its source at Pond Head, four miles from the finish. The Walk passes through Strensall, Sheriff Hutton, Crayke and Oulston.

Start	York, N Yorks	SE603522
Finish	Easingwold, N Yorks	SE528698
On OS maps	100, 105	
Waymark	Named signposts and named arrows with frog logo	

Publication(s)
Booklet: *The Foss Walk* by Mark W Jones (Maxiprint). 1994\210 x 135\16pp\£2.35(incl p+p).

Founders Footpaths 164

Surrey	40 km / 25 miles

A route around the Surrey Hills visiting sites associated with the founding of the LDWA, including Steer's Field and Blatchford Down, both named in memory of the founders of the Association.

Start and finish	Steer's Field, Surrey	TQ141504
OS maps	186, 187	

Publication(s)
Leaflet: *Founders Footpaths* (Ann Sayer). 1997\12pp\Free(+9" x 6" SAE).
Certificate (£1.00/post free) available from Ann Sayer.

Four Pikes Hike 165

Gtr Man, Lancs, W Yorks	72 km / 45 miles

A route over moors and farmland via the Pikes of Rivington, Hoglaw, Thievely and Stoodley.

Start	Great House Barn, Lancs	SD628139
Finish	Hebden Bridge, W Yorks	SD992273
OS maps	103, 109	

Publication(s)
Looseleaf: *The Four Pikes Hike* (Derek Magnall). Free(+SAE).
Badge and certificate (£1.50/ - /SAE) available from Derek Magnall.

Frome Valley Walkway 166

Avon	22 km / 14 miles

The Walkway links the northern outskirts of Bristol to the Cotswold Way by way of Frampton Cotterell, Yate and Chipping Sodbury. It passes through sandstone gorges, and by old mills, before rising to the Jurassic limestone of the Cotswolds.

Start	Frenchay, Avon	ST640772
Finish	Old Sodbury, Avon	ST752812
On OS maps	172	
Waymark	Kingfisher logo	

Publication(s)
Booklet: *Frome Valley Walkway* (Bristol City Council). 1993\100 x 180\28pp\Free.

Furness Way 167

Cumbria	121 km / 75 miles

A coast to coast across southern Lakeland linking with the Westmorland Way, Cumberland Way and Cumbria Way and exploring High Furness, it passes through the Lyth Valley, Cartmel, Coniston, the Duddon Valley and Eskdale.

Start	Arnside, Cumbria	SD455787
Finish	Ravenglass, Cumbria	SD083963
OS maps	89, 96, 97	

Publication(s)
Paperback: *Furness Way* by Paul Hannon (Hillside Publications). ISBN:187014127X. 1994\175 x 115\104pp\£5.50.

Gallo Way Round 168

Dumfries & Gall, Ayrshire	80 km / 50 miles

A high-level route, with 12,500ft of ascent over 30 tops in the three main ranges of the Galloway Hills. Views are extensive from the route which dips into the skirts of the forestry plantations three times. The bulk of the way is over the tops with only odd traces of path, and will test navigation skills. The mixed terrain can be very tough through heather, bog and rocks with short turf above 2,000ft.

Start and finish	Bruce's Stone, L Trool, Dumfries & Gall	NX415803
OS maps	77	

Publication(s)
Looseleaf: *Gallo Way Round* (Glyn Jones). Free(+SAE).

Certificate (£1.00/SAE) available from Glyn Jones.

Gipping Valley River Path   169

Suffolk	27 km / 17 miles

Connecting with the Mid Suffolk Footpath at Stowmarket, this path mainly follows the towpath of the former Ipswich to Stowmarket Navigation. The remains of eleven locks can be viewed as well as water meadows, gravel pits and water mills.

Start	Stowmarket, Suffolk	TM050588
Finish	Ipswich, Suffolk	TM163439
On OS maps	155, 169	
Waymark	Poppy logo	

Publication(s)
Leaflet: *The Gipping Valley River Path* (Suffolk County Council). A5 \ Free(+SAE).

Glamorgan Heritage Coast   170

Vale of Glamorgan, Bridgend	22 km / 14 miles

A coastal route of ecological diversity taking in rocky and sandy beaches, sand dunes and cliffs.

Start	Gileston, Vale of Glamorgan	SS026672
Finish	Newton Point, Bridgend	SS836775
OS maps	170	

Publication(s)
Leaflet: *Glamorgan Heritage Coast* (Glamorgan Heritage Coast Centre). 1996 \ A4/3 \ free(+SAE).

Glevum Way   171

Glos	42 km / 26 miles

A route around the outskirts of the City of Gloucester, It was devised by the Gloucester Ramblers Group as part of the RA Diamond Jubilee celebrations.

Start and finish	Castle Meads, Glos	SO826185
OS maps	162	
Waymark	Named discs with letters GW	

Publication(s)
Leaflet: *The Glevum Way* (John Street). 1995 \ A3/6 \ £0.50(+40p).

Gloucestershire Way 172

Glos, Monmouth	161 km / 100 miles

A route through the Forest of Dean, Severn Plain and Cotswolds. Links with the Wye Valley Walk at Chepstow, the Wychavon Way at Winchcombe and the Severn Way at Tewkesbury. The guide also provides details of a suggested link with the Worcestershire Way.

Start	Chepstow Castle, Monmouth	ST534941
Finish	Tewkesbury, Glos	SO891324
On OS maps	150, 162, 163	
Waymark	Gloucester Cathedral,river and tree topped hill	

Publication(s)
Paperback: *The Gloucestershire Way* by Gerry Stewart (Countryside Matters). ISBN:0952787008. 1996\210 x 140\128pp\£4.95.

Glyndwr's Way/Ffordd Glyndwr 173

Powys	195 km / 121 miles

Named after Owain Glyndwr, the 15th century warrior/statesman who attempted to establish an independent Welsh nation, the route is by, or close to, many sites connected with his rebellion. It links with Offa's Dyke Path at both ends and passes through Abbey Cwmhir, Llanidloes, Machynlleth, Llangadfan and Hope. There are plans for the Way to become a National Trail with existing road walking vastly reduced.

Start	Knighton, Powys	SO283724
Finish	Welshpool, Powys	SJ229071
On OS maps	125, 126, 135, 136, 137, 147, 148	
Waymark	Yellow arrow on named plaques	

Publication(s)
Softback: *Owain Glyndwr's Way* by Richard Sale (Constable and Co Ltd). ISBN:0094713103. 1992\116x172\206pp\£9.95.
Paperback: *Owain Glyndwr's Way: A Pocket Companion Guide* by Gillian Walker (Management Update Ltd). ISBN:0946679398. 1990\A5\80pp\£4.95(+95p).
Folder: *Glyndwr's Way/Ffordd Glyndwr* (Powys County Council). 1998\A4/3\16pp\£4.00.
Leaflet: *Glyndwr's Way Accommodation List* (Powys County Council). Annual\A4/3\£0.10(+SAE).

Gordon Way   174

| Aberdeenshire | 34 km / 21 miles |

From Bennachie the route takes in forests, farmland and moorlands across several hills. Currently the available publication covers to Suie car park, with the intention to extend the route to Rhynie in due course.

Start	Bennachie Centre, Aberdeenshire	NJ700217
Finish	Rhynie, Aberdeenshire	NJ500270
On OS maps	37, 38	
Waymark	Hexagonal logo with letters GW	

Publication(s)
Leaflet: *Bennachie and The Gordon Way* (Bennachie Project). 1996\A4/3\£0.50.

Grafton Way   175

| Bucks, Northants | 21 km / 13 miles |

This route follows the Grand Union Canal towpath and then through undulating farmland and villages. At Greens Norton there is a link with the way-marked Knightley Way (12 miles), but for which a publication is not available. See North Bucks Way.

Start	Wolverton, Bucks	SP807413
Finish	Greens Norton, Northants	SP671490
On OS maps	152	
Waymark	White circles, black arrows	

Publication(s)
Leaflet: *Grafton Way* (Northamptonshire County Council). 1984\A5\£0.25(+30p).

Grand Union Canal Walk   176

| Bucks, Gtr London, Herts, Northants, W Midlands, Warks | 234 km / 145 miles |

This first national waterways walk was created as part of the celebrations of the 200th anniversary of the creation of the canal companies that later formed the Grand Union Canal. Being almost entirely towpath, it provides much for those interested in canal history. From the centre of London at Little Venice, the canal heads to Slough and then through Hertfordshire and the Chilterns to Tring. Apart from the stretch through Milton Keynes, the route is then largely rural, passing the Canal Museum at Stoke Bruerne, to Leamington Spa and Warwick. The final stretch is through the suburbs of Birmingham. At Startop End near Marsworth the

Aylesbury Arm (6 miles) provides a link to that town, with a similar connection at Bulbourne, the Wendover Arm (6 miles), into Wendover. The Two Ridges Link (8 miles) at Leighton Buzzard gives access to the Ridgeway and the Greensand Ridge Walk. A letterbox scheme of ten checkpoints exists where a special passport can be stamped - details from the Grand Union Canal Project Officer at Braunston. See Beeches Way, Jurassic Way and Colne Valley - Way and Trail.

Start	Little Venice, Paddington, Gtr London	TQ260818
Finish	Birmingham, Gas Street Basin, W Midlands	SP062867
On OS maps	139, 151, 152, 165, 166, 175, 176	
Waymark	Named posts at regular intervals	

Publication(s)
Softback: *Grand Union Canal Walk* by Anthony Burton and Neil Curtis (Aurum Press). ISBN:1854102443. 1993\210 x 130\168pp\ £9.99.
Paperback: *The Grand Union Canal Walk* by Clive Holmes (Cicerone Press). ISBN1852842067. 1996\120pp\£6.99.
Booklet: *Accommodation Guide* (British Waterways - Braunston). 1995/6\A5\52pp\£1.50.
Leaflet: *Exploring the Grand Union Canal* (British Waterways - Braunston). 1996\A5\Free(+SAE).
Leaflet: *The Aylesbury Arm* (Buckinghamshire County Council). A4/3\Free(+SAE).
Leaflet: *Two Ridges Link* (Buckinghamshire County Council). A4/3\Free(+SAE).
Leaflet: *The Wendover Arm* (Buckinghamshire County Council). A4/3\Free(+SAE).
Stripmap: *Grand Union Canal 1: Northen Section* (GEOprojects). ISBN:0863510213. 1995\945 x 428\£3.75.
Stripmap: *Grand Union Canal 2: Central Section* (GEOprojects). ISBN:0863510221. 1995\810 x 428\£3.75.
Stripmap: *Grand Union Canal 3: Southern Section* (GEOprojects). ISBN:086351023X. 1995\810 x 428\£3.75.

Grand Western Canal 177

Devon, Somerset	38 km / 24 miles

A route along the course of the Grand Western Canal which is water filled between Tiverton and Lowdells. Along the dry section, use is made in parts of the actual canal bed. The area abounds in flora and fauna.

Start	Tiverton, Devon	SS955124
Finish	Taunton, Somerset	ST228255
On OS maps	181, 192, 193	

Publication(s)
Booklet: *Grand Western Canal - Mid-Devon Section* (Mid-Devon District Council). A5\16pp\£1.00(+A5 SAE).
Leaflet: *Grand Western Canal Country Park - Devon Section* (Devon County Council). A3/4\£0.25(+SAE).
Booklet: *Exploring the Grand Western Canal in Somerset* (J.Hall and J.Yeates). 1992\A5\24pp\£1.50(incl p+p).
Folder: *In Search of the Grand Western Canal - Somerset Section* (Taunton Deane Borough Council). 1996\168 x 220\20pp\ £3.95(incl p+p).

Grantham Canal 178

Leics, Lincs, Notts	53 km / 33 miles

The Grantham Canal was opened in 1797, and was built to link Grantham with the River Trent at Nottingham. Although the canal is no longer navigable the towpath provides an opportunity to enjoy the countryside in the East Midlands, running through the heart of the Vale of Belvoir and passing through many unspoilt villages. Part of the Leicestershire section has been designated an SSSI.

Start	Nottingham, Notts	SK569392
Finish	Grantham, Lincs	SK908355
OS maps	129, 130	

Publication(s)
Paperback: *Discover the Grantham Canal in Nottinghamshire - full route* (Nottinghamshire County Council). A5\84pp\ £3.75(+35p).

Grasmere Skyline Classic Walk 179

Cumbria	32 km / 20 miles

A high level route taking in Heton Pike, Fairfield, Calf Crag and Blea Rigg.

Start and finish	White Moss Common, Cumbria	NY348065
OS maps	90	

Publication(s)
Looseleaf: *Grasmere Skyline Classic Walk* (Brian Richmond). Free (+9" x 4" SAE).
Badge and certificate (£0.85/£0.15/SAE) available from Brian Richmond.

Great English Walk 180

Numerous	969 km / 602 miles

A journey across England from south-east Wales to north-east England. The route takes in the Forest of Dean, Wenlock Edge, the Cheshire Plain, the Peak District, the lesser used parts of the Yorkshire Dales, Allendale and the Northumbrian towns of Rothbury and Wooler.
Not included in map section.

Start	Chepstow, Monmouth	ST535942
Finish	Berwick-upon-Tweed, Northumb	NT996533
OS maps	75, 80, 81, 87, 92, 99, 103, 104, 110, 117, 118, 119, 126, 138, 149, 150, 162	

Publication(s)
Softback: *The Great English Walk - Volume One. Chepstow to Hathersage* by Margaret & Brian Nightingale (Nightingale Publications). ISBN:0952949016. 1996\210 x 148\192pp\£7.95.
Softback: *The Great English Walk - Volume Two. Hathersage to Berwick-upon-Tweed* by Margaret & Brian Nightingale (Nightingale Publications). ISBN:0952949024. 1997\210 x 148\192pp\ £7.95 (Both volumes together - £15).

Great Glen Way 181

Highland	101 km / 63 miles

A proposed Scottish Long Distance Route which would link the west coast, the end of the West Highland Way at Fort William, along the Great Glen (and Loch Ness) with the east coast at Inverness. The existing route uses forest tracks, the Caledonian canal towpath, and various minor roads avoiding the busy A82 as much as possible.

Start	Fort William, Highland	NN105742
Finish	Inverness, Highland	NH667452
OS maps	26, 34, 35, 41	

Publication(s)
Hardback: *The Great Glen Way* by Heather Connon and Paul Roper (Mainstream Publishing Co Ltd). ISBN:1851588647. 1997\215 x 125\192pp\£9.99.
Paperback: *Scottish Glens - Book 6: The Great Glen* by Peter D Koch-Osbourne (Cicerone Press). ISBN:1852842369. 1997\116 x 175\144pp\£5.99.
Leaflet: *The Great Glen Cycle Route* (Forest Enterprise Northern Scotland). 1993\A4/3\Free.
Stripmap: *Caledonian Canal & the Great Glen* (GEOprojects). ISBN:0863510434. 1997\£3.75.

Great North Forest Trail   182

Tyne & Wear	105 km / 65 miles

The Trail is part of an initiative to improve the countryside in this former mining area. For the present three of the six intended sections are open, covering eastwards from Causey Arch to Hetton-le-Hole. Part of this route connects with the shorter walks, Coalfield Way (10 miles) and Stephenson Trail (10 miles).

Start and finish	Causey Arch, Tyne & Wear	NZ204564
OS maps	88	
Waymark	Name & leaf	

Publication(s)
Leaflet: *Great North Forest Trail - Causey Arch to Pelton* (Great North Forest). 1996\A5\3pp\Free.
Leaflet: *Great North Forest Trail - Pelton to Bournmoor* (Great North Forest). 1996\A5\3pp\Free.
Leaflet: *Great North Forest Trail - Bournmoor to Hetton-le-Hole* (Great North Forest). 1996\A5\3pp\Free.
Folder: *Coalfield Way* (Sunderland City Council). 1997\A4/3\5pp\£1.50(+50p).
Folder: *Stephenson Trail* (Sunderland City Council). 1997\A4/3\5pp\£1.50(+50p).

Green Chain Walk   183

Gtr London	62 km / 39 miles

The Green Chain Walk provides a link between the river Thames and many of the open spaces in South-East London. There are alternative starting points on the Thames and several variations to the route itself and which passes through Oxleas Wood and Mottingham before terminating at Crystal Palace or Chiselhurst. Though there is inevitably some street walking, there is a surprising amount of woodland, grassland, park and garden.

Start	Thamesmead, Gtr London	TQ472813
Finish	Crystal Palace, Gtr London	TQ343705
OS maps	177	
Waymark	GC in form of chain links	

Publication(s)
Booklets: *Green Chain Walk. Thamesmead to Crystal Palace* (Green Chain Working Party). 1995\100 x 210\set of four\20-28pp\Free(+38p A5 SAE).

Green London Way 184

Gtr London	150 km / 93 miles

An urban walk through London suburbs utilising rivers, canals, disused railway lines, alley-ways, parks, commons, woods, and heaths. It descends to the Lea Valley, and thence to East Ham, crossing the river at Woolwich and passing Shooters Hill, Crystal Palace, Streatham Common, Richmond Park, Kew and following a brief stretch along the River Brent, it rises to Harrow-on-the-Hill and Hampstead.

Start and finish	Finsbury Park, Gtr London	TQ315869
OS maps	176, 177	

Publication(s)
Paperback: *Green London Way* by Bob Gilbert (Lawrence and Wishart Ltd). ISBN:0853157464. 1991\155 x 234\195pp\£9.99.

Greensand Ridge Walk 185

Beds, Bucks, Cambs	64 km / 40 miles

A route taking in woods and farmland along the dissected Greensand Ridge passing Woburn Abbey and Ampthill Park where it connects with the Bunyan Trail. At Leighton Buzzard, the Two Ridges Link provides a link via the Grand Union Canal to Ivinghoe Beacon and the Ridgeway/Icknield Way. See Clopton Way.

Start	Leighton Buzzard, Beds	SP915251
Finish	Gamlingay, Cambs	TL226533
On OS maps	152, 153, 165	
Waymark	Letters GRW and deer emblem	

Publication(s)
Leaflet: *Greensand Ridge Walk* (Bedfordshire County Council). A4/3\£0.65(+25p).
Leaflet: *Two Ridges Link* (Buckinghamshire County Council). A4/3\Free(+SAE).

Greensand Way 186

Kent, Surrey	173 km / 107 miles

The Way follows the Greensand ridge across Surrey and Kent. It passes the Devil's Punch Bowl, crosses Hascombe Hill and Winterfold Heath before descending to Dorking. In Kent it crosses Toy's and Ide Hills, descends to Sevenoaks Weald and crosses the Medway Valley to Yalding. Then ascending the ridge, passing through villages, orchards and hop gardens, views over the Weald are achieved. The ridge becomes indistinct beyond Great Chart but the route crosses a rolling landscape of farmland and woodland. The Way meets the Saxon Shore Way at Hamstreet near to the Royal Military Canal.

Start	Haslemere, Surrey	SU898329
Finish	Hamstreet, Kent	TR019349
On OS maps	186, 187, 188, 189	
Waymark	Letters GW in Surrey/oast-house in Kent	

Publication(s)
Booklet: *Along and Around the Greensand Way* by Bea Cowan (Kent County Council or Surrey County Council). ISBN: 1873010915. 1997\210 x 215\132pp\£6.95.

Greenway Challenge Walk 187

Essex	51 km / 32 miles

A walk around Basildon and Billericay, linking country parks and nature reserves, including Westley Heights, Little Burstead Common and Norsey Wood.

Start and finish	Wat Tyler Country Park, Essex	TQ738867
OS maps	178	
Waymark	Standard arrows	

Publication(s)
Leaflet: *Greenway Challenge Walk* (Basildon Greenways). A4\ Free(+SAE).

Gritstone Edge Walk 188

Derbys, S Yorks	43 km / 27 miles

Linear walk running generally downhill along the eastern edge system of the Peak District, taking in Derwent, Stanage, Burbage, Froggatt, Baslow and Chatsworth Edges.

Start	Flouch Inn, S Yorks	SE197016
Finish	Baslow, Derbys	SK256725
OS maps	110, 119	

Publication(s)
Paperback: *Peak District End to End Walks* by John Merrill (Happy Walking International Ltd). ISBN: 0907496393. A5\52pp\£3.00. Badge and certificate (£3.00/post free) available from Happy Walking International Ltd.

Gritstone Trail 189

Cheshire, Staffs	29 km / 18 miles

The Trail follows the gritstone edge providing views of the Peak District and Cheshire Plain with much of the upland walking above 1000ft. The route takes in Sponds Hill, Tegg's Nose Country Park, Croker Hill and the Minns. At Lyme Park the Trail connects with the Ladybrook Valley Walk (10 miles) which in turn, running east to west, crosses the Macclesfield Canal and the Middlewood Way (11 miles). It links with the Staffordshire Way/Mow Cop Trail at Rushton Spencer.

Start	Lyme Park, Cheshire	SJ962823
Finish	Rushton Spencer, Staffs	SJ935625
On OS maps	109, 118	
Waymark	Black bootmark & yellow letter G	

Publication(s)
Paperback: *Gritstone Trail and Mow Cop Trail* by Carl Rogers (Mara Publications). ISBN:0952240947. 1995\135 x 210\68pp\ £4.25.
Booklet: *Gritstone Trail* (Cheshire County Council). 1986\212 x 200\12pp\£1.50(+31p).
Leaflet: *Ladybrook Valley* (Stockport Metropolitan Borough Council). A4/3\6 leaflets\Free.
Leaflet: *Middlewood Way* (Stockport Metropolitan Borough Council). A4/3\Free.

Hadrian's Wall Path 190

Cumbria, Northumb, Tyne & Wear	130 km / 81 miles

Approved for National Trail status, the route will not be fully open until the year 2001 at the earliest. It is intended to create footpaths where none currently exist in order to achieve a route as close to the Wall as is possible, but avoiding interference with remains. For the present, a crossing is available by way of resorting to road walking and/or deviating from the wall using rights of way and minor roads.

Start	Wallsend, Tyne & Wear	NZ304660
Finish	Bowness-on-Solway, Cumbria	NY225628
OS maps	85, 86, 87, 88	

Publication(s)
Paperback: *Guide to Walking Hadrian's Wall* by Graham Mizon (Hendon Publishing Co). ISBN:0860670120. 1993\210 x 135\ 48pp\£2.60(+45p).

Paperback: *Hadrian's Wall: Vol I: The Wall Walk* by Mark Richards (Cicerone Press). ISBN:1852841281. 1993\116 x 176\224pp\ £7.99.
Leaflet: *The Hadrian's Wall Path* (Countryside Commission Postal Sales). 1996\A5/6\Free(+SAE).

Hadrian's Way   191

Tyne & Wear	20 km / 12 miles

A route along the north bank of the River Tyne through the centre of Newcastle to the City Boundary, from where it can be extended along former railway lines to Wylam Bridge. The Keelman's Way (13 miles), an on and off-road route, links Wylam Bridge with Bill Quay City Farm in Gateshead along the south bank of the river. It is anticipated that the Way will ultimately form part of the Hadrian's Wall Path National trail. See Tyne-Wear Trail.

Start	Segendum Fort, Tyne & Wear	NZ301661
Finish	Tyne Riverside Country Park, Tyne & Wear	NZ160657
OS maps	88	
Waymark	Named signs	

Publication(s)
Leaflet: *Hadrian's Way* (Newcastle City Council). Details TBA Summer, 1998.
Looseleaf: *The Keelman's Way* (Gateshead Metropolitan Borough Council). 1994\2pp\Free(+SAE).

Haematite Trail   192

Cumbria	29 km / 18 miles

The Trail was devised to explore some of the remains of the iron mining industry which brought about the industrial expansion of Furness and the subsequent emergence of Barrow. In its heyday the Furness mining industry was an equivalent to the American Gold Rush and provided some of the richest iron ore worked in Britain. The route passes Newton, Little Urswick, Lindal, Marton and Askam.

Start and finish	Barrow-in-Furness, Cumbria	SD190688
OS maps	96	
Waymark	Pithead logo and named posts	

Publication(s)
Leaflet: *The Haematite Trail* (Barrow Tourist Information Centre). A4/3\Free.

Hambleton Hobble 193

N Yorks	50 km / 31 miles

A strenuous route with 2,500ft of ascent based on Black Hambleton, to the west of the North York Moors National Park. It passes through the villages of Osmotherley, Hawnby and Boltby.

Start and finish	Osmotherley, N Yorks	SE461985
OS maps	100	

Publication(s)
Leaflet: *Hambleton Hobble* (Lyke Wake Club). £0.25(+SAE).
Badge (£1.25/SAE) available from Lyke Wake Club.

Hangers Way 194

Hants	34 km / 21 miles

Named after the series of steep-sided hills, the Hampshire Hangers, the route is through wooded and grassed areas and the village of Selborne. It meets with the South Downs Way and Staunton Way at the southern end.

Start	Alton, Hants	SU723397
Finish	QE Country Park, Hants	SU718182
On OS maps	186, 197	
Waymark	Tree on hill	

Publication(s)
Leaflet: *Hangers Way* (Hampshire County Council). A4/3\Free (+SAE).

Hanslope Circular Ride 195

Bucks	32 km / 20 miles

A bridle route to the north of Milton Keynes, the Ride runs through open countryside centred on the village of Hanslope, with its distinctive spire, and gives extensive views over the Ouse and Tove Valleys.

Start and finish	Great Linford, Bucks	SP846424
On OS maps	152	
Waymark	Named standard discs and posts	

Publication(s)
Leaflet: *Hanslope Circular Ride* (Buckinghamshire County Council). Free(+SAE).

Harcamlow Way 196

Cambs, Essex, Herts	227 km / 141 miles

A figure-of-eight walk, mainly on tracks and green lanes passing many places of historic interest, crossing low hills, woods and arable land via Standon and Manuden to meet the cross-over point at Newport. It continues through Saffron Walden and over the low Bartlow Hills to Horseheath and the Fleam Dyke, to enter Cambridge, the return route passing through Melbourn and Chrishall to Newport, continuing via Debden, Thaxted, Takeley and Hatfield Forest.

Start and finish	Harlow, Essex	TL445113
On OS maps	153, 154, 166, 167	

Publication(s)
Booklet: *Harcamlow Way* by Fred Matthews and Harry Bitten (Ways through Essex). A5 \ 52pp \ £2.50.
Badge (£1.00) available from Ways through Essex.

Harden Hike 197

W Yorks	40 km / 25 miles

Using a mix of woodland, fields and moorland paths/tracks, the walk makes a complete circuit of Rombald's Moor, giving extensive views of Airedale and Wharfedale.

Start and finish	Golden Fleece Inn, Harden, W Yorks	SE085084
OS maps	104	

Publication(s)
Looseleaf: *Harden Hike* (Peter Bashforth). Free(+9" x 4" SAE).
Badge and certificate (£1.25/£0.25/9" x 6" SAE) available from Peter Bashforth.

Hardy Way 198

Dorset, Wilts	342 km / 212 miles

The Way explores Thomas Hardy's Wessex and visits many Hardy locations beginning at his birthplace near Dorchester and takes in the Piddle and Frome valleys, an outstanding stretch of coast between Lulworth Cove and the Encombe Valley, to Corfe Castle and Dorchester, ending in Stinsford churchyard where his heart lies buried.

Start	Higher Bockhampton, Nr Dorchester, Dorset	SY728925
Finish	Stinsford Church, Dorset	SY712910
OS maps	183, 184, 193, 194, 195	

Waymark	Named signs

Publication(s)
Paperback: *The Hardy Way - A 19th Century Pilgrimage* by Margaret Marande (Dorset Publishing). ISBN:0948699531. 1995\210 x 148\208pp\£11.50.
Leaflet: *The Hardy Way* (Dorset County Council). 1997\A4/3\ Free(+SAE).

Harrogate Ringway 199

N Yorks	34 km / 21 miles

A trail encircling the spa town at a radius of 3-4 miles, mostly on attractive country paths. Can be divided into shorter stages or linked with Knaresborough Round to form a 36 mile route.

Start and finish	Pannal, N Yorks	SE307514
On OS maps	104	
Waymark	Named signposts	

Publication(s)
Folder: *Harrogate Ringway* (Harrogate Borough Council). 1997\ A4/3\6pp\£2.50.
Leaflet: *Harrogate Ringway* (RA Harrogate Group). A5\4pp\ £0.30(+SAE).
Badge (£1.50/SAE) available from RA Harrogate.

Haslemere Circular Walk 200

Hants, Surrey, W Sussex	36 km / 22 miles

A circuit around Haslemere, with a large proportion of the route crossing National Trust woodland and heathland, including Gibbet Hill, Blackdown, Marley Common, Waggoners Wells and the Devil's Punch Bowl.

Start and finish	Devil's Punch Bowl, Surrey	SU890358
OS maps	186	

Publication(s)
Looseleaf: *Haslemere Circular Walk* by Elizabeth Pamplin (Elizabeth Pamplin). A4\3pp\Free(+SAE).

Haworth-Hebden Bridge Walk 201

W Yorks	30 km / 19 miles

Basically a 14.5 miles circular taking in Leeshaw Reservoir, Hardcastle Crags, Walshaw Dean Reservoirs, Top Withins and Bronte

Bridge, but with extensions into Haworth (1.5 miles) and/or Hebden Bridge (3 miles) catered for.

Start	Haworth, W Yorks	SE032370
Finish	Hebden Bridge, W Yorks	SD993272
On OS maps	103, 104	
Waymark	Named posts	

Publication(s)
Leaflet: *Two Walks Linking Haworth and Hebden Bridge* (Hebden Bridge Tourist Information Centre). A4/3 \ £0.45(+26p).

Heart of Arden Walk   202

Warks	42 km / 26 miles

A route with an historic theme in the Forest of Arden passing through Henley in Arden, Alcester, Ullenhall and other villages/places of interest. It is coincident in parts with the Heart of England Way between Henley and south of Alcester.

Start and finish	Henley-in-Arden, Warks	SP151658
On OS maps	150, 151	
User group	Heart of England Way Association	

Publication(s)
Leaflet: *The Heart of Arden Way* (Peter Ibbotson). A5 \ 2pp \ Free(+9" x 6" SAE).
Certificate (£1.00+SAE) available from Peter Ibbotson.

Heart of Bowland Walk   203

Lancs, N Yorks	29 km / 18 miles

A varied circuit of moorland, steep-sided valleys, rivers and forests in the picturesque Forest of Bowland.

Start and finish	Slaidburn, Lancs	SD714523
OS maps	103	

Publication(s)
Looseleaf: *Heart of Bowland Challenge Walk* (Robert Waller). Free (+9" x 4" SAE).
Badge and certificate (£1.50/10" x 8" SAE) available from Robert Waller.

Heart of England Way 204

Glos, Staffs, Warks	161 km / 100 miles

The Way follows a curving route through gently undulating farm-land, woodland and riverside paths. It takes in Cannock Chase, Lichfield, Kingsbury Water Park, the Arden countryside, the Avon Valley and the northern aspects of the Cotswolds to Chipping Campden, Swell and Low Slaughter. At Bourton-on-the-Water, it connects with the Oxfordshire Way and the Avon Valley Walk (10 miles) provides a link from Stratford-upon-Avon to the Way at Bidford-on-Avon.

Start	Milford, Staffs	SJ975212
Finish	Bourton-on-the-Water, Glos	SP170209
On OS maps	127, 128, 139, 140, 150, 151, 163	
Waymark	Green and white HEW Logo	
User group	Heart of England Way Association	

Publication(s)
Paperback: *Heart of England Way* by John Roberts (Walkways/Quercus). ISBN:0947708316. 1995\210 x 145\124pp\£6.45.
Leaflet: *Heart of England Way* (Heart of England Way Association). A4/3\Free(+9" x 4" SAE).
Looseleaf: *Heart of England Way Accommodation List* (Walkways/Quercus). Free(+SAE).
Leaflet: *Avon Valley Walk* (Stratford-upon-Avon District Council). 1993\A4/3\Free(+SAE).
Badge and certificate (£1.20/£1.00/SAE) from Heart of England Way Association.

Helm Wind Walk 205

Cumbria	32 km / 20 miles

The Walk takes its name from the notorious Helm Wind which often rages fiercely on the summit of Cross Fell, at 2,960ft the highest point on the route. Care should be taken when attempting the Walk, especially in poor weather conditions.

Start and finish	Garrigill, Cumbria	NY744417
OS maps	87, 91	

Publication(s)
Looseleaf: *Helm Wind Walk* (LDWA Cumbria Group). Free(+SAE).
Badge and certificate (£1.30/SAE/£0.40/SAE) available from LDWA Cumbria Group.

Hereward Way
206

Cambs, Leics, Lincs, Norfolk, Northants, Suffolk	166 km / 103 miles

The Way links the Viking Way (at Okeham) with the Peddars Way (near to Knettishall Heath). It passes through Stamford, Peterborough and Ely to reach the Brecklands heaths and forests at Brandon and Thetford. There are areas of flat open fenland. See St Edmund Way.

Start	Oakham, Leics	SK861088
Finish	Harling Road Station, Norfolk	TL978879
On OS maps	141, 142, 143, 144	
Waymark	Tiger face, named posts in Leics, double sword logo in Cambs	

Publication(s)
Booklet: *Hereward Way* (Trevor Noyes). 1998. Details from Trevor Noyes.
Leaflet: *Hereward Way - Peterborough to Ely* (Cambridgeshire County Council). 1989\A5\£0.30(A5 SAE).
Leaflet: *Hereward Way - Oakham to Stamford* (Leicestershire County Council). A4/3\£0.50(9" x 4" SAE).

Herriot Way
207

N Yorks	88 km / 55 miles

A route taking in many of the locations referred to in the James Herriot book and based on the Youth Hostels at Aysgarth, Grinton, Keld and Hawes.

Start and finish	Aysgarth Falls Youth Hostel, N Yorks	SE012885
OS maps	92, 98	

Publication(s)
Booklet: *The Herriot Way* (Norman F Scholes). ISBN:0953035700. 1997\A5\40pp\£3.00.
Leaflet: *The Herriot Way - Introduction & Booking Form* (YHA Northern Region). 1997\A4/3\Free(+SAE).

Hertfordshire Chain Walk
208

Gtr London, Herts	140 km / 87 miles

A chain of linking circular walks which stretch from near Crews Hill Station in the London Borough of Enfield to Ashwell Station in Cambridgeshire. Though each walk is complete in itself, they can be combined to provide a walk from London to Cambridgeshire and back. The route runs in a generally northerly direction, passing Cuffley, Little Berkhamsted, Hertingfordbury, Watton at Stone, Cottered and Therfield.

Start and finish	Whitewebbs Park, Gtr London	TQ329998
On OS maps	153, 154, 166, 176, 177	

Publication(s)
Paperback: *Hertfordshire Chain Walk* by East Herts Footpath Society (Castlemead Publications). ISBN:094855536X. 1994\A5\80pp\£4.00.

Hidden Valley Walk 209

Lancs	35 km / 22 miles

This walk around Sabden Valley south of Pendle Hill runs from the centre of Whalley via Nick of Pendle and Newchurch to Blacko, returning via Sabden.

Start and finish	Whalley, Lancs	SD732362
OS maps	103	

Publication(s)
Booklet: *The Hidden Valley Walk* by David Phipps (Carnegie Press). ISBN:1874181063. 1994\135 x 214\28pp\£2.75.

High Hunsley Circuit 210

E Yorks	39 km / 24 miles

A route supported by the Beverley Group of the RA which takes in wooded valleys and a number of villages. It is coincident with sections of the Wolds Way and Beverley 20.

Start and finish	Walkington, E Yorks	SE999368
On OS maps	106, 107	
Waymark	Named signs	

Publication(s)
Leaflet: *High Hunsley Circular* (RA Beverley Group). A4\Free(+9" x 4" SAE).
Badge (£1.00/6" x 4" SAE) available from RA Beverley Group.

High Peak 60 211

Derbys	96 km / 60 miles

A circular walk designed by the New Mills Group to celebrate the RA Diamond Jubilee. The landscape varies from farmland and river valleys to bleak exposed moorland, with a number of steep ascents. See the Ten Church Challenge.

Start and finish	New Mills, Derbys	SK999855
OS maps	110, 119	

Publication(s)
Paperback: *High Peak Hikes* by David Frith (Sigma Leisure).
ISBN:1850584591. 1996\A5\160pp\£6.95.

High Peak Way 212

Derbys, S Yorks	~ 45 km / 28 miles

A walk including 6500ft of ascent over moorland, through Hope, Hathersage and along the Great Ridge between Mam Tor and Lose Hill. The route is not recommended in adverse weather conditions.

Start	Chinley, Derbys	SK038826
Finish	Padley, Derbys	SK251788
OS maps	109, 110, 119	

Publication(s)
Looseleaf: *The High Peak Way* (Alan S Edwards). 20pp\Free(+A5 SAE).
Badge and certificate (£2.25/post free) available from Alan S Edwards.

High Pennine Trail 213

Cumbria	161 km / 100 miles

Devised to celebrate the 25th anniversary of the LDWA and 20th of the West Yorkshire group, a Trail through the heart of the North Pennines traversing some of the wildest terrain in England and visiting 20 Cumbrian fells. The actual manner of completion of this challenge is down to personal choice, there being no fixed route between the fells.

Start	Sedbergh, Cumbria	NY657921
Finish	Alston, Cumbria	NY718465
OS maps	86, 90, 91, 98	

Publication(s)
Looseleaf: *High Pennine Trail* (Tony Wimbush). A5\Free(+SAE).
Certificate available, details from Tony Wimbush.

High Street Stroll 214

Cumbria	48 km / 30 miles

A scenic high-level route over the mountains of the central and eastern Lake District, avoiding tourist spots and visiting Harter Fell, Nabs Moor, Swindale, Mardale and High Street.

Start and finish	Ambleside, Cumbria	NY376045
OS maps	90	

Publication(s)
Looseleaf: *High Street Stroll* (Joyce Sidebottom). Free(+9" x 4" SAE).
Badge and certificate (£2.50/9" x 7" SAE) available from Joyce Sidebottom.

High Weald Landscape Trail 215

Kent, E Sussex, W Sussex	144 km / 89 miles

A walking route through the unique landscape of the High Weald, the centre of the 16th Century iron industry and still the most wooded area of England. The Trail takes in hop gardens, orchards, villages and historic gardens. The route is expected to be completed in 1998 with a route guide available for the whole route from Kent County Council later in the year.

Start	Horsham, W Sussex	TQ179309
Finish	Rye, Kent	TQ918205
OS maps	187, 188, 189	
Waymark	Green named signs with tree & church	

Publication(s)
Leaflet: *The High Weald: Landscape Heritage Trails in West Sussex* (West Sussex County Council). 1997\A5\Free.

High Weald Walk 216

E Sussex, Kent	45 km / 28 miles

The Walk explores the variety of unspoilt countryside around Royal Tunbridge Wells on the borders of Kent and East Sussex and is within the High Weald AONB passing through a rolling landscape of ridges and valleys with a patchwork of small fields, hedges and broadleaved woodland. In addition to the long distance path there are four linked routes from the centre of Royal Tunbridge Wells.

Start and finish	Southborough Common, Kent	TQ575427
On OS maps	188	
Waymark	Hill, path and trees	

Publication(s)
Booklet: *Along and Around the High Weald Walk* by Bea Cowan (Kent County Council). ISBN:1873010443. 1994\210 x 210\56pp\£4.45.

Hillingdon Trail   217

Gtr London	32 km / 20 miles

This route spans the London Borough of Hillingdon from south to north via Ruislip and Harefield.

Start	Cranford Park, Gtr London	TQ043929
Finish	Springwell Lock, Gtr London	TQ103782
OS maps	176	
Waymark	Fingerposts and trail logo	

Publication(s)
Folder: *The Hillingdon Trail* (Hillingdon Borough Council). 1994 \
A5 \ 6pp \ £2.00(+50p).

Holme Valley Circular Challenge Walk   218

W Yorks	38 km / 24 miles

Not the same route as detailed in the next entry, this one involves almost 4,000ft of ascent.

Start and finish	Meltham Infants School, W Yorks	SE093111
OS maps	110	

Publication(s)
Looseleaf: *Holme Valley Circular Challenge Walk* (Norman F Scholes). Free(+9" x 4" SAE).
Badge and certificate (£1.00/9" x 4" SAE) available from Norman F Scholes.

Holme Valley Circular Walk   219

W Yorks	39 km / 24 miles

A walk along the heights around the Holme Valley, it takes in Castle Hill, the villages of Farnley Tyas, Thurstonland, Hepworth, Netherthong and Honley. There is a variety of scenery including many viewpoints.

Start and finish	Berry Brow, W Yorks	SE136137
On OS maps	110	

Publication(s)
Paperback: *Holme Valley Circular Walk* by E S Boocock (Holme Valley Civic Society). 135 x 200 \ 32pp \ £2.00(+50p).

Howden 20   220

E Yorks	32 km / 20 miles

From Howden the walk heads west along the bank of the river Ouse, and north across flat farmland and along the Derwent valley via Asselby and Wressle to Bubwith, from where it meanders southwards over farmland back to Howden.

Start and finish	Howden, E Yorks	SE748283
On OS maps	105, 106	
Waymark	Standard arrows with H20	

Publication(s)
Looseleaf: *Howden 20* (Goole Rambling Club). Free(+9" x 4" SAE). Badge and certificate (£0.50/ - /6" x 4" SAE) available from Goole Rambling Club.

Howdenshire Way   221

E Yorks	26 km / 16 miles

A route around the market town of Howden, the route passes from Eastrington to Saltmarshe and then along the River Ouse to Boothferry where it turns to Asselby and Newsholme.

Start and finish	Eastrington, E Yorks	SE786298
OS maps	105	
Waymark	Standard arrows with white spot	

Publication(s)
Looseleaf: *The Howdenshire Way* (Don Sweeting). A4\5pp\Free (+9"x4" SAE).
Badge and certificate (£1.20/ - /+6"x4" SAE) available from Don Sweeting.

Hyndburn Clog   222

Lancs	50 km / 31 miles

A route around Accrington passing through pastures, moorland villages and close to reservoirs.

Start and finish	Oswaldtwistle, Lancs	SD723277
OS maps	103	

Publication(s)
Leaflet: *Hyndburn Clog* (JJ Allen). A5\£0.20(+9" x 6" SAE).
Badge and certificate (£0.50/£0.60/SAE) available from JJ Allen.

Icknield Way   223

Beds, Bucks, Cambs, Essex, Herts, Suffolk	166 km / 103 miles

From The Ridgeway and using green lanes, farm and forestry tracks the Way follows, as far as is possible, the group of prehistoric trackways which form the Icknield Way along the chalk spine from the Chilterns to Norfolk. Many sights of archeological interest are passed on the route through Luton, Baldock, Royston, Great Chesterfield and Icklingham meeting the Peddars Way at the finish. An alternative route exists avoiding Dunstable and Luton. See St Edmund Way/ Bunyan Trail/ Greensand Ridge Walk/Stour Valley Path (East Anglia) and Lea Valley Walk.

Start	Ivinghoe Beacon, Bucks	SP960168
Finish	Knettishall Heath, Suffolk	TL944807
On OS maps	144, 153, 154, 155, 165, 166	
Waymark	Named disc with neolithic flint axe emblem	
User group	Icknield Way Association	

Publication(s)
Paperback: *Icknield Way Path* (Icknield Way Association). 1993\210 x 148\£4.50.
Paperback: *The Icknield Way Path* by Elizabeth Barrett (Wimpole Books). ISBN:0951601121. A5\48pp\£3.50(+31p).
Booklet: *Accommodation List* (Icknield Way Association). £1.00(+SAE).
Leaflet: *The Icknield Way - Walkers Route* (Cambridge County Council). A4/3\Free(+SAE).

Imber Range Perimeter Path   224

Wilts	48 km / 30 miles

This route is around the perimeter of a military training firing range on Salisbury Plain mainly following the escarpment above Westbury White Horse and passing several Iron Age hill forts. Warning notices must be adhered to.

Start and finish	Westbury, Wilts	ST893510
On OS maps	183, 184	
Waymark	Name of route with cannon logo	

Publication(s)
Looseleaf: *Imber Range Path* (Richard Archard). Free(+9"x6" SAE).
Badge and certificate (£1.50/£0.50/9"x6" SAE) available from Richard Archard.

Inn Way   225

N Yorks	122 km / 76 miles

A walk taking in many Yorkshire Dales attractions, catering for overnight stops at Buckden, Askrigg, Reeth, West Burton, Kettlewell and Grassington. Twenty-six traditional English inns are passed along the Way.

Start and finish	Grassington, N Yorks	SE003641
OS maps	98	

Publication(s)
Paperback: *The Inn Way* by Mark Reid (Ashridge Press). ISBN:1901214052. 1997\A5\136pp\£7.95(+£1.00 p+p).

Irwell Valley Way   226

Gtr Man, Lancs	48 km / 30 miles

The Way links the centre of Manchester with the moors above Bacup and makes use of a former railway line, follows the former Bolton - Bury Canal and through Bury, Ramsbottom and Rawtenstall to the finish where it links with the Rossendale Way.

Start	Manchester (Castlefield), Gtr Man	SJ833976
Finish	Deerplay, Lancs	SD866264
On OS maps	103, 109	
Waymark	Dragonfly	

Publication(s)
Booklet: *The Irwell Valley Way* (Rossendale Borough Council). A4/3\28pp\£0.51.

Isle of Man Coast Path   227

IOM	145 km / 90 miles

The path, circuits the island and, with a few exceptions, stays close to the shoreline and along the clifftops which provide spectacular views and nesting sites for a rich variety of birdlife. Contrasting sections follow roads and promenades through the harbour and resort towns.

Start and finish	Douglas, IOM	SC379754
OS maps	95	
Waymark	White gull and lettering on blue background	

Publication(s)
Paperback: *Isle of Man Coastal Walk: Raad ny Foillan* by Aileen Evans (Cicerone Press). ISBN:0902363956. 1988\116 x 176\ 144pp\£5.99.
Booklet: *Walking the Isle of Man Coastal Path* by John Merrill (Happy Walking International Ltd). ISBN:1874754535. £3.95.
Looseleaf: *Raad ny Foillan: Coastal Footpath & Accommodation List* (Isle of Man Department of Tourism & Leisure). A4\1pp\Free.
Maps: *Isle of Man: North & South - 1:25000* (Isle of Man Department of Tourism & Leisure). 1995\£6.00.
Badge and certificate (£3.00/post free) available from Happy Walking International Ltd.

Isle of Wight Coast Path   228

IOW	104 km / 65 miles

The coastal path completely encircles the island and, with the exception of detours to the west of Thorness Bay and round the Osborne Crown Property at Osborne Bay, stays close to the coast. It is a very varied walk over chalk and sandstone cliffs, through popular holiday resorts and the less crowded inlets, bays, marshes and saltings.

Start and finish	Cowes, IOW	SZ500956
On OS maps	196	
Waymark	Named signs	

Publication(s)
Paperback: *A Walker's Guide to the Isle of Wight* by Martin Collins & Norman Birch (Cicerone Press). ISBN:1852842210. 216pp\ £9.99(+75p).
Paperback: *The Isle of Wight Coast Path* by John Merrill (Happy Walking International Ltd). ISBN:0907496687. 56pp\£3.25.
Paperback: *Isle of Wight Coastal Path Notebook* by Russell & Suzanne Mills (Island Tourist Products). A5\63pp\£5.45(incl p&p).
Folder: *Isle of Wight Coastal Path* (Isle of Wight County Council). 1997\A4/3\4pp\£1.50(+30p).
Badge and certificate (£3.00/post free) available from Happy Walking International Ltd.

Ivanhoe Way   229

Leics	56 km / 35 miles

A route around the north-western area of the county. The castle at Ashby and the surrounding countryside were the setting for the novel of the same name. The route links with the Leicestershire Round at Bagwith/Shakerstone.

Start and finish	Ashby-de-la-Zouch, Leics	SK361165

OS maps	128, 129
Waymark	Named signs

Publication(s)
Leaflet: *Ivanhoe Way* (Leicestershire County Council). A4/3\£0.50
(+9" x 4" SAE).

Jack Mytton Way   230

Shrops	116 km / 72 miles

From the northern edge of Wyre Forest, the Way follows a disused
railway to Highley and the Severn Valley and goes across rolling
farmland to Much Wenlock where it then follows the escarpment
of Wenlock Edge and descends to Church Stretton. It climbs to the
Long Mynd via the Cardingmill Valley, to reach Plowden and Clun
Forest. It runs for a stretch alongside Offa's Dyke before finishing
on the Shropshire/Powys border.

Start	Billingsley, Shrops	SO715835
Finish	Llanfair Waterdine, Shrops	SO246760
On OS maps	127, 137, 138	
Waymark	Horseshoe motif with horse and rider	

Publication(s)
Folder: *The Jack Mytton Way* (Shropshire County Council).
A5\13pp\ £4.99(+£1.00 p&p) - cheques payable to Shropshire
County Council. Available from Shropshire Books.
Booklet: *Jack Mytton Way* by Ian R Jones (Ian R Jones). 1995\
A5\22pp\£1.00(+30p).
Leaflet: *Jack Mytton Way: Shropshire's Long Distance Bridleway*
(Shropshire County Council). 1996\A5\Free.

Jorvic Way   231

N Yorks	104 km / 65 miles

A low-level route around Greater York, the Way passes the sites of
the former Healaugh Priory and the Battle of Marston Moor, Moor
Monkton - the confluence of the Rivers Nidd and Ouse,and the
Moorlands Nature Reserve. Many villages are incorporated into
the walk, with 24 pubs providing ample opportunities for refresh-
ment.

Start and finish	Tadcaster, N Yorks	SE488435
On OS maps	105	
Waymark	Named signs	

Publication(s)
Folder: *Walking in the Countryside around York* (Yorkshire Footpath Trust). 1995\210 x 147\13pp\£3.45.

Jubilee Way (South Gloucestershire)   232

Glos	26 km / 16 miles

Devised to celebrate the RA Golden Jubilee, the Way links the Cotswold Way with the Severn Bridge and hence Offa's Dyke Path. From the Cotswolds, the route skirts to the north of Chipping Sodbury and south of Thornbury, following fieldpaths for most of the way.

Start	Old Sodbury, Glos	ST752812
Finish	Severn Bridge, Glos	ST573893
On OS maps	162, 172	
Waymark	RA rucksack logo with number 50	

Publication(s)
Booklet: *Jubilee Way* (South Gloucestershire County Council). 1992\100 x 178\28pp\Free.

Jurassic Way   233

Lincs, Northants, Oxon	142 km / 88 miles

The Way follows the band of Jurassic Limestone that runs along the northern boundary of Northamptonshire running first along the Oxford Canal and then via Middleton Cheney and Woodford Halse to Braunston on the Grand Union Canal. Here it turns to pass between Market Harborough and Corby, following the Welland Valley to Rockingham with its castle.

Start	Banbury, Oxon	SP462402
Finish	Stamford, Lincs	TF041075
On OS maps	140, 141, 151, 152	
Waymark	Ammonite logo	

Publication(s)
Folder: *Jurassic Way* (Northamptonshire County Council). 1994\ A4/3\3 x leaflets\£1.75(+30p).

Kennet and Avon Walk   234

Avon, Berks, Wilts	135 km / 84 miles

A route linking the Thames at Reading with the west coast and also the Thames Path to the Cotswold Way, following the canal through Thatcham, Hungerford, Pewsey, Devizes, Bradford-on-Avon, Bath and Bristol where advantage is then taken of the Avon Walkway to the finish.

Start	Reading, Berks	SU731738
Finish	Pill, Avon	ST525759

OS maps	172, 173, 174, 175
Waymark	AW logo on Avon Walkway section.

Publication(s)

Paperback: *The Kennet & Avon Walk* by Ray Quinlan (Cicerone Press). ISBN:1852840900. 1991\116 x 176\200pp\£6.99.
Paperback: *Exploring the Kennet and Avon Canal* by Nigel Vile (Countryside Books). ISBN:1853061247. 210 x 150\96pp\£4.95.
Leaflet: *Explore the Kennet & Avon Canal* (British Waterways - Kennet & Avon). 1997\A5\16pp\Free(+A5 SAE).
Leaflet: *Kennet & Avon Canal - Accommodation Guide* (British Waterways - Kennet & Avon). Annual\A5\16pp\Free(+A5 SAE).
Stripmap: *Kennet & Avon Canal* (GEOprojects. ISBN:0863510140. 1995\1260 x 426\£3.75.

Kerry Ridgeway   235

Powys, Shrops	25 km / 16 miles

This route provides scenic walking along the crest of the Kerry Hills, following the line of a prehistoric ridge track known as the Old Road and passing earthworks, tumuli and a motte and bailey castle at Bishopsmoat.

Start	Kerry Hill, Powys	SJ100840
Finish	Bishop's Castle, Shrops	SJ329890
On OS maps	136, 137	

Publication(s)

Leaflet: *Kerry Ridgeway* (Powys County Council). A4/3\£0.40(+9" x 4" SAE).

Kesteven 25   236

Lincs	42 km / 26 miles

A route linking 12 villages in North and South Kesteven districts of Lincolnshire. The walk meanders south and east along or close to the River Witham.

Start and finish	Beckingham, Lincs	SK875538
OS maps	121, 130	

Publication(s)

Looseleaf: *Kesteven 25* (Mike Surr). £0.20(+SAE).
Badge and certificate (£1.50/SAE/£0.20/SAE) available from Mike Surr.

Kett's Country Walk 237

Norfolk	32 km / 20 miles

A walk based on the 16th Century activities of Robert Kett taking in a number of churches, along a meandering route. By using the Norwich Riverside Walk - no publication, a link can be achieved to Marriott's Way. See Upper Tas Valley Walk.

Start	Cringleford, Norfolk	TG200595
Finish	Wymondham, Norfolk	TM109012
On OS maps	134, 144	

Publication(s)
Booklet: *Kett's Country* (Norfolk County Council). 1997\A5\ 12pp\Free(+SAE).

Kielder Water Circuit Challenge Walk 238

Northumb	42 km / 26 miles

A route encircling Kielder Water following paths and forest tracks.

Start and finish	Leaplish Waterside Park, Northumb	NY660877
OS maps	80	
Waymark	Red pawprint inside yellow arrow	

Publication(s)
Folder: *The Kielder Water Circuit Challenge Walk* (Northumbrian Water). 1994\£2.00.
Certificate (£1.00) available from Northumbrian Water.

King's Way 239

Hants	72 km / 45 miles

A walk devised by the Hampshire Area RA in memory of Allan King, one of their early members. The route links the old Roman strongholds of Portchester and Winchester.

Start	Portchester, Hants	SU625044
Finish	Winchester, Hants	SU487293
On OS maps	185, 196	

Publication(s)
Booklet: *King's Way* (RA Hampshire Area). ISBN:086146091X. 1995\A5\48pp\£3.25(+40p).

Kinver Clamber 240

Worc	32 km / 20 miles

From the edge of the Black Country, this walk uses forestry tracks, canal paths, open fieldpaths and ridge paths. It passes Enville with its Hall, Kinver Edge with its rock dwellings, Caunsall and Whittingham. It picks up the Roman Road to return to Stourbridge.

Start and finish	Stourbridge, Worc	SO882840
OS maps	138, 139	

Publication(s)
Looseleaf: *Kinver Clamber* (Eric Perks). Free(+9" x 6" SAE).
Badge and certificate (£2.00/£0.75/9" x 6" SAE) available from Eric Perks.

Kirklees Way 241

W Yorks	118 km / 73 miles

The Way presents a large circle around Huddersfield and mixes the exposed moorland tops with the industrial towns in the valleys crossing the Spen Valley to Oakwell Hall, Dewsbury, Clayton West and the Holme Valley to Marsden.

Start and finish	Scholes, W Yorks	SE167259
On OS maps	104, 110	
Waymark	Named discs and blue letter K	

Publication(s)
Booklet: *A Stroller's Guide to Walks along the Kirklees Way* by C Dexter Ellis (C Dexter Ellis). 1991\A5\40pp\£2.70.
Folder: *The Kirklees Way* (Huddersfield Examiner). 12pp\ £7.50(+£1.00 p+p).

Knaresborough Round 242

N Yorks	32 km / 20 miles

A route passing through the Nidd Gorge and a succession of villages to the north and east of this historic town. Can be divided into two stages or linked with the Harrogate Ringway to form a 36-mile route.

Start and finish	Knaresborough, N Yorks	SE350565
On OS maps	99, 104, 105	
Waymark	Named signposts	

Publication(s)
Leaflet: *Knaresborough Round* (RA Harrogate Group). A5\4pp\
£0.30(+SAE).
Badge (£1.50/SAE) available from RA Harrogate.

Lady Anne's Way   243

N Yorks, Cumbria	161 km / 100 miles

Lady Anne Clifford was born at Skipton Castle in 1590, the last in
line of the great Clifford family. This walk is based on some of the
routes taken by her whilst visiting the many important buildings
of her estate. From the castle, the valleys of Wharfedale and
Wensleydale are explored before traversing the high-level Lady
Anne's Highway at Abbotside Fells, to Mallerstang and the Eden
Valley, passing the castles of Pendragon, Brough and Brougham
Castle, where she died.

Start	Skipton, N Yorks	SD990519
Finish	Penrith, Cumbria	NY515305
OS maps	90, 91, 98, 103, 104	

Publication(s)
Paperback: *Lady Anne's Way* by Sheila Gordon (Hillside Publica-
tions). ISBN:1870141350. 1995\115 x 175\96pp\£5.50(+40p).
Paperback: *Wharfedale to Westmorland* by Aline Watson (Sigma
Leisure). ISBN:1850583676. 1994\150pp\£6.95
Badge (£2.25/post free) available from Sheila Gordon.

Lake District Boundary Walk   244

Cumbria	244 km / 152 miles

A route basically following the boundary of the Lake District
National Park, and generally avoiding the more popular central
areas. *The Lakeland Fringe* publication describes a similar route
(147 miles) from Newby Bridge.

Start and finish	Gilpin Bridge, Cumbria	SD471854
OS maps	89, 90, 96, 97	

Publication(s)
Paperback: *The Lake District Boundary Walk* by Graham K Dug-
dale (Westmorland Gazette). ISBN:0902272950. 1996\A5\
105pp\£4.95.
Paperback: *Exploring The Lakeland Fringe* by R H Gambles and
B Richardson (A G Publications). ISBN:0951473204. 1989\210 x
144\190pp\£3.75(+85p).

Lakeland Challenge Walk   245

Cumbria	29 km / 18 miles

A tough 6,000ft ascent of ten Lakeland peaks in a circular walk from Langdale, firstly via Stickle Tarn and the Langdale Pikes to Esk Hause, followed by the ascent of Scafell Pike, returning via Bowfell, Crinkle Crags and Pike of Blisco.

Start and finish	Dungeon Ghyll, Cumbria	NY295066
OS maps	89, 90	

Publication(s)
Paperback: *John Merrill's Lakeland Challenge Walk* by John Merrill (Happy Walking International Ltd). ISBN 0907496504. 140 x 210 \ 32pp \ £3.00.
Badge and certificate (£3.00/post free) available from Happy Walking International Ltd.

Lakeland Heritage Trail   246

Cumbria	27 km / 17 miles

A route designed to be completed in stages, following paths and fells, and visiting Grange in Borrowdale, Castle Crag, Ashness Bridge and Surprise View. Proceeds of sales to charity.

Start and finish	Moot Hall, Keswick, Cumbria	NY266235
OS maps	89	

Publication(s)
Booklet: *Lakeland Trails* (Tony Wimbush). 1998 \ 210 x 138 \ £5.95(incl p+p).
Badge and certificate available, details from Tony Wimbush.

Lakeland Round   247

Cumbria	203 km / 126 miles

Climbing almost 40,000ft in visiting high fells and waters, the route takes in such as Grasmere, Coniston, Elterwater, Wasdale Head, Buttermere, Braithwaite, Threlkeld and Glenridding.

Start and finish	Grasmere, Cumbria	NY336076
OS maps	89, 90, 96	

Publication(s)
Hardback: *Walking the Lakeland Round* by Tom Lawton (Ward Lock). ISBN:0706372093. 265 x 200 \ 176pp \ £16.99.
Softback: *Walking the Lakeland Round* by Tom Lawton (Ward Lock). ISBN:0706374657. 265 x 200 \ 176 \ £10.99.

Paperback: *Tom Lawton's Lakeland Round* by Tom Lawton (Ward Lock). ISBN:0706374215. 235 x 155 \ 144pp \ £9.99.

Lakeland Top Ten   248

Cumbria	91 km / 57 miles

A route taking in 30,100ft of ascent in reaching the ten highest tops of the Lake District, a challenge not to be under-estimated.

Start and finish	Thirlmere Bridge End, Cumbria	NY315192
OS maps	89, 90	

Publication(s)
Paperback: *The Lakeland Top Ten* by Brian G Smailes (Challenge Publications). ISBN:0952690039. 1997 \ 124 x 185 \ 72pp \ £6.50.
Badge and certificate (£3.50/£0.50/9" x 6" SAE) available from Challenge Publications.

Lakeland Tour   249

Cumbria	167 km / 104 miles

A route taking in Patterdale, Derwentwater, Ennerdale, Eskdale, Borrowdale and Dunnerdale. The publication describes the main (high level) route, and also includes a low level alternative (98 miles).

Start	Staveley, Cumbria	SD469982
Finish	Ambleside, Cumbria	NY376045
OS maps	89, 90, 97	

Publication(s)
Paperback: *A Walking Tour of Lakeland* by Paul Buttle (Amadorn). ISBN:0951934511. 1997 \ 198 x 128 \ 96pp \ £4.99.

Lambourn Valley Way   250

Berks	35 km / 22 miles

The Way runs from the Berkshire Downs near the Uffington White Horse to Newbury along the valley of the River Lambourn connecting the Ridgeway with the Kennet valley. The terrain can be bleak in winter. The route passes through the villages of Lambourn, East Garston, Great Shefford and Boxford.

Start	Uffington Castle, Berks	SU300863
Finish	Newbury, Berks	SU471671
On OS maps	174	
Waymark	Named discs and posts	

Publication(s)
Leaflet: *Lambourn Valley Way* (Berkshire County Council). 1994\
A4/3\Free(+SAE).

Lancashire Coastal Way 251

Lancs	106 km / 66 miles

As the name suggests, a route by and large along the coast with
the odd diversion where necessary. It is intended to link the Way
with the Sefton Coast Path.

Start	Silverdale, Lancs	SD461749
Finish	Freckleton, Lancs	SD437297
On OS maps	97, 102	
Waymark	Gull & wave logo	

Publication(s)
Folder: *Lancashire Coastal Way* (Lancashire County Council).
Details TBA Spring, 1998.
Map: *Lancashire Coastal Way* (Lancashire County Council).
A5\£1.50(+31p).

Lancashire Loop 252

Lancs	209 km / 130 miles

This route keeps to the fields and hills despite passing close to some
densely populated areas, taking in the wild Trough of Bowland, the
attractive Pendle area and historic Ribchester, returning across
the West Pennine Moors.

Start and finish	Croston, Lancs	SD490185
OS maps	103, 108, 109	

Publication(s)
Folder: *The Lancashire Loop* (Frank Atkinson). 1996\A4\50\
£4.30(+70p).

Lancashire Trail 253

Gtr Man, Lancs, Merseyside, N Yorks	113 km / 70 miles

A route linking industrial Lancashire with the Pennine Way, the
Trail passes Billinge, Abbey Lakes, the viewpoints of Ashurst
Beacon and Harrock Hill, Coppull Moor, Blackrod and Rivington
Pike. A relatively low-lying section follows via Abbey village and
Mellor before reaching Whalley and the climb to Pendle Hill, from
where the route descends to Barley. Link routes from the centres
of Wigan, Bolton and Burnley, to and from the Ribble Way at
Sawley, and to the Sandstone Trail are described.

Start	St Helens, Merseyside	SJ512956
Finish	Thornton-in-Craven, N Yorks	SD906484
OS maps	102, 103, 108, 109	

Publication(s)
Paperback: *The Lancashire Trail* (A Richmond). 1990\A5\28pp\ £2.75.

Lancashire Way   254

Cumbria, Gtr Man, Lancs	195 km / 121 miles

A tour of Lancashire with a mixture of moorland, farmland, canal, riverside and coastal area passing Barley, Pendle Hill and Lancaster Castle as well as the towns of Bolton and Burnley..

Start	Bolton, Gtr Man	SD719087
Finish	Arnside, Cumbria	SD461788
OS maps	97, 103, 109	

Publication(s)
Looseleaf: *The Lancs Way Footpath* (Frank Hodson). A4\3pp\2 x 20p stamps.
Certificate (£0.50/SAE) available from Frank Hodson.

Lancashire-Lakeland Link   255

Lancs, Cumbria	114 km / 71 miles

The route takes in canal towpaths, former railway lines, parkland and riverside, providing easy access to castles, pele towers and mansions. The route links with the Dales Way at Burneside.

Start	Preston, Lancs	SD542297
Finish	Windermere, Cumbria	SD414986
OS maps	97, 102	

Publication(s)
Paperback: *The Lancashire-Lakeland Link* by Jack Jowett (Owl Books). ISBN:1873888600. 1994\122 x 182\96pp\£4.99(+50p).

Lancaster Canal   256

Cumbria, Lancs	91 km / 57 miles

A towpath walk from the Ribble across the Fylde and through Lancaster and Carnforth to the Lake District. The Waterwitch 100 looseleaf describes an extension south from Eccles, along the Leeds and Liverpool Canal to Chorley and across country to Preston.

Start	Preston, Lancs	SD526303

Finish	Kendal, Cumbria	SD520931
OS maps	97, 102	

Publication(s)
Paperback: *A Walker's Guide to the Lancaster Canal* by Robert Swain (Cicerone Press). ISBN:1852840552. 1990\116 x 176\ 124pp\£5.50.
Leaflet: *The Lancaster Canal (Lancaster to Kendal)* (South Lakeland District Council). A4/3\12pp\Free(+9"x4" SAE).
Looseleaf: *The Waterwitch 100* (Frank Hodson). 2 x 20p stamps.
Badge and certificate for Waterwitch 100 (£1.00/£0.50/SAE) available from Frank Hodson.

Landsker Borderlands Trail 257

Pembrokeshire   96 km / 60 miles

Landsker is an old Norse word for frontier. The route explores the rural area on the Pembrokeshire/Carmarthenshire border from Llanboidy and Efailwen in the north via Canaston Bridge on the Daugleddau to Landshipping and Lawrenny in the south, returning via Reynalton and Ludchurch. See South of Landsker Trail

Start and finish	Canaston Bridge, Pembrokeshire	SN067152
On OS maps	145, 157, 158	
Waymark	Named disc with Celtic design for logo	

Publication(s)
Leaflet: *The Landsker Borderlands Trail* (SPARC). 1993\A5\Free.

Land's End Round 258

Cornwall   80 km / 50 miles

A walk combining coastal scenery with an attractive rural link to create a challenging circuit. Starting from the south Cornish coast, the route crosses the county to the north coast at St Ives. The South West Coast Path is then followed around Land's End back to Mousehole.

Start and finish	Mousehole, Cornwall	SW470264
OS maps	203	

Publication(s)
Looseleaf: *The Land's End Round* (Dave and Anne Carrivick). A4\ Free(+9" x 4" SAE).
Certificate (£1.00 post free) available from Dave and Anne Carrivick.

Land's End to John O'Groats   259

Numerous	1368 km / 850 miles

There is no set route to this, one of the ultimate walking challenges
in the UK and whatever the chosen route, it will not be less than
850 miles. There are inherent dangers in using lanes/roads but
there are various established long distance routes which can be
taken advantage of to avoid such hazards. The publication listed
describes alternatives and the Land's End to John O'Groats Association is prepared to offer route advice. A second publication from
Andrew McCloy (listed) describes a walk around the coast of
England & Wales (approx 2970 miles/4780 km) which provides
additional alternatives in reaching the border with Scotland. See
Land's End Trail.

Not included in map section.

Start	Land's End, Cornwall	SW343251
Finish	John O'Groats, Highland	ND379734
OS maps	Numerous	
User group	Land's End to John O'Groats Association	

Publication(s)
Paperback: *Land's End to John O'Groats* by Andrew McCloy (Coro-
net). ISBN:0340637501. 1995\128 x 198\285pp\£6.99.
Paperback: *Coastwalk: Walking the Coastline of England & Wales*
by Andrew McCloy (Coronet). ISBN:0340657405. 1997\128 x
198\266pp\£7.99.
Certificate available - details from Lands End to John O'Groats
Association.

Land's End Trail   260

Cornwall, Devon, Somerset, Wilts	480 km / 298 miles

A route from the Ridgeway at Avebury connecting with other long
distance routes as it takes an inland generally high level line
through the South West peninsula. It provides an alternative
option to those routes often used in linking Land's End with
England's central ways.

Not included in map section.

Start	Avebury, Wilts	SU909696
Finish	Land's End, Cornwall	SW343251
OS maps	173, 180, 181, 182, 183, 185, 191, 200, 201, 203, 204	
Waymark	Yellow chevron	

Publication(s)
Booklet: *The Land's End Trail* (R. Preston). 1998\details TBA
Summer 1998.

Booklet: *The Land's End Trail - Accommodation Guide* (R. Preston). 1998\details TBA.

Langbaurgh Loop 261

Cleveland	61 km / 38 miles

The route is along sandy coastland paths; high cliff edges; rich agricultural land; high rugged moors, thick with heather; dense pine forests; and ancient woods. Parts of the route are over little-used footpaths and rights of way, and some knowledge of map reading is required.

Start and finish	Saltburn-by-the-Sea, Cleveland	NZ668216
OS maps	93, 94	
Waymark	Ellipse and callipers	

Publication(s)
Leaflet: *Langbaurgh Loop* (Langbaurgh Loop). A4/3\Free(+9"x4" SAE).
Badge and certificate (£2.50/ - /SAE) available from Langbaurgh Loop.

Lea Valley Walk 262

Beds, Gtr London, Herts	80 km / 50 miles

A route on riverside paths, linking London's Docklands with Dunstable Downs and the Icknield Way, following the course of the river, which is variously spelt Lee and Lea. It incorporates the Lee Navigation towpath, the Upper Lea Valley Walk, and the Cole Green Way west of Hertford. It passes the numerous reservoirs that line the valley through North London. At Hoddesdon, the Stort Navigation branches off to Harlow and Bishop's Stortford and at Ware, the river turns to Hertford before heading to Harpenden and Luton. An urban stretch through Luton finishes on the Icknield Way. The Beane Valley Walk (14 miles) from Walkern, near Stevenage provides a route south to Hertford where it can be linked to the Lea Valley Walk.

Start	Bow Locks, Gtr London	TQ382828
Finish	Luton, Beds	TL061249
On OS maps	166, 176, 177	
Waymark	Named discs with swan logo	

Publication(s)
Folder: *Lea Valley Walk* (Lee Valley Regional Park Authority). 1993\A5\5 leaflets\£1.50(+60p).
Leaflet: *Beane Valley Walk* (Hertfordshire County Council). A4/3\Free(+SAE).

Lead Mining Trail 263

Durham	38 km / 24 miles

A convoluted walk through the Durham moors and valleys, visiting lead mining sites, using the tracks of the old packhorse trails.

Start	Cowshill, Durham	NY856407
Finish	Edmundbyers, Durham	NZ018501
OS maps	87	
Waymark	Named posts	

Publication(s)
Folder: *Lead Mining Trail* (Durham County Council). 1996\125 x 210\3 leaflets\£2.25(+£0.50 p&p).

Leeds Country Way 264

W Yorks	96 km / 60 miles

A route around Leeds some 5-6 miles from the city centre with much of it over green belt land. It takes in the Harewood estate, Barwick-in-Elmet and the outskirts of Wakefield.

Start and finish	Golden Acre Park, W Yorks	SE267417
On OS maps	104, 105	
Waymark	Yellow owl and letters LCW on olive green plaque	

Publication(s)
Leaflets: *Leeds Country Way* (Leeds City Council). A5\4 leaflets\ Free.

Leicestershire Jubilee Way 265

Leics, Lincs	25 km / 16 miles

The Way devised to mark the Queens Silver Jubilee, connects Melton Mowbray with the Viking Way, following a meandering course across pasture and woodland and past old ironstone workings near Eaton, before climbing through woods to Belvoir castle from where there are fine views over the Vale of Belvoir.

Start	Melton Mowbray, Leics	SK756191
Finish	Woolsthorpe, Lincs	SK846387
On OS maps	129, 130	
Waymark	Orb, yellow on brown	

Publication(s)
Leaflet: *Leicestershire Jubilee Way* (Leicestershire County Council). A4/3\£0.20(+9" x 4" SAE).

Leicestershire Round 266

Leics	163 km / 101 miles

The Round is within easy reach of the market towns of Oakham, Melton Mowbray, Loughborough, Hinkley and Lutterworth and through some of the most beautiful and historically interesting parts of the county: including Burrough Hill, Foxton Locks, High Cross, Bosworth battlefield and Charnwood Forest.

Start and finish	Burrough Hill, Leics	SK766115
On OS maps	129, 140, 141	
Waymark	Circle of brown arrows on standard waymarks	

Publication(s)
Paperback: *The Leicestershire Round* (Leicestershire Footpath Association). ISBN:0850223903. 1996\176 x 115\126pp\£5.00.
Badge (£2.50/SAE) available from Leicestershire Footpath Association.

Leland Trail 267

Somerset	45 km / 28 miles

A route through the rolling hills of Somerset from near Stourhead to near Stoke-sub-Hamdon following the route traversed by John Leland during his 16th century survey of Britain. It connects with the Liberty Trail at Ham Hill. See River Parrett Trail.

Start	Alfred's Tower, Somerset	ST745352
Finish	Ham Hill, Somerset	ST478172
On OS maps	183, 193	
Waymark	Bust of John Leland	

Publication(s)
Folder: *Leland Trail* (South Somerset District Council). 1992\A5\14pp\£4.25(+50p).
Leaflet: *An Introduction to the Leland Trail* (South Somerset District Council). 1997\210 x 150\Free(+SAE).

Liberty Trail 268

Dorset, Somerset	45 km / 28 miles

Linking the Leland Trail with the Dorset Coast Path, this route follows the footsteps of people who, in 1685, walked to join the protestant Monmouth rebellion at Lyme taking in Crewkerne and Forde Abbey. For the last stretch through Dorset into Lyme Regis via the Iron Age hillforts of Lamberts and Coneys Castles, it is coincident with the Wessex Ridgeway. See River Parrett Trail.

Start	Ham Hill, Somerset	ST478172
Finish	Lyme Regis, Dorset	SY347922
On OS maps	193	
Waymark	Named signs	

Publication(s)
Folder: *The Liberty Trail* (South Somerset District Council). 1996\
160 x 210\£4.25(+50p).
Leaflet: *An Introduction to the Liberty Trail* (South Somerset
District Council). 1996\210 x 150\Free.

Limestone Dale Walk 269

Derbys, S Yorks	39 km / 24 miles

A route through the limestone dales of the White Peak, via Cun-
ning, Woo, Deep and Horseshoe Dales to Earl Sterndale, and then
Dovedale to Hartington, Milldale and Mapleton.

Start	Buxton, Derbys	SK060735
Finish	Ashbourne, Derbys	SK178469
OS maps	119, 128	

Publication(s)
Paperback: *Peak District End to End Walks* by John Merrill (Happy
Walking International Ltd). ISBN: 0907496393. 140 x 210\52pp\
£3.00.
Badge and certificate (£3.00/post free) available from Happy Walk-
ing International Ltd.

Limestone Link 270

Cumbria	21 km / 13 miles

The Link runs across the limestone country of South Cumbria with
its nationally important flora, through the low wooded hills of the
Arnside area, across the flat open mosses between Hale and
Holme, and over the rocky fells of Clawthorpe and Hutton Roof.

Start	Arnside, Cumbria	SD461788
Finish	Kirkby Lonsdale, Cumbria	SD611789
On OS maps	97	
Waymark	Named discs	

Publication(s)
Leaflet: *The Limestone Link* (South Lakeland District Council).
1994\A4/3\12pp\Free(+9"x4" SAE).

Limestone Link Path 271

Glos, Somerset	58 km / 36 miles

A route from the Cotswold Way at Cold Ashton through St Catherine's valley, along the Kennet and Avon Canal to Dundas Aqueduct and then to the Mendip escarpment past Burrington Combe and Dolebury Warren to the finish where it links with the West Mendip Way (Mendip Ways).

Start	Cold Ashton, Glos	ST751728
Finish	Shipham, Somerset	ST443572
On OS maps	172, 182	
Waymark	Ammonite logo	

Publication(s)
Booklet: *The Limestone Link* (Yatton Ramblers). ISBN: 0951134248. 1995\145 x 205\66pp\£2.50(+£0.40 p&p).

Limestone Lion 272

N Yorks	56 km / 35 miles

A route linking some of the finest limestone features of the Yorkshire Dales, taking in Ingleborough Cave, Horton-in-Ribblesdale, Attermire Cave, Malham and Kilnsey.

Start	Ingleton, N Yorks	SC695730
Finish	Grassington, N Yorks	SE003638
OS maps	98	

Publication(s)
Booklet: *Limestone Lion Walk* by J. Ginesi (Pen-y-ghent Cafe). £1.00(9" x 6" SAE.
Badge (£1.90/SAE) available from Pen-y-ghent Cafe.

Limestone Way 273

Derbys, Staffs	80 km / 50 miles

A recently extended route, the former finish point of Matlock is now the end of a spur to the main Way with a second link created to Ashbourne. Many of the more well known locations of the Peak District are accommodated such as Monyash, Miller's Dale and Robin Hood's Stride. A connection with the Pennine Way can easily be achieved from Castleton and at Rocester it connects with the Staffordshire Way.

Start	Castleton, Derbys	SK150829
Finish	Rocester, Staffs	SK108392
OS maps	110, 119, 128	

Waymark	Derby ram

Publication(s)
Paperback: *Walking the Limestone Way* by R & E Haydock and B & D Allen (Scarthin Books). ISBN:0907758924. 1997\A5\80pp\ £5.50.
Leaflet: *The Limestone Way* (Derbyshire Dales District Council). 1997\A4/3\Free(+SAE).
Badge (£1.00/SAE) available from Derbyshire Dales District Council.

Limey Way   274

Derbys	64 km / 40 miles

A meandering traverse of the limestone countryside of the White Peak area visiting twenty dales including Cave Dale, Monsal Dale, Deep Dales, Lathkill Dale and Dove Dale.

Start	Castleton, Derbys	SK151828
Finish	Thorpe, Derbys	SK157505
OS maps	110, 119	

Publication(s)
Paperback: *Limey Way* by J N Merrill (Happy Walking International Ltd). ISBN:0907496830. 185 x 122\48pp\£3.50.
Badge and certificate (£3.00/post free) available from Happy Walking International Ltd.

Lindsey Loop   275

Lincs	161 km / 100 miles

A figure-of-eight loop, devised by the Lincoln Group of the RA, over the rounded chalk hills of the Lincolnshire Wolds and lowland farmland. It links the six market towns of Market Rasen, Spilsby, Alford, Caistor, Horncastle and Louth.

Start and finish	Market Rasen, Lincs	TF111897
OS maps	113, 121, 122	

Publication(s)
Folder: *Lindsey Loop* (Brett Collier). A4\9pp\£1.80(+SAE).
Badge (£1.25/SAE) available from Brett Collier.

Lipchis Way   276

Hants, W Sussex	42 km / 26 miles

A route across the heaths, woods and farmland of the western Weald over Older Hill and Woolbeding Common to Midhurst and

Heyshott, and across the South Downs via The Trundle to Lavant and Chichester.

Start	Liphook, Hants	SU842309
Finish	Chichester, W Sussex	SU858043
OS maps	186, 197	

Publication(s)
Leaflet: *The Lipchis Way* (Liphook Ramblers). 1985\A4/3\£1.00.

Little John Challenge Walk 277

Notts	45 km / 28 miles

A walk through Sherwood Forest, the heart of Robin Hood country, which includes forests, gorges, meandering rivers and historic houses, and passes Church Warsop, Cuckney, Cresswell Crags, Clumber Park, Bothamsall and Ollerton.

Start and finish	Edwinstowe, Notts	SK626669
OS maps	120	

Publication(s)
Paperback: *The Little John Challenge Walk* by John Merrill (Happy Walking International Ltd). ISBN: 0907496466. 132 x 210\32pp\£3.00.
Badge and certificate (£3.00/post free) available from Happy Walking International Ltd.

London Countryway 278

Berks, Bucks, Essex, Gtr London, Kent, Surrey	331 km / 206 miles

A complete circuit around London keeping from between 13 to 31 miles from the centre. The Way is over the woodlands and heathlands of Surrey and Berkshire, along canal towpaths to Windsor, from where the river Thames is followed to Maidenhead and Marlow. Here it turns to the Chiltern hills to West Wycombe and Great Missenden, and then follows a meandering route to Kings Langley, St Albans, Broxbourne, the Lea valley, Epping Forest and Theydon Bois. The route continues to Brentwood, over the Essex fens to cross the Thames via the Tilbury to Gravesend Ferry, before heading south and then west along the sandstone and chalk hills of Kent and Surrey.

Start and finish	Box Hill, Surrey	TQ173513
OS maps	165, 166, 167, 175, 176, 177, 186, 187, 188	

Publication(s)
Softback: *Guide to the London Countryway* by Keith Chesterton
(Constable and Co Ltd). ISBN:0094639604. 1981\171 x 114\
280pp\£5.95.

London Loop & Capital Ring   279

Gtr London   222 km / 138 miles

Two routes introduced by the London Walking Forum, a group
comprising among others, representatives from all London local
authorities. The Loop (138 miles) will provide a countryside route,
through such as Epping Forest, the Ring (72 miles) an inner
London route linking parks, commons and open spaces. These are
ongoing developments and for the present, publications are available for just four parts of the Loop alone.

Start and finish	Various	Various
OS maps	166, 167, 176, 177, 187	
Waymark	Hovering kestrel (Loop); Big Ben/arrows (Ring)	

Publication(s)
Leaflet: *London Loop - West Wickham Common to Hamsey Green*
(London Walking Forum). 1996\A4/3\Free(+SAE).
Leaflet: *London Loop - Hamsey Green to Farthing Down* (London
Walking Forum). 1996\A4/3\Free(+SAE).
Leaflet: *London Loop - Elstree to Cockfosters* (London Walking
Forum). 1996\A4/3\Free(+SAE).
Leaflet: *London Loop - Jubilee Country Park, Bromley to West
Wickham Common, Bromley* (London Walking Forum). 1997\
A4/3\Free(+SAE).
Leaflet: *Overview of London Loop* by London Walking Forum
(Corporation of London). 1998\Full details TBA.

Longshaw Limber   280

Derbys   48 km / 30 miles

A high level route taking in Stanage Edge, Win Hill, Curbar Edge
and White Edge.

Start and finish	Longshaw, Derbys	SK267801
OS maps	110, 119	

Publication(s)
Booklet: *The Longshaw Limber* (Paul Pugh). A5\Free(+9" x 6"
SAE).
Badge and certificate(£1.80/9" x 6"SAE) available from Paul Pugh.

Lost Lancs Way   281

Cumbria	80 km / 50 miles

A route along the old boundary of Lancashire with Cumberland and Westmorland visiting Duddon Valley, Wrynose Pass, Windermere and Winster Valley.

Start	Green Road Station, Cumbria	SD190840
Finish	Grange-over-Sands, Cumbria	SD412781
OS maps	89, 90, 96, 97	

Publication(s)
Looseleaf: *Lost Lancs Way* (Frank Hodson). 2 x 20p stamps.
Badge and certificate (£1.00/£0.50/SAE) available from Frank Hodson.

Lower Dales Three Hostels Walk   282

N Yorks	51 km / 32 miles

A route based on the youth hostels at Kettlewell, Linton and Malham taking in some of the finest scenery in this popular part of the Yorkshire Dales National Park.

Start and finish	Kettlewell, N Yorks	SD971724
OS maps	98	

Publication(s)
Looseleaf: *Lower Dales Three Hostels Walk* by Martyn Hanks (YHA Northern Region). A4\8pp\£1.00.

Lune Valley Walk   283

Cumbria, Lancs	127 km / 79 miles

A route following the course of the River Lune from its source to the sea, starting from north of the Howgills near to Newbiggin-on-Lune. The River Lune leaflet provides details of links from Lancaster to Morecambe and Glasson.

Start	Greenside, Cumbria	NY712038
Finish	Sunderland Point, Lancs	SD423552
OS maps	91, 97, 102	
Waymark	Named signposts	

Publication(s)
Paperback: *Walking Down The Lune* by Robert Swain (Cicerone Press). ISBN:1852841036. 1992\116 x 176\160pp\£6.99.
Booklet: *Lune Valley Ramble* (Lancaster City Council). A5\12pp\Free(+SAE).

Leaflet: *River Lune* (Lancaster City Council). A4/3\Free(+SAE).
Leaflet: *Lune Valley - Mini guide and accommodation* (Lancaster City Council). A5/Free(+SAE).

Lyke Wake Walk   284

N Yorks	63 km / 39 miles

This classic route was pioneered by the late Bill Cowley in 1955 when much of the route was undefined and whilst this is not now the case, the route provides a strenuous challenge. In the early stages it is coincident in parts with the Cleveland Way and the Coast to Coast route. It has suffered from over-use and subsequent erosion. In an effort to ease the use of the route, alternative challenges are described in the Bill Cowley publication, they being; the *Lyke Wake Way* (50 miles) - a linear route also from Osmotherley to Ravenscar, and the *Shepherds Round* (40 miles) - a strenuous circular route from Scarth Nick.

Start	Osmotherley, N Yorks	SE469994
Finish	Ravenscar,N Yorks	NZ971012
OS maps	93, 94, 99	

Publication(s)
Paperback: *Lyke Wake Walk* by Bill Cowley (Dalesman Publishing Ltd). ISBN: 1855680726. 1993\205 x 135\72pp\£5.95.
Paperback: *The Novices Guide to Completing The Lyke Wake Walk* by Brian G Smailes (Challenge Publications). ISBN:0952690012. A5\£3.25.
Paperback: *The Lyke Wake Walk in Quarter Mile Steps* by Jim Goodman (Minerva Press). ISBN:1861063687. 1997\A5\54pp\£7.99.
Leaflet: *Shepherd's Round* (Lyke Wake Club). A4/3\£0.25(+SAE).
Badge and certificate - Lyke Wake Walk - (£1.25/£0.25/SAE) available from Lyke Wake Club.
Badge - Shepherd's Round - (£1.25/SAE) available from Lyke Wake Club.

Macmillan Way   285

Dorset, Glos, Lincs, Leics, Northants, Oxon, Somerset, Warks, Wilts	467 km / 290 miles

A route devised to raise funds for the Macmillan Cancer Relief and to which all proceeds are donated. It runs along sea banks and river banks, across the Lincolnshire fens via Stamford to Abbotsbury on the Dorset Coast. It provides a link with the Viking Way at Oakham, the Thames Path near Thames Head and with the South-West Coast Path at the finish.

Start	Boston, Lincs	TF327442

Finish	Abbotsbury, Dorset	SY560845
On OS maps	130, 131, 141, 151, 152, 162, 163, 172, 173, 183, 194	
Waymark	Green bow, walk name and the words - Across Country for Cancer Care (both directions)	
User group	Macmillan Way Association	

Publication(s)
Booklet: *The Macmillan Way - Boston to Oakham - Guide & Accommodation* by Peter Titchmarsh (Macmillan Way Association). 1997\130 x 210\28pp\£3.25(incl p+p).
Paperback: *The Macmillan Way Guidebook - Oakham to Abbotsbury* by Peter Titchmarch (Macmillan Way Association). ISBN:0952685108. 1996\130 x 210\96pp\£6.50(incl p+p).
Booklet: *The Macmillan Way Planner & Accommodation Guide - Oakham to Abbotsbury* by Peter Titchmarch (Macmillan Way Association). 1996\12pp\£2.25(no postage if obtained with guide).
Badge and certificate (£2.50\Free\SAE) available from Macmillan Way Association.

Maelor Way 286

Cheshire, Wrexham, Shrops	38 km / 24 miles

The Way links the Sandstone Trail, South Cheshire Way, Marches Way and Shropshire Way at Grindley Brook, to the Offa's Dyke Path at Chirk. It crosses farmland to Hanmer Mere and Overton, then follows woodland trails alongside the Rivers Dee and Ceiriog to Chirk.

Start	Grindley Brook, Cheshire	SJ522433
Finish	Bronygarth, Shrops	SJ263375
On OS maps	117, 126	
Waymark	MW monogram as arrow	

Publication(s)
Paperback: *Guide to the Maelor Way* by Gordon Emery (Gordon Emery). ISBN:1872265987. 1991\A5\126pp\£6.95\Annual update available\Free(+SAE).
Leaflet: *The Maelor Way* (Wrexham County Borough Council). 1997\A4/3\Free.

Maldon Millennium 287

Essex	35 km / 22 miles

Inaugurated as part of the celebrations for the millennium of the town of Maldon in 1991, the Way is a circular around the town at the head of the Blackwater estuary. It visits the site of the battle of Maldon in 991 at the end of the causeway to Northey Island and also the villages of Woodham Mortimer, Woodham Walter, Langford, Great and Little Totham, and Heybridge.

Start and finish	Maldon, Essex	TL853072
OS maps	168	

Publication(s)
Folder: *Walking in and around Maldon* (Ways through Essex).
1992\£2.00.

Malvern Hills Challenge Walk   288

Heref & Worc	32 km / 20 miles

Involving 3,000ft of ascent, this walk around the Malvern Hills
heads south via Little Malvern on the lower slopes and returns
north along the ridge.

Start and finish	Old Wyche, Malvern, Heref & Worc	SO773442
OS maps	150	

Publication(s)
Paperback: *The Malvern Hills Challenge Walk* by John Merrill
(Happy Walking International Ltd). ISBN: 0907496954. A5\32pp\
£3.00.
Badge and certificate (£3.00/post free) available from Happy Walking International Ltd.

Malvern Link   289

Heref & Worc	64 km / 40 miles

This route links the North Worcestershire Path with the Worcestershire Way, with a blend of fieldpaths, country lanes, woodland,
parkland, canal and riverside scenery.

Start	Forhill, Heref & Worc	SP055755
Finish	Cowleigh Park Farm, Heref & Worc	SO766476
OS maps	139, 150	

Publication(s)
Looseleaf: *Malvern Link* by Dave Irons (Dave Irons). 1994\A4\
9pp\£1.50(incl p+p).

Mansell Way   290

Essex	32 km / 20 miles

The Way is dedicated to the memory of Dennis Mansell, photographer, journalist and hill walker. A circular walk, never more than
three miles from the centre of Braintree, visiting the valleys
through which the rivers Pant, Blackwater and Brain flow.

Start and finish	Braintree, Essex	TL761228

OS maps   167

Publication(s)
Booklet: *The Mansell Way* by Edgar Eastall and John Spratling (Braintree & District Outdoor Pursuits). 1993\A5\18pp\ £1.00(+A5 SAE).

Marches Way   291

Cardiff, Cheshire, Heref & Worc, Monmouth, Newport, Powys, Shrops	329 km / 204 miles

A route through the borderland between England and Wales linking the two Roman forts which guarded the Welsh border, Chester and Caerleon. It takes in towns and villages such as Wem, Shrewsbury, Leominster, Abergavenny and Pontypool, mainly following the course of the Whitchurch - Newport railway lines. See also Maelor Way.

Start	Chester, Cheshire	SJ413670
Finish	Cardiff	ST180765
OS maps	117, 126, 138, 149, 161, 171	
Waymark	Named discs in Cheshire only	

Publication(s)
Softback: *The Marches Way* by Les Lumsdon (Sigma Leisure). ISBN:1850582696. 1992\A5\160pp\£6.95.

Marriott's Way   292

Norfolk	34 km / 21 miles

A peaceful and secluded walk along a former railway line near to the River Wensum. At Hellesdon it can be linked with the Norwich Riverside Walk (5 miles) - no publication, and at Aylsham to the Bure Valley Walk (9 miles). The Bickling Hall link path (1 mile) - no publication, near Cawston can be used to connect with the Weavers Way. See Kett's Country Walk.

Start	Hellesdon Bridge, Norfolk	TG198000
Finish	Aylsham, Norfolk	TG195265
On OS maps	133, 134	
Waymark	Brown and cream coloured logo	

Publication(s)
Leaflet: *Marriott's Way* (Norfolk County Council). 1996\A4/3\ Free(+SAE).
Leaflet: *The Bure Valley Walk* (Norfolk County Council). 1995\ A4/3\Free(+SAE).

Medlock Valley Way 293

Gtr Man	20 km / 12 miles

One of several routes developed along Manchester's rivers, the Medlock Valley Way runs from Ducie Street near Piccadilly Station via Clayton Vale, Daisy Nook and Strines Dale to finish at Bishop Park north east of Oldham. The landscape varies from canal stretches through reclaimed areas to clough woodland and open country near the finish.

Start	Manchester (Ducie St), Gtr Man	SJ848981
Finish	Bishop Park, Gtr Man	SD962084
On OS maps	109	
Waymark	Named discs with valley logo	

Publication(s)
Folder: *The Medlock Valley Way* (Oldham Countryside Ranger Service). A5 \ 13pp \ £1.50.

Medway Valley Walk 294

Kent	45 km / 28 miles

A valley walk in west Kent, the route is of interest for its landscape, natural history and archaeology. It passes through a varied landscape of downland, woodland, orchards, hop gardens; meadows and farmland; lakes and marshland; unspoilt villages and historic towns. Links are made with the Eden Valley Walk/Greensand Way/High Weald Walk/North Downs Way/Saxon Shore Way and Wealdway.

Start	Tonbridge, Kent	TQ590465
Finish	Rochester, Kent	TQ741688
On OS maps	178, 188	
Waymark	Kingfisher logo & walk name	

Publication(s)
Booklet: *Medway Valley Walk* by Kev Reynolds (Kent County Council). ISBN:1873010524. 210 x 210 \ 92pp \ £4.95.

Mendip Ways 295

Somerset	79 km / 49 miles

Comprising the *West Mendip* (30 miles) and the *East Mendip* (19 miles) *Ways*, there was involvement in their creation by Rotary Club members. The route of the West passes close to Cheddar Gorge and takes in Wookey Hole, that of the East passing Shepton Mallet. See Limestone Link Path.

Start	Uphill, Somerset	ST315585
Finish	Frome, Somerset	ST777481
OS maps	172, 182, 183	
Waymark	West = Rotary International logo, East = Ash key logo	

Publication(s)
Booklet: *West Mendip Way* by Andrew Eddy (Weston-super-Mare Civic Society). 1998\A5\50pp\Price TBA.
Leaflet: *East Mendip Way* (Somerset Tourism). £1.25.

Mercian Way 296

Cardigan, Powys, Shrops, Staffs	241 km / 150 miles

A route linking castles at either end and crossing the ancient Kingdom of Mercia. The major conurbations such as Birmingham, Ludlow and Bridgnorth are avoided. The Armed Services - The Not Forgotten Association, benefits from sales of the publication.

Start	Tamworth, Staffs	SK213045
Finish	Aberystwyth, Cardigan	SN580816
OS maps	127, 128, 136, 137, 138, 139	

Publication(s)
Looseleaf: *The Mercian Way* (Clive Lungmuss). A4\30pp\£5.00 (+£1.50).

Mid Suffolk Footpath 297

Suffolk	32 km / 20 miles

The path connects the end of the Gipping Valley Path at Stowmarket with the Angles Way on the River Waveney at Hoxne. It broadly follows the valleys of the Rivers Dove and Gipping via Eye, Thorndon and Mendlesham.

Start	Hoxne, Suffolk	TM184782
Finish	Stowmarket Greens Meadow, Suffolk	TM042599
OS maps	155, 156	
Waymark	Named discs with poppy logo	

Publication(s)
Leaflet: *The Mid Suffolk Footpath* (Mid Suffolk District Council). 1998\Price TBA.

Middlesex Greenway 298

Essex, Gtr London, Surrey	69 km / 43 miles

A route across almost the whole of the territorial county passing West Drayton, Uxbridge, Ruislip, Pinner, Mill Hill, Finchley and Enfield. It was designed to heighten public awareness of the county and to help safeguard the Green Belt.

Start	Staines, Surrey	TQ032725
Finish	Waltham Abbey, Essex	TL376005
OS maps	166, 176, 177	

Publication(s)
Looseleaf: *The Middlesex Greenway* by Stephen J. Collins (Stephen J Collins). 1990 \ A4 \ 16pp \ £1.00(+SAE).

Middlewich Challenge Walk 299

Cheshire	35 km / 22 miles

A figure of eight route taking in the Middlewich Canal which links the Trent & Mersey and Shropshire Union Canals.

Start and finish	Church Minshull, Cheshire	SJ667606
OS maps	118	

Publication(s)
Booklet: *The Middlewich Challenge Walk* by John Merrill (Happy Walking International Ltd). ISBN:1874754623. A5 \ £3.25.
Badge and certificate (£3.00/incl p+p) available from Happy Walking International Ltd.

Midshires Way 300

Bucks, Derbys, Gtr Man, Leics, Northants, Notts	362 km / 225 miles

The Way, designed for multi-use, links the Ridgeway with the Trans Pennine Trail. For the most part it follows bridleways and quiet lanes with, wherever possible alternative waymarked footpath routes provided for walkers. In Derbyshire particularly, the bridleway development for other users has yet to be completed. From the end of the Derbyshire section at Whaley Bridge, the route north is coincident with the Goyt Way, (10 miles) - Whaley Bridge to Compstall - and from Compstall, with part of the Etherow-Goyt Valley Way, (12 miles) - Stockport to Woolley Bridge - into Stockport. The Brampton Valley Way (14 miles) is used between Northampton and Market Harborough.

Start	Bledlow, Bucks	SP770012
Finish	Stockport, Gtr Man	SJ893903

On OS maps	109, 110, 119, 128, 129, 141, 152, 165
Waymark	Named discs with letters MW in linked acorn form

Publication(s)
Folder: *The Midshires Way* (Derbyshire County Council). 1994\
A5\12pp\£3.00.
Booklet: *Etherow - Goyt Valley Way* (Stockport Metropolitan Borough Council). A5\16pp\£0.50(+SAE).
Leaflet: *The Goyt Way* (Stockport Metropolitan Borough Council).
A4/3\Free(+SAE).
Leaflet: *Brampton Valley Way* (Northamptonshire County Council). 1993\A4/3\£0.60(+30p).

Millennium Way   301

IOM	45 km / 28 miles

Developed to celebrate the Manx Millennium, the 1000th anniversary of the establishment of Tynwald, the Island's Parliament, the route is based on the Royal Way, an ancient high-level route between Ramsey, and the former capital, Castletown. The Way crosses the island, climbing to open heather moorland on the western slopes of Snaefell to reach the Way's highest point at 1,500ft. From here it descends to Crosby, and follows lowland paths, roads and the banks of the Silverburn river through Ballasalla to the medieval castle of Rushen. From Castletown the waymarked Herring Road/Bayr ny Skiddan (14 miles) provides a link to Peel.

Start	Sky Hill, IOM	SC432945
Finish	Castletown, IOM	SC265675
OS maps	95	
Waymark	Disc waymark with arrow	

Publication(s)
Paperback: *Isle of Man Coastal Walk: Raad ny Foillan* by Aileen Evans (Cicerone Press). ISBN:0902363956. 1988\116 x 176\144pp\£5.99. Includes details of Millennium Way.
Looseleaf: *Millennium Way* (Isle of Man Department of Tourism & Leisure). Free.
Looseleaf: *Raad ny Foillan & Bayr ny Skeddan* (Isle of Man Department of Tourism & Leisure). Free.
Maps: *Isle of Man: North & South - 1:25000* (Isle of Man Department of Tourism & Leisure). 1995\£6.00.

Mini-Alps   302

Worc	32 km / 20 miles

The route takes in Worcestershire Beacon, Old Hollow, Whithams Hill, Hatfield Coppice and Herefordshire Beacon where it follows the ridge path.

Start and finish	Old Wyche, Malvern, Worc	SO773442
OS maps	150	

Publication(s)
Looseleaf: *Mini-Alps* (Eric Perks). Free(+9" x 6" SAE).
Badge and certificate (£2.00/£0.75/9" x 6" SAE) available from Eric Perks.

Minster Way   303

E Yorks, N Yorks	80 km / 50 miles

The Way, linking the two famous medieval Minsters at Beverley and York, crosses farmland and the chalk hills of the Yorkshire Wolds. It follows the Wolds Way across Sylvan Dale before diverting to Millington, Bishop Wilton and Stamford Bridge. Here the River Derwent is followed before the Plain of York is crossed on field and woodland paths to meet and follow the River Ouse to the centre of York.

Start	Beverley, E Yorks	TA038393
Finish	York, N Yorks	SE603522
On OS maps	105, 106, 107	
Waymark	Letters MW on standard waymarks plus named signposts	

Publication(s)
Looseleaf: *The Minster Way* (Ray Wallis). A4 \ 3pp \ £0.50.
Badge (£1.25/SAE) available from Ray Wallis.

Monarch's Way   304

Avon, Devon, Dorset, E Sussex, Glos, Hants, Heref & Worc, Shrops, Somerset, Staffs, Warks, Wilts	981 km / 609 miles

The Way is based on the route taken by Charles II during his escape after the battle of Worcester in 1651, taking in Stratford upon Avon, the Cotswolds, Mendips and the South Coast from Charmouth to Shoreham. The route takes in many historic buildings, features of interest and antiquity, with connections to numerous other long distance routes.

Start	Worcester, Heref & Worc	SO852544
Finish	Shoreham, E Sussex	TQ237046

On OS maps	127, 138, 139, 150, 151, 163, 172, 173, 183, 184, 185, 193, 194, 196, 197, 198
Waymark	Name + crown in oak tree surmounted by ship
User group	Monarch's Way Association

Publication(s)

Paperback: *The Monarch's Way: Worcester to Stratford-upon-Avon* by Trevor Antill (Meridian Books). ISBN:1869922271. 1995\229 x 145\112pp\£5.95(+£1).

Paperback: *The Monarch's Way: Stratford-upon-Avon to Charmouth* by Trevor Antill (Meridian Books). ISBN:186992228X. 1995\229x145\136pp\£6.95(+£1).

Paperback: *The Monarch's Way: Charmouth to Shoreham* by Trevor Antill (Meridian Books). ISBN:1869922298. 1996\229x145\136pp\£6.95(+£1).

Leaflet: *The Monarch's Way Accommodation List* (Monarch's Way Association). 1996\Free(+SAE).

Certificate (Free+9" x 6" SAE) available from Monarch's Way Association.

Montgomery Canal 305

Powys, Shrops	56 km / 35 miles

This partially restored canal runs from a junction with the busy Llangollen Canal to Newtown. The northern section crosses the North Shropshire Plain and the southern section goes through the Severn valley. Although work is progressing to fully restore the canal, some parts are still dry and others are unnavigable because of lowered bridges.

Start	Frankton Junction, Shrops	SJ371318
Finish	Newtown, Powys	SO135925
OS maps	126, 136	

Publication(s)

Leaflet: *The Montgomery Canal* (Montgomery Waterway Restoration Trust). A4/3\Free.

Leaflet: *Montgomery Canal* (Powys County Council). A4/3\£0.10 (+SAE).

Stripmap: *Llangollen and Montgomery Canals* (GEOprojects). ISBN: 0863510337. 1997\945 x 428\£3.75.

Mortimer Trail 306

Heref & Worc, Shrops	48 km / 30 miles

The Trail starts in Shropshire, but soon enters Herefordshire, crossing the rivers Teme, Lugg and Arrow taking in the Mary Knoll Valley, the High Vinnals, Orleton Common, Croft Ambrey and Wapley hill fort, visiting a number of villages on the route.

Start	Ludlow, Shrops	SO510746
Finish	Kington, Heref & Worc	SO295567
On OS maps	137, 138, 148, 149	
Waymark	Green/brown/yellow named disc with crown & shield logo	

Publication(s)
Booklet: *The Mortimer Trail* (Ian R Jones). A5 \ 18pp \ £1.00(+30p).
Booklet: *The Mortimer Trail Walker's Guide* (Herefordshire County
Council). ISBN:185301219. 1997 \ 44pp \ £4.50(incl p+p).

Moyle Way   307

Moyle	29 km / 18 miles

Starting on the Antrim coast, the route heads round the forested
slopes of Knocklayd and follows Glenshesk River upstream. An
ascent of Slieveanorra is followed by the boggy shoulder of Trostan.

Start	Ballycastle, Moyle	IJ115407
Finish	Glenariff, Moyle	IJ200208
OS maps	(OSNI) 5, 9	
Waymark	Wooden markers with yellow arrows	

Publication(s)
Folder: *The Moyle Way* (Moyle District Council). 205 x 95 \ 8pp \
£2.00.

Myrtle Meander   308

W Yorks	40 km / 25 miles

To the south of Bingley, the walk combines rarely used paths with
more popular routes. Places visited include Egypt, World's End,
Queensbury and Haworth.

Start and finish	Myrtle Park School, Bingley, W Yorks	SE108387
OS maps	104	

Publication(s)
Looseleaf: *Myrtle Meander* (Peter Bashforth). Free(+9" x 4" SAE).
Badge and certificate (£1.75/£0.25/9" x 6" SAE) available from
Peter Bashforth.

Nar Valley Way   309

Norfolk	54 km / 34 miles

The Way passes through pleasant countryside in the watershed of
the River Nar, visiting many attractive villages and historical
sites. The walk links with the Peddars Way at Castle Acre.

Start	King's Lynn, Norfolk	TF616198
Finish	Gressenhall, Norfolk	TF975169
On OS maps	132	
Waymark	Named signposts & white named discs	

Publication(s)
Booklet: *Nar Valley Way* by C Andrews & D Dear (Pathway Publishing). ISBN:095266285X. 1996\A5\28pp\£2.00.
Leaflet: *Nar Valley Way* (Norfolk County Council). 1995\A3/6\ Free(+SAE).

Navigation Way 310

W Midlands   161 km / 100 miles

A meandering towpath walk which passes through a mixture of urban and rural areas and follows sections of the many canals in the area. The first loop follows the towpaths of the Birmingham and Fazeley, Grand Union, Stratford-upon-Avon, and Worcester and Birmingham Canals, returning to Gas Street Basin, with the second loop along towpaths of parts of the Birmingham, Dudley, Stourbridge, Staffordshire and Worcestershire, and Tame Valley Canals. The final section is along the Rushall and Wyrley and Essington canals.

Start	Birmingham, Gas Street Basin, W Midlands	SP062867
Finish	Chasewater, W Midlands	SK040070
OS maps	138, 139	

Publication(s)
Paperback: *The Navigation Way* by Peter Groves and Trevor Antill (Meridian Books). ISBN:1869922190. 1993\A5\40pp\£4.95.

Nene Way 311

Cambs, Lincs, Northants   177 km / 110 miles

A route along the Nene Valley including canalised riverbank passing through Northampton, Wellingborough, Oundle, Peterborough and Wisbech. At Sutton Bridge there is a link with the Peter Scott Walk. See also Fen Rivers Way.

Start	Badby, Northants	SP560587
Finish	Sutton Bridge, Lincs	TF482210
On OS maps	131, 141, 142, 143, 152, 153	
Waymark	Named signposts	

Publication(s)
Leaflet: *Nene Way: A Cambridgeshire Country Walk* (Cambridgeshire County Council). A5\£0.30(+50p).

Folder: *Nene Way: A Northamptonshire County Path* (Northamptonshire County Council). 1990\A5\£1.75(+40p).
Leaflet: *Nene Way: A Peterborough Country Walk* (Peterborough City Council). A5\8pp\Free(+A5 SAE).

Nev Cole Way 312

Lincs	93 km / 58 miles

The Way passes from the Jurassic scarp overlooking the River Trent, via the south bank of the Humber to Immingham and Grimsby. Here it turns inland into the gently sloping Lincolnshire Wolds, passing through several villages to Nettleton which provides a link with the Viking Way and which could be used to return north to Barton-upon-Humber.

Start	Burton upon Stather, Lincs	SE870178
Finish	Nettleton, Lincs	TA112001
OS maps	112, 113	
Waymark	Named discs	

Publication(s)
Booklet: *Nev Cole Way* (Wanderlust Rambling Club). ISBN: 0951109227. 1991\147 x 206\40pp\£1.50(+SAE 50p).
Badge and certificate (£2.00/£0.50/9" x 4" SAE) available from Wanderlust Rambling Club.

New Five Trig Points Walk 313

Gtr Man, W Yorks	29 km / 18 miles

The circuit along lanes, tracks and footpaths over the Pennine moors, and in parts coincident with the Pennine Way, was designed as a companion walk to the Saddleworth Five Trig Points Walk. It visits the trig points on Bishop Park, Tame Scout, Blackstone Edge, White Hill and Standedge.

Start and finish	Delph, Gtr Man	SD985079
OS maps	109, 110	

Publication(s)
Looseleaf: *The New Five Trig Points Walk* (Bob Tait). A4\Free (+SAE).
Badge and certificate (£1.00/£0.20/9" x 5" SAE) available from Bob Tait.

Newtondale Trail 314

| N Yorks | 32 km / 20 miles |

This walk links together the terminal stations of the North Yorkshire Moors Railway, which follows Newton Dale northwards from Pickering across the moors to Grosmont, some sections going close to the Railway and others following forest tracks and crossing the open moors high above the valley.

Start	Pickering, N Yorks	SE797842
Finish	Grosmont, N Yorks	NZ828053
OS maps	94, 100	

Publication(s)
Leaflet: *Newtondale Trail* (Mike Teanby). A4/3 \ Free(+SAE).

Nidd Vale Circuit 315

| N Yorks | 42 km / 26 miles |

Based mainly on Nidderdale, the route takes in the high moors to the River Cover, and Caldbergh passing close to Roundhill Reservoir.

Start and finish	Lofthouse, N Yorks	SE101737
OS maps	99	

Publication(s)
Looseleaf: *Nidd Vale Circuit* (Simon Townson). Free(+10" x 7" SAE).
Badge and certificate (£1.50/13" x 9" SAE) available from Simon Townson.

Nidd Valley Link 316

| N Yorks | 45 km / 28 miles |

A route connecting the Nidderdale Way at Hampsthwaite with the confluence of the rivers Nidd and Ouse near to Nun Monkton, from where a link can be made into the centre of York by way of the banks of the River Ouse (8 miles).

Start	Hampsthwaite, N Yorks	SE259587
Finish	Nidd-Ouse Confluence, N Yorks	SE513578
OS maps	104, 105	

Publication(s)
Looseleaf: *Nidd Valley Link* (John Eckersley). 1997 \ A4 \ 4pp \ £1.00.
Certificate (£1.00) available from John Eckersley.

Nidderdale Way 317

N Yorks	85 km / 53 miles

A long established route from the lowland pastures to the open fells near the source of the River Nidd. The Way follows the northern side of the dale passing the gritstone outcrops of Brimham Rocks high above the dale, and the old lead mill at Smelthouses, before following paths close to the Nidd from Pateley Bridge to Lofthouse. Here the Way loops round the head of the valley to Scar House Reservoir. The route returns along the south side of the dale, looping away from the Nidd to visit Merryfield Mines and Heyshaw Moor. See the Nidd Valley Link.

Start and finish	Hampsthwaite, N Yorks	SE259587
On OS maps	99, 104	
Waymark	Named signposts	

Publication(s)
Folder: *Nidderdale Way* by J.K.E. Piggin (Yorkshire Footpath Trust). Details/price TBA.
Badge (£1.50+SAE) available from Yorkshire Footpath Trust.

North Bowland Traverse 318

Lancs, N Yorks	50 km / 31 miles

A low-level walk through the countryside of the Bowland Forest, crossing farmland and meadow land. Although it is a fairly easy walk, it is best to go well-prepared, as much of the route is well away from any good roads and conditions can change rapidly. Links with the Witches Way at Slaidburn.

Start	Slaidburn, Lancs	SD714523
Finish	Stainforth, N Yorks	SD821673
OS maps	97, 98, 103	

Publication(s)
Paperback: *North Bowland Traverse* by David Johnson (Hillside Publications). ISBN:1870141016. 1987 \ 175 x 115 \ 56pp \ £4.50.
Badge and certificate (£1.50/ - /9"x4" SAE) available from David Johnson.

North Bucks Way 319

Bucks	56 km / 35 miles

A walk from the Ridgeway at Chequers Nature Reserve crossing the Vale of Aylesbury and taking in a number of villages, it connects with the Cross Bucks Way at Addington and with the Grafton Way at Wolverton. The Tramway Trail (6 miles) provides an alternative

connection between Quainton and Waddesdon, the route taking to
the Brill Tramway and the grounds of Waddesdon Manor. See
Aylesbury Ring/Thame Valley Walk.

Start	Great Kimble, Bucks	SP830053
Finish	Wolverton, Bucks	SP807413
On OS maps	152, 165	
Waymark	Orange arrows	

Publication(s)
Leaflet: *North Bucks Way* (Buckinghamshire County Council).
A4/3\Free(+SAE).
Leaflet: *The Tramway Trail* (Buckinghamshire County Council).
A4/3\Free(+SAE).

North Cotswold Diamond Way 320

Glos	96 km / 60 miles

A route devised by the North Cotswold Group of the RA to commemorate the Association's Diamond Jubilee. A roughly diamond
shaped walk visiting many small villages using quiet footpaths.

Start and finish	Moreton-in-Marsh, Glos	SP204325
OS maps	150, 151, 163	
Waymark	Blue diamond	

Publication(s)
Softback: *North Cotswold Diamond Way* by Elizabeth Bell (RA
Gloucestershire Area). ISBN:0900613912. 1995\A5\£3.50(+70p).

North Downs Way 321

Kent, Surrey	229 km / 142 miles

The North Downs Way National Trail broadly follows the historic
Pilgrims Way along the Downs to Canterbury. The first 14 miles
are over sandy countryside to the south. The Downs are first
reached at Newlands Corner, east of Guildford and from there on,
the Way mainly follows the crest of the southern escarpment of the
North Downs, or footpaths and tracks along their lower slopes.
There are views over the Weald to the South Downs and several
steepish ascents where the ridge is cut by valleys, notably those of
the Mole at Box Hill, the Darent at Otford, the Medway at Roch-
ester, and the Stour near Wye. Generally, the route provides
comparatively easy walking through woods, over chalk grassland
and, especially in Kent, through orchards and farmland. At
Boughton Lees there is a choice of routes. The direct one goes
through Wye, over the Downs to Folkestone and along the cliffs to
Dover. The alternative follows hills to the west of the river Stour
and passes through orchards and the picturesque village of Chil-

ham to Canterbury. From the cathedral city it heads south-east via Barham Downs, Shepherdswell and Waldershare Park to Dover. See Downs Link and Thames Down Link.

Start	Farnham, Surrey	SU844468
Finish	Dover, Kent	TR308399
On OS maps	178, 179, 186, 187, 188, 189	
Waymark	National Trail Acorn	

Publication(s)
Softback: *North Downs Way* (Official Guide) by Neil Curtis and Jim Walker (Aurum Press). ISBN:1854105370. 1998\210 x 130\ £10.99.
Softback: *Guide to the Pilgrims' Way and North Downs Way* by Christopher John Wright (Constable and Co Ltd). ISBN: 0094722307. 1993\171 x 114\316pp\£10.95.
Booklet: *North Downs Way: A Practical Handbook* (Kent County Council). 1997\210 x 100\6pp\£1.95.
Leaflet: *North Downs Way* (Countryside Commission Postal Sales). 1992\A4/3\Free.

North to South Surrey Walk 322

Berks, Surrey   66 km / 41 miles

A route pioneered by the Surrey Group of the LDWA, crosses the varied Surrey countryside taking in flooded gravel pits and passing Runnymede Memorial, Windsor Park and Gibbet Hill.

Start	Colnbrook, Berks	TQ030771
Finish	Haslemere Edge, Surrey	SU914312
OS maps	176, 186	

Publication(s)
Looseleaf: *North-South Surrey* (Keith Chesterton). A4\Free (+SAE).

North Wales Path 323

Aberconwy, Caernarfon, Denbigh   96 km / 60 miles

The path is only partly coastal and significant stretches explore the hilly hinterland, but with the larger resorts accessible. It links with the Offa's Dyke Path at Prestatyn, and the book by Jan Harris details a link with the Cambrian and Lleyn Coast Path.

Start	Prestatyn, Denbigh	SJ081838
Finish	Bangor, Caernarfon	SH592720
On OS maps	115, 116	
Waymark	Named discs with stylised hills and sea	

Publication(s)
Paperback: *Walking the North Wales Path* by Jan Harris (Walking Routes). ISBN:0951814850. 1997\A5\56pp\£4.95.
Folder: *North Wales Path* (Conwy Borough Council). 1997\ A5\16pp\£3.00(+31p).

North Western Fells 324

Cumbria	80 km / 50 miles

A route visiting all the peaks described in the book, North Western Fells (A. Wainwright) and which involves 18,000ft of ascent.

Start and finish	Rannerdale Knotts, Cumbria	NY162182
OS maps	89	

Publication(s)
Looseleaf: *North Western Fells* (A G Foot). Free(+SAE).
Certificate (£1.50/post free) available from A G Foot.

North Wolds Walk 325

E Yorks	32 km / 20 miles

An undulating route across the chalk hills and valleys of the Yorkshire Wolds passing through the villages of Millington, Great Givendale, Bishop Wilton, Kirby Underdale and Thixendale.

Start and finish	Millington Road End, E Yorks	SE836567
On OS maps	100, 106	

Publication(s)
Looseleaf: *North Wolds Walk* (R.H. Watson). A4\Free(+9" x 4" SAE).
Badge (£1.50/SAE) available from R.H. Watson.

North Worcestershire Hills Marathon 326

Heref & Worc	42 km / 26 miles

The route passes through Burcot, Linthurst and Lickey Beacon to the Clent Hills, and returns via Belbroughton, Pepper Wood, Dodford, Park Gate and Sander Park.

Start and finish	Bromsgrove, Heref & Worc	SO960707
OS maps	139	

Publication(s)
Looseleaf: *North Worcestershire Hills Marathon* (Dave Irons). 1994\A4\£1.00(incl p&p).

North Worcestershire Path 327

Worc	43 km / 27 miles

A route linking four country parks in north-east Worcestershire providing contrasting views of Birmingham and the Black Country in the north with the Vale of Worcester and Severn Valley to the south. It meets with the Worcestershire and Staffordshire Ways at Kinver Edge. See also Malvern Link.

Start	Kingsford, Worc	SO836821
Finish	Major's Green, Worc	SP101782
On OS maps	138, 139	
Waymark	Coloured arrows - pine cone logo	

Publication(s)
Paperback: *North Worcestershire Path Guide* (Worcestershire County Council). 1997\38pp\£4.50.
Leaflet: *North Worcestershire Path* (Worcestershire County Council). 1992\A4/3\Free.

North York Moors Challenge Walk 328

N Yorks	40 km / 25 miles

A strenuous walk in the North York Moors National Park which includes high moorland.

Start and finish	Goathland, N Yorks	NZ838014
OS maps	94	

Publication(s)
Paperback: *John Merrill's North Yorkshire Moors Challenge Walk* by John Merrill (Happy Walking International Ltd). ISBN 0907496369. 32pp\£3.00.
Badge and certificate (£3.00/post free) available from Happy Walking International Ltd.

North York Moors Walk 329

N Yorks	158 km / 98 miles

From the start on the Esk Valley Railway, the route goes to Danby Rigg, Rosedale Abbey, Osmotherley, the Hambleton Drove Road and Rievaulx Abbey. It then goes on to Kirkbymoorside, Hutton-le-Hole, the Cawthorn Roman camps, Levisham and Hole of Horcum to the finish at Goathland, where the North Yorkshire Moors Railway can connect the walker with the Esk Valley Railway.

Start	Danby, N Yorks	NZ707084
Finish	Goathland, N Yorks	NZ838014

OS maps   93, 94, 99, 100

Publication(s)
Paperback: *Footpath Touring: North York Moors* by Ken Ward (Footpath Touring). ISBN:0711704260. 221 x 114\64pp\£3.50.

North York Moors Wobble   330

N Yorks	51 km / 32 miles

A route taking in Rudland Rigg, Farndale, Rosedale Abbey, Rosedale Moor, Cropton, Appleton-le-Moors and Hutton-le-Hole, aimed at raising funds for a locally based search and rescue team.

Start and finish	Gillamoor, N Yorks	SE684801
OS maps	100	

Publication(s)
Booklet: *North York Moors Wobble* (George Davies). 12pp\£5.00 (+A4 SAE).
Certificate (Free/9" x 4" SAE) available from George Davies.

Northern Fells   331

Cumbria	84 km / 52 miles

A demanding route visiting such as Skiddaw, Bowscale Fell, High Pike and Mungrisdale Common. Map reading and compass skills are essential.

Start and finish	Mosedale, Cumbria	NY356322
OS maps	90	

Publication(s)
Looseleaf: *The Northern Fells* (Doreen Viney). Free(+9" x 4" SAE).
Certificate(£0.50+SAE) available from Doreen Viney.

Northumbrian Coastline   332

Northumb, Tyne & Wear	96 km / 60 miles

A coastal route with many interesting features including Berwick fortifications, Holy Island, Bamburgh Castle, Farne Islands, Dunstanburgh Castle, Warkworth Castle and Tynemouth Castle and Priory. Links with the St Cuthbert's Way.

Start	Berwick-upon-Tweed, Northumb	NT994534
Finish	North Shields, Tyne & Wear	NZ356678
OS maps	75, 81, 88	

Publication(s)
Paperback: *Northumbrian Coastline* by Ian Smith (Sandhill Press Ltd). ISBN:0946098328. 175 x 125 \ £3.95(+65p).

Offa's Dyke Path   333

Denbigh, Glos, Heref & Worc, Monmouth, Powys, Shrops	287 km / 178 miles

For over sixty miles the route of this National Trail runs along or close to the 8th century dyke passing many other historical sites. The Path meanders along the east side of the Wye Valley to Monmouth, crosses lowland farmland to Pandy and Hatterrall Ridge which is followed to Hay-on-Wye. The Radnorshire Hills are crossed to Knighton as is the hill country of Clun. The next part of the route is across the plain of Montgomery, along the Severn Valley and across the vale of Llangollen to the Clwydian Hills. An alternative route (31 miles) along higher terrain between Monmouth and Hay-on-Wye is described in the publication, The Offa's Dyke Path Castles Alternative. It passes the medieval castles of Pembridge, Skenfrith, Grosmont and Longtown. See Cestrian Link Walk/Wysis Way/Maelor Way/North Wales Path.

Start	Sedbury Cliffs, Glos	ST552927
Finish	Prestatyn, Denbigh	SJ081838
On OS maps	116, 117, 126, 137, 148, 161, 162	
Waymark	National Trail Acorn	
User group	Offa's Dyke Association	

Publication(s)
Softback: *Offa's Dyke Path North* (Official Guide) by Ernie and Kathy Kay and Mark Richards(Aurum Press). ISBN:1854103229. 1995 \ 210 x 130 \ 144pp \ £9.99.
Softback: *Offa's Dyke Path South* (Official Guide) by Ernie and Kathy Kay and Mark Richards(Aurum Press). ISBN:1854102958. 1995 \ 210 x 130 \ 144pp \ £10.99.
Softback: *Guide to Offa's Dyke Path* by Christopher John Wright (Constable and Co Ltd). ISBN:0094691401. 1990 \ 171 x 114 \ 320pp \ £10.95.
Paperback: *Walking Offa's Dyke Path* by David Hunter (Cicerone Press). ISBN:1852841605. 1995 \ 224 \ £8.99.
Paperback: *Langton's Guide to the Offa's Dyke Path* by Andrew Durham (Langton's Guides). ISBN:1899242023. 1996 \ 210 x 130 \ 224pp \ £12.99.
Folder: *Offa's Dyke Path - North to South* (Offa's Dyke Association). 1994 \ £1.20(+£0.30 p&p).
Folder: *Offa's Dyke Path - South to North* (Offa's Dyke Association). 1994 \ £1.20(+£0.30 p&p).
Booklet: *Offa's Dyke Path Accommodation Guide* (Offa's Dyke Association). 1997 \ A6 \ £1.50(+30p).
Folder: *Strip Maps of Offa's Dyke Path* by Ian Dormer (Offa's Dyke Association). 1997 \ 8pp \ £2.50(+50p).

Leaflet: *The Offa's Dyke Path / Llwybr Clawdd Offa* (Countryside Council for Wales). 1994\A4/3\Free.
Paperback: *Offa's Dyke Path Castles Alternative* (Offa's Dyke Association). 1987\A5\24pp\£0.80.
Badge and certificate (£0.95/30p/£1.35 /30p) available from Offa's Dyke Association.

Offa's Hyke   334

Denbigh	32 km / 20 miles

A walk on and around the Clwydian Hills providing distant views. It is coincident with parts of the Offa's Dyke Path. Profits from the sale of badges/certificates go to Hope House Childrens Hospice.

Start and finish	Bwlch Penbarra, Denbigh	SJ161605
OS maps	116	

Publication(s)
Looseleaf: *Offa's Hyke* (Michael Skuse). A4\1pp\Free(+SAE).
Badge and certificate (£1.50/SAE/£0.50/SAE) available from Michael Skuse.

Ogwr Ridgeway Walk   335

Bridgend, Rhondda	21 km / 13 miles

Part of a long ridge walk across South West Wales, the Ogwr Ridgeway links the Taff-Ely Ridgeway Walk (Ffordd y Bryniau) with the Coed Morgannwg Way. It largely follows the tops of the southern Lower Pennant Sandstone ridge from Mynydd y Gaer and Bryn y Wrach, to Mynydd Baeden and Mynydd Margam, taking in the valleys of the Ogwr Fawr and Fach, Garw and Llynfi. The scenery varies from windswept heights with fine views to the woodlands and arable farms of the valley sides and floors.

Start	Bodvic Stone, Bridgend	SS832880
Finish	Mynydd Maendy, Rhondda	ST977861
On OS maps	170	
Waymark	Arrows with named hill logo	

Publication(s)
Leaflet: *Ogwr Ridgeway Walk* (Bridgend County Borough Council). 1991\A4/3\Free.

Old Sarum Challenge   336

Wilts	40 km / 25 miles

A route from Amesbury over chalk downland linking Old Sarum and intervening villages.

Start and finish	Amesbury, Wilts	SU161417
OS maps	184	

Publication(s)
Looseleaf: *Old Sarum Challenge* (Richard Archard). Free(+9" x 4" SAE).
Badge and certificate (£2.00/9" x 6" SAE) available from Richard Archard).

Oldham Way 337

Gtr Man	64 km / 40 miles

A walk around the borough, the landscape varies from moorland to urban canal. It starts at Dove Stone Reservoir near Greenfield, and continues over Saddleworth Moor to Diggle and Castleshaw Moor to Denshaw. It then skirts the north of Shaw and Royton to meet the Rochdale Canal at Chadderton Hall Park. It follows the canal south through Chadderton to Failsworth, after which it joins the Medlock Valley to Daisy Nook and Park Bridge before climbing over Hartshead Pike to Quick.

Start and finish	Dove Stone Reservoir, Gtr Man	SE002036
On OS maps	109, 110	
Waymark	Owl	

Publication(s)
Folder: *The Oldham Way* (Oldham Metropolitan Borough Council). A4/3 \ 9 leaflets \ £1.99.

Ouse Valley Way 338

Cambs	42 km / 26 miles

The Way follows the River Great Ouse through St Neots, Godman-chester and St Ives with significant areas of meadowland and elevated bank views from north of Holywell.

Start	Eaton Socon, Cambs	TL173587
Finish	Earith, Cambs	TL394746
On OS maps	142, 153, 154	
Waymark	Standard waymarks with swan, water and tree logo	

Publication(s)
Folder: *Ouse Valley Way* (Huntingdon District Council). A4/3 \ 7pp \ £1.00.

Ox Drove Way 339

Hants	40 km / 25 miles

The Ox Drove itself is part of an old cross-country route on the Downs to the northeast of Winchester called the Lunway, a name recalled in the Lunways Inn at Itchen Wood. This bridle route forms a figure of eight using the Ox Drove and passing Preston Down, Bentworth, Upper Wield, and Old Alresford.

Start and finish	Abbotstone Down, Hants	SU585361
On OS maps	185	
Waymark	Standard arrows with ox logo	

Publication(s)
Leaflet: *The Ox Drove Way* (Hampshire County Council). A4/3 \ Free(+SAE).

Oxbridge Walk 340

Beds, Bucks, Cambs, Oxon	185 km / 115 miles

A route connecting the famous University cities of Oxford and Cambridge and making use of the Cross Bucks Way, Thames Valley Way, Greensand Ridge Walk and Clopton Way.

Start	Head of River Pub, Oxford, Oxon	SP055514
Finish	The Backs, Cambridge	TL586445
OS maps	153, 154, 164, 165	

Publication(s)
Paperback: *An Oxbridge Walk* by James A Lyons (Cicerone Press). ISBN:1852841664. 1995 \ 180 x 120 \ 168pp \ £7.99(£0.75 p+p).

Oxford Canal Walk 341

Northants, Oxon, Warks, W Midlands	133 km / 83 miles

A walk connecting the cathedral cities of Oxford and Coventry using the continuous canal towpath, passing 43 locks, many bridges, one tunnel and crossing only one road. See Jurassic Way.

Start	Coventry, W Midlands	SP370840
Finish	Oxford, Oxon	SP516060
On OS maps	140, 151, 164	
Waymark	Multi-coloured diamond	

Publication(s)
Leaflet: *The Oxford Canal Walk* (British Waterways - Braunston). 1995 \ A4/3 \ Free.

Leaflet: *Exploring the Oxford Canal* (British Waterways - Braunston). 1996\A5\Free(+SAE).
Booklet: *Oxford Canal Walk - Accommodation Guide* (British Waterways - Braunston). 1996/7\A5\20pp\£1.50.
Stripmap: *The Oxford Canal Map* (GEOprojects). ISBN: 0863510035. 426 x 875\£3.75.

Oxfordshire Trek   342

Oxon	103 km / 64 miles

The Trek is a route around the city of Oxford with several access points. Starting at Bladon, the site of Sir Winston Churchill's grave, the route passes Blenheim Palace, Dorchester Abbey and crosses both the Oxford Canal and the River Thames.

Start and finish	Bladon, Oxon	SP449149
OS maps	164	

Publication(s)
Paperback: *Guide to the Oxfordshire Trek* by Laurence Main (Halsgrove Press). ISBN:0702809152. 1989\210 x 120\64pp\ £3.95(+55p).

Oxfordshire Way   343

Glos, Oxon	104 km / 65 miles

The Way, a traverse of Oxfordshire from the Cotswolds to the Chilterns, links the Heart of England Way with the Thames Path across the rolling limestone countryside of the Cotswold Hills, passing through Shipton-under-Wychwood, Charlbury and other villages before crossing Otmoor to Studley, north of Oxford. Here it turns to Tetsworth and Pyrton, and crosses the open farmland and woods of the chalk hills of the Chilterns to reach the Thames. See Cross Bucks Way/Thame Valley Way/Wardens's Way/Windrush Way.

Start	Bourton-on-the-Water, Glos	SP170209
Finish	Henley-on-Thames, Oxon	SU757833
On OS maps	163, 164, 165, 175	
Waymark	Letters OW on standard waymarks	

Publication(s)
Paperback: *Oxfordshire Way* by Alison Kemp (Oxfordshire County Council). 1993\£5.99(£0.50 p+p).
Paperback: *The Oxfordshire Way* by Faith Cooke and Keith Wheal (Sutton Publishing Ltd). ISBN:0750903562. 1993\A5\90pp\ £5.99(+50p).

Painters Way 344

Essex, Suffolk	45 km / 28 miles

The Way crossing meadows and arable land, follows the hills flanking the River Stour and its tributaries and passes many places associated with the painters Thomas Gainsborough and John Constable. From Sudbury, where Gainsborough's house can be visited, the Way passes through Bures, Nayland and Stratford St Mary. A short diversion from the direct route takes in Dedham Mill and East Bergholt, Constable's birthplace, before passing Flatford Mill.

Start	Sudbury, Suffolk	TL877410
Finish	Manningtree, Essex	TM094322
OS maps	155, 168	

Publication(s)
Booklet: *A Guide to The Painters Way* (Hugh Turner). 1992 \ A5 \ 12pp \ £1.25.

Peak District High Level Route 345

Derbys, S Yorks, Staffs	147 km / 91 miles

This route around the Peak National Park is particularly strenuous taking in the limestone plateau to Dove Dale, the Roaches, Shining Tor, Chinley Churn, the southern edge of Kinder to the Ladybower reservoir and the whole of the eastern gritstone edges from Stanage to Beeley before following the Derwent Valley to the finish.

Start and finish	Matlock, Derbys	SK298603
OS maps	110, 119	

Publication(s)
Paperback: *The Peak District High Level Route* by John Merrill (Happy Walking International Ltd). ISBN:0907496555. 60pp \ £3.00.
Badge and certificate (£3.00/post free) available from Happy Walking International Ltd.

Peak District Round 346

Derbys	172 km / 107 miles

Climbing 12,300ft in the Peak District area, the route takes in such as Edale, Hathersage, Baslow, Winster, Monyash, Ilam, Longnor and Castleton.

Start and finish	Edale, Derbys	SK123860

OS maps	110, 119

Publication(s)
Hardback: *Walking Around the Peak District* by Tom Lawton (Ward Lock). ISBN:070637441X. 265 x 200 \ 176pp \ £17.99.

Peakland Way   347

Derbys	156 km / 97 miles

This route through the National Park visits Ilam, Longnor, Blackwell, Mam Tor, Kinder Scout, Snake Pass and Tissington where it joins the Tissington Trail.

Start and finish	Ashbourne, Derbys	SK178469
OS maps	110, 119	

Publication(s)
Paperback: *The Peakland Way* by John Merrill (Happy Walking International Ltd). ISBN:0907496849. 1989 \ 130 x 210 \ 64pp \ £3.50.
Badge and certificate (£3.00/post free) available from Happy Walking International Ltd.

Peddars Way & Norfolk Coast Path   348

Norfolk, Suffolk	151 km / 94 miles

The first part of this National Trail follows tracks, footpaths and minor roads along, or as near as possible to, the Peddars Way (a Romanised section of the prehistoric Icknield Way, the extant sections of which are a scheduled ancient monument). From the wooded, sandy Breckland, it passes Castle Acre (linking with the Nar Valley Way) and the ruins of the priory and castle to reach the North Norfolk coast at Holme-next-the-Sea. Here a short section of the Coast Path leads west to Hunstanton, while the main path heads east along or near to the shoreline over low cliffs, sand dunes, coastal defences enclosing marshes and mud flats, passing woodland, bird sanctuaries and harbours. Near to Great Hockham, the Great Eastern Pingo Trail (8 miles) provides a circular route through a SSSI in the Thompson Common area. See also Angles Way/Weavers Way and Hereward Way.

Start	Knettishall Heath, Suffolk	TL944807
Finish	Cromer, Norfolk	TG215420
On OS maps	132, 133, 144	
Waymark	National Trail Acorn	

Publication(s)
Softback: *Peddars Way and Norfolk Coast Path* (Official Guide) by
Bruce Robinson (Aurum Press). ISBN:185410408X. 210 x 130\
£10.99.
Paperback: *Langton's Guide to the Peddars Way and Norfolk Coast
Path* by Andrew Durham (Langton's Guides). ISBN:1899242007.
1994\210 x 130\128pp\£6.95.
Paperback: *East Anglian Trackways - Peddars Way* by Elizabeth
Barrett (Wimpole Books). ISBN:0951601105. A5\129pp\£7.95
(+50p).
Booklet: *Peddars Way and North Norfolk Coast Path Guide* by Ian
Mitchell (RA Norfolk). 1997\A5\24pp\£2.10(+26p).
Leaflet: *Peddars Way and Norfolk Coast Path* (Countryside Com-
mission Postal Sales). 1991\A4/3\Free.
Leaflet: *The Great Eastern Pingo Trail* (Norfolk County Council).
A5\Free(+SAE).

Pembrokeshire Coast Path 349

Pembrokeshire	299 km / 186 miles

With the exception of Milford Haven and several MOD estab-
lishments, the route of this National Trail follows the coastline
around the county of Pembrokeshire and the Pembrokeshire Coast
National Park. Once the resorts of Tenby, Pembroke and Milford
Haven have been passed, only small settlements and relatively few
obtrusive holiday developments are encountered. The scenery
provides an interesting contrast between the softer sedimentary
rocks of the south coast, with its fine beaches, and the more
resistant rocks of the rugged northern coast. The area is rich in
prehistoric remains and is noted for its sea birds and seals.

Start	Amroth, Pembrokeshire	SS168071
Finish	St Dogmaels, Pembrokeshire	SN163469
On OS maps	145, 157, 158	
Waymark	National Trail Acorn	

Publication(s)
Softback: *Pembrokeshire Coast Path* (Official Guide) by Brian John
(Aurum Press). ISBN:1854104594. 1997\210 x 130\168pp\
£10.99.
Softback: *Guide to the Pembrokeshire Coast Path* by Christopher
John Wright (Constable and Co Ltd). ISBN:0094692602. 1990\171
x 114\391pp\£9.95.
Paperback: *The Pembrokeshire Coast Path* by John Merrill (Happy
Walking International Ltd). ISBN:0907496695. 1993\84pp\£4.50.
Paperback: *Walking the Pembrokeshire Coast Path* by Patrick
Stark (Gomer Press). ISBN:0863836860. 1995\84pp\£3.75(+50p).
Paperback: *The Pembrokeshire Coastal Path* by Dennis R. Kelsall
(Cicerone Press). ISBN:1852841869. 1996\200pp\£9.99.
Folder: *Coast Path Cards* (Pembrokeshire Coast National Park).
10pp\£2.50(+43p).

Leaflet: *Coast Path Accommodation Guide* (Pembrokeshire Coast National Park). £1.50(+36p).
Leaflet: *Coast Path Mileage Chart* (Pembrokeshire Coast National Park). £0.10(+29p).
Leaflet: *Explore the Pembrokeshire Coast Path - Children's Leaflet* (Pembrokeshire Coast National Park). A4/3\Free(+SAE).
Leaflet: *Flowers of the Pembrokeshire Coast Path* (Pembrokeshire Coast National Park). A4/3\Free(+SAE).
Leaflet: *Llwybr Arfordir Sir Benfro/The Pembrokeshire Coast Path* (Countryside Council for Wales). 1992\A4/3\Free.
Leaflet: *Accommodation Booking Service* (YHA Northern Region). Free(+SAE).
Badge and certificate available on proof of completion - details from Pembrokeshire Coast National Park.

Pendle and Ribble Round 350

Lancs	32 km / 20 miles

A route crossing Pendle Hill and visiting Downham before returning by riverside and farm paths.

Start and finish	Whalley, Lancs	SD732362
OS maps	103	

Publication(s)
Booklet: *Bronte Round/Pendle and Ribble Round* by Derek Magnall (Derek Magnall). 1994\A5\36pp\£1.85.
Badge and certificate (£1.50/SAE) available from Derek Magnall.

Pendle Marathon 351

Lancs	43 km / 27 miles

A route over Pendle Hill visiting Foulridge and Barley. An alternative linear route to Slaidburn is available.

Start and finish	Earby YH, Lancs	SD915469
OS maps	103	

Publication(s)
Looseleaf: *Pendle Marathon* (Frank Hodson). 2 x 20p stamps.
Badge and certificate (£1.00/£0.50/SAE) available from Frank Hodson.

Pendle Way 352

Lancs	72 km / 45 miles

A route through contrasting scenery, ranging from moorland to river valleys visiting Barnoldswick, Thornton-in-Craven, Wycoller,

Reedley, Newchurch and Pendle Hill. The latter part of the route has associations with the Pendle Witches.

Start and finish	Barrowford, Lancs	SD863398
On OS maps	103	
Waymark	Black witch	

Publication(s)
Paperback: *Pendle Way* by Paul Hannon (Hillside Publications). ISBN:1870141671. 1997\175 x 115\48pp\£3.50.
Folder: *The Pendle Way* (Pendle Borough Council). 1987\A4/3\8 leaflets\£2.50(+50p).

Pennine Bridleway 353

Cumbria, Derbys, Durham, N Yorks, Northumb, W Yorks	335 km / 208 miles

This proposed National Trail will follow a route through varied countryside, from the green pastures of Derbyshire and the Ribble Valley to the rugged and remote hills of Cumbria as it approaches its northern terminus at the Fat Lamb Inn, near Kirkby Stephen. Tracks rarely rising above 300 metres, except in the later stages in Cumbria, provide excellent opportunities for horse rider, cyclist and walker. The target date for opening the route is the year 2000.

Start	Carsington Reservoir, Derbys	SK249530
Finish	Fat Lamb Inn, Kirkby Stephen, Cumbria	NY739023
OS maps	86, 87, 91, 92, 98, 99, 103, 104	

Publication(s)
Leaflet: *Pennine Bridleway* (Countryside Commission Postal Sales). 1995\A4/3\Free.

Pennine Way 354

Borders, Cumbria, Derbys, Durham, Gtr Man, N Yorks, Northumb, W Yorks	404 km / 251 miles

This first National Trail was formally opened after a 30-year campaign led by Tom Stephenson of the RA. It follows the central upland spine of England from Derbyshire to the Scottish Borders, crossing a wide variety of terrain. The Way crosses the peaty expanse of the gritstone moorlands of the Kinder Plateau, the Bronte country, the predominantly limestone areas of the Yorkshire Dales National Park which is traversed via Malham, Pen-y-ghent, Great Shunner Fell and Keld. The Way descends from the high fells to reach the River Tees which is followed past High Force and Cauldron Snout waterfalls then crossing the fells to High Cup, Great Dunfell and Cross Fell then descending to Alston to reach the Northumberland National Park and Hadrian's Wall. The Wall is followed to Housesteads Fort before turning north across the Kielder Forest to Redesdale and the often boggy uplands of the Cheviot Hills. The English-Scottish border fence is then followed before gradually descending to Kirk Yetholm, where it can be linked with the St Cuthbert's Way. At Alston the Way links with the South Tyne Trail (10 miles) providing a low-level alternative up the valley towards Hadrian's Wall. The publication, The Alternative Pennine Way, describes a 268 miles long route from Ashbourne to Jedburgh which does not keep to the hill tops, thereby entailing more climbing. This alternative coincides with the main Way on very few occasions. A register is maintained at the Pen-y-ghent Cafe, Horton-in-Ribblesdale for signature/comments from those involved in walking the Way. See Central Scottish Way/Cestrian Link Walk and Limestone Way.

Start	Edale, Derbys	SK125858
Finish	Kirk Yetholm, Borders	NT827282
On OS maps	74, 75, 80, 86, 87, 91, 92, 98, 103, 109, 110, 119	
Waymark	National Trail Acorn	
User group	Pennine Way Association	

Publication(s)
Softback: *Pennine Way North* (Official Guide) by Tony Hopkins (Aurum Press). ISBN:1854104608. 1997\210 x 130\168pp\ £10.99.
Softback: *Pennine Way South* (Official Guide) by Tony Hopkins (Aurum Press). ISBN:1854103210. 1995\210 x 130\£9.99.
Hardback: *Pennine Way Companion* by A Wainwright (Michael Joseph). ISBN:0717140710. 1994\175 x 117\224pp\£9.99.
Softback: *Guide to the Pennine Way* by Christopher John Wright (Constable and Co Ltd). ISBN:0094706409. 1991\171 x 114\ 240pp\£10.95.
Paperback: *Pennine Way* by Terry Marsh (Dalesman Publishing Ltd). ISBN:1855681080. 1997\165 x 100\192pp\£7.99.
Paperback. *The Pennine Way* by Martin Collins (Cicerone Press). ISBN:1852842628. 1998.
Hardback: *Wainwright on the Pennine Way* by A Wainwright (Michael Joseph). ISBN:0718124294. 250 x 215\224pp\£17.99.
Paperback: *Wainwright on the Pennine Way* by A Wainwright (Michael Joseph). ISBN:0718128389. 1992\250 x 215\224pp\ £13.99.
Paperback: *The Alternative Pennine Way* by Denis Brook and Paul Hinchliffe (Cicerone Press). ISBN: 1852840951. 1992\116 x 176\ 272pp\£8.99.
Stripmap: *The Pennine Way, Part One: Edale to Teesdale* (Footprint). £2.95.
Stripmap: *The Pennine Way, Part Two: Teesdale to Kirk Yetholm* (Footprint). £2.95.
Booklet: *Pennine Way Association Accommodation and Camping Guide* (Pennine Way Association). Annual\£0.90(+SAE).
Leaflet: *The Pennine Way - Accommodation and Service* (Pennine Way Coordination Project). Annual\A3/6\Free.

Leaflet: *Accommodation Booking Service* (YHA Northern Region). 1997 \ Free(+SAE).
Leaflet: *The Pennine Way* (Countryside Commission Postal Sales). A4/3 \ Free.
Leaflet: *South Tyne Trail* (Northumberland County Council). 1997 \ A4/3 \ Free(+SAE).
Badge (enamel) and certificate(£2.00/ strong SAE/£2.50/post free) available from Pennine Way Association.
Badge and certificate (£3.00/post free) available from Happy Walking International Ltd.

Pennington Round 355

Cumbria	40 km / 25 miles

A walk over moorland countryside visiting the John Barrow monument overlooking the delightful market town of Ulverston. It is partly coincident with the Cumbria Way.

Start and finish	Beckside, Cumbria	SD235822
OS maps	96	

Publication(s)
Looseleaf: *The Pennington Round* (Brian Richmond). 1pp \ £0.20 (+9" x 4" SAE).
Badge and certificate (£0.85/£0.15/SAE) available from Brian Richmond.

Pioneers Round 356

Gtr Man, Lancs	32 km / 20 miles

A route devised to mark the 150th anniversary of the Co-operative Movement, starts from Toad Lane, the birthplace of the movement and takes in Healey Dell, Watergrove Reservoir, Hollingworth Lake, Milnrow and the Rochdale Canal.

Start and finish	Rochdale, Gtr Man	SD896136
OS maps	109	

Publication(s)
Booklet: *The Pioneers Round* by Derek Magnall (Rochdale Pioneers Museum). 1994 \ A5 \ 34pp \ £1.85.
Badge and certificate (£1.50/SAE) available from Rochdale Pioneers Museum.

Plogsland Round 357

Lincs, Notts	72 km / 45 miles

A walk around the city of Lincoln with the cathedral in view for much of the route. It links many villages following paths and green lanes across the flat, drained arable land and along the banks of the River Witham.

Start and finish	Fiskerton, Lincs	TF058715
OS maps	121	

Publication(s)
Folder: *The Plogsland Round* (Brett Collier). 5pp \ £1.00(+SAE).
Badge (£1.25/SAE) available from Brett Collier.

Poppyline Marathon 358

Norfolk	42 km / 26 miles

An undulating route in North Norfolk, which includes inland paths and parts of the North Norfolk Coast Path. There is also an option for a 17 miles route.

Start and finish	Sheringham, Norfolk	TG159430
OS maps	133	

Publication(s)
Looseleaf: *Poppyline Marathon* (Bobbie Sauerzapf). A4 \ 1pp \ Free (+SAE).
Badge and certificate (£1.50/A4 SAE) available from Bobbie Sauerzapf.

Pride of the Peak Walk 359

Derbys	48 km / 30 miles

This route takes in a wide variety of scenery including limestone dales, gritstone edges, woodland, a number of villages and historical features such as Monsal Viaduct, Crossbrook Mill and Chatsworth House. There is 3700ft of ascent.

Start and finish	Bakewell, Derbys	SK217685
OS maps	119	

Publication(s)
Booklet: *Pride of the Peak Walk* by Alan S Edwards (Alan S Edwards). 1991 \ A5 \ 30pp \ £2.55.
Badge and certificate (£2.25/post free) available from Alan S Edwards.

Purbeck Plodder Challenges 360

Dorset, IOW, Wilts Various km

A series of challenge walks devised on behalf of the Purbeck Plodders Walkers Club, comprising: the *Hardy Hobble* (27 miles) - Hardy Monument to Corfe Castle, *A Ridge Too Far* (22 miles) - Maiden Newton circular, *West Dorset Enigma* (19 miles) - Litton Cheney circular, *Day Return To Charmouth* (18 miles) - circular, *Purbeck Steam Package* (24 miles) - Swanage to Corfe Castle, *Cross Wight Traverse* (29 miles) - Isle of Wight coast to coast, *Inter-City Challenge* (20 miles) - Wool to Weymouth, *Majesty Of the Wiltshire Downs* (18 miles) - Broad Chalke circular, *Locus Classicus* (26 miles) - Bradbury Rings to Salisbury, and the *Tesrod Elddod* (33 miles) - Weymouth to Swanage. All included in the one publication.

Start	Various	Various
Finish	Various	Various
OS maps	184, 193, 194, 195, 196	

Publication(s)
Booklet: *A Ridge Too Far* (Garth H Gunn). A5 \ 40pp \ £5.95.

Ramblers Route 361

Berks 42 km / 26 miles

A figure-of-eight route allowing for circuits of 19 or 13 miles through farmland, heaths, coniferous forests and visiting several country parks.

Start and finish	The Look Out, Berks	SU875661
OS maps	175	
Waymark	Black arrow on named white disc	

Publication(s)
Leaflet: *Bracknell Forest Ramblers Route* (Bracknell Forest Borough Council). A4/3 \ Free.

Ramsbottom Round 362

Lancs 32 km / 20 miles

A route around Ramsbottom over moorland, riverside and farm paths taking in the Irwell Valley, Irwell Vale and Summerseat.

Start and finish	Ramsbottom, Lancs	SD792168
OS maps	103, 109	

Publication(s)
Booklet: *Ramsbottom Round / Spanners Round* (Derek Magnall).
1992\A5\36pp\£1.85.
Badge and certificate (£1.50/SAE) available from Derek Magnall.

Red Kite Trail 363

Powys, Cardigan	119 km / 74 miles

A route taking in Tregaron, Rhayader and Pumsaint traversing the southern Cambrian Mountains, the home of the red kite and other birds of prey. Good navigational skills are required and the route between the four towns is self devised.

Start and finish	Llanwrtyd Wells, Powys	SN879467
OS maps	146, 147	

Publication(s)
Looseleaf: *Red Kite Trail* (Neuadd Arms Hotel). A4/3 \ Free(+SAE).
Badge and certificate (£2.00/SAE/ - /A4 SAE) available from Neuadd Arms Hotel.

Red Rose Walk 364

Cumbria, Gtr Man, Lancs	188 km / 117 miles

A route through the old and new counties of Lancashire, using footpaths, old packhorse routes, bridleways and Roman roads, and passing on a meandering course through Rossendale and the Forest of Bowland, Wardle, Holcombe Brook, Whalley, Sawley, Slaidburn and Hornby.

Start	Uppermill, Gtr Man	SD997057
Finish	Arnside, Cumbria	SD461788
OS maps	97, 102, 109	

Publication(s)
Paperback: *The Red Rose Walk* by Tom Schofield (Sigma Leisure).
ISBN:1850583420. 1993\A5\90pp\£6.95.

Reiver's Way 365

Northumb	242 km / 150 miles

A meandering route across Northumberland, starting in the Tyne Valley passing the finest remains of Hadrian's Wall, and then heading northwest to Rothbury, over the Cheviots to Wooler, and finishing with the coast path from Budle Bay to Alnmouth.

Start	Corbridge Station, Northumb	NZ989635
Finish	Alnmouth, Northumb	NU248108

OS maps	75, 80, 81, 87

Publication(s)
Paperback: *The Reiver's Way* by James Roberts (Cicerone Press).
ISBN:1852841303. 1993\116 x 176\112pp\£5.99.

Rhymney Valley Ridgeway Walk 366

Caerphilly	45 km / 28 miles

A route winding its way across the hills encircling the unique and often spectacular scenery of the Rhymney Valley. The walk follows quiet countryside paths and lanes, where steep beech woodlands merge into panoramic mountain tops. Mynydd Machen is the highest point. It links with the Taff-Ely Ridgeway Walk at Caerphilly Common, and in the east is partly coincident with the Sirhowy Valley Walk. The Northern Rhymney Valley Ridgeway Walk (12 miles) links with the main valley walk at Gelligaer finishing at Bryn Bach Park.

Start and finish	Gelligaer, Caerphilly	ST137969
On OS maps	171	
Waymark	Ridgeway Walk logo and standard arrows	

Publication(s)
Leaflet: *Rhymney Valley Ridgeway Walk* (Caerphilly Mountain Countryside Service). 1993\A4/3\Free.
Leaflet: *Northern Rhymney Valley Ridgeway Walk* (Caerphilly County Borough Council). A4/3\Free.

Ribble Way 367

Lancs, N Yorks	118 km / 73 miles

The Way follows the valley of the River Ribble from the mouth to the source near to the Pennine Way on Gayle Moor. From the tidal marshes, the route passes Preston, Ribchester, Clitheroe, with views of Pendle Hill, Settle and Horton-in-Ribblesdale. At Horton, the Pen-y-ghent Cafe maintains a register for signature/comments by those taking part in the walk.

Start	Longton, Lancs	SD458255
Finish	Gayle Moor, N Yorks	SD813832
On OS maps	98, 102, 103	
Waymark	Blue and white letters RW/wave logo	

Publication(s)
Softback: *The Ribble Way* by Gladys Sellers (Cicerone Press).
ISBN:1852841079. 1993\116 x 176\102pp\£5.99.
Badge (£1.90/SAE) available from Pen-y-ghent Cafe.

Ridgeway   368

Berks, Bucks, Herts, Oxon, Wilts	137 km / 85 miles

The western part of this National Trail largely follows the route of a prehistoric ridge track along the crest of the North Wessex Downs and passes many historic sites, including Liddington, Segsbury, Barbury and Uffington Castles (hill forts), Uffington White Horse and Wayland's Smithy (long barrow). Much of the Trail is along a broad rutted track. At Streatley the route crosses and then follows the river Thames, continuing over the Chiltern Hills, mainly along the north-western escarpment. The walking on the eastern half is far more varied, along tracks and paths, across open downland, and through farm and woodland, passing Nuffield, Swyncombe, Princes Risborough (see Swan's Way), Wendover and Pitstone. The Ridgeway is linked at Ivinghoe Beacon with the Greensand Ridge Walk by the Two Ridges Link (8 miles) and where it also connects with the Icknield Way. See South Bucks Way.

Start	Overton Hill, Wilts	SU118681
Finish	Ivinghoe Beacon, Bucks	SP960168
On OS maps	165, 173, 174, 175	
Waymark	National Trail Acorn	
User group	Friends of Ridgeway	

Publication(s)
Softback: *The Ridgeway* (Official Guide) by Neil Curtis (Aurum Press). ISBN:185410490X. 1997\210 x 130\144pp\£10.99.
Paperback: *Discovering the Ridgeway* by Howard Clarke and Vera Burden (Shire Publications). ISBN:074780267X. 1995\112 x 177\80pp\£3.95(ı£1.00).
Booklet: *Ridgeway Information and Accommodation Guide* (Ridgeway Trail Officer). Annual\A5\40pp\£1.50(+40p).
Booklet: *The Ridgeway Public Transport Guide* (Ridgeway Trail Officer). Annual\A5\36pp\Free(+SAE).
Stripmap: *The Ridgeway* (Footprint). £2.95.
Leaflet: *The Ridgeway* (Countryside Commission Postal Sales). 1997\A4/3\Free.
Leaflet: *Two Ridges Link* (Buckinghamshire County Council). A4/3\Free(+SAE).

Ripon Rowel   369

N Yorks	80 km / 50 miles

A route around the ancient City of Ripon, visiting villages, sites of special and historical significance, wooded valleys, rivers, lakes and streams.

Start and finish	Ripon, N Yorks	SE319705
On OS maps	99	

| Waymark | Rowel logo - (circular part of a spur) |

Publication(s)
Booklet: *The Ripon Rowel Walk* by Les Taylor (RA Ripon). 1996\
210 x 145\70pp\£4.95(+49p).
Badge (£1.50 + SAE) available from RA Ripon.

River Parrett Trail 370

| Dorset, Somerset | 80 km / 50 miles |

A route which follows the River Parrett from source to mouth winding through the Somerset Levels, moors, ecologically sensitive areas and some of England's richest pasture land where there is an abundance of history and wildlife. The Trail crosses the Liberty Trail near Haselbury and Ham Hill, where it also meets up with the Leland Trail.

Start	Chedington, Dorset	ST490059
Finish	Steart, Somerset	ST281469
OS maps	182, 193	
Waymark	Name & two eels	

Publication(s)
Booklet: *The River Parrett Trail* (South Somerset District Council). ISBN:1899983309. 216 x 216\26pp\£5.25(+55p).
Leaflet: *An introduction to the River Parrett Trail* (South Somerset District Council). 1997\210 x 150\Free.

Rivers Way 371

| Derbys, Staffs | 69 km / 43 miles |

A meandering route through the Peak District National Park, the Way links the five principal rivers - the Noe, Derwent, Wye, Dove and Manifold - and passes the villages of Hope, Grindleford, Baslow, Bakewell, Flagg, Hartington and Wetton.

Start	Edale, Derbys	SK124853
Finish	Ilam, Derbys	SK135509
OS maps	119	

Publication(s)
Paperback: *The Rivers Way* by John Merrill (Happy Walking International Ltd). ISBN:0907496415. 140 x 210\36pp\£3.00.
Badge and certificate (£3.00/post free) available from Happy Walking International Ltd.

Roach Valley Way 372

Essex	37 km / 23 miles

A route around south-east Essex which takes in a variety of landscapes including the ancient woodlands of Hockley and the coastal margins of the Roach and Crouch estuaries.

Start and finish	Rochford, Essex	TQ873905
On OS maps	178	
Waymark	Blue/yellow river scene & name	

Publication(s)
Booklet: *Roach Valley Way* (Ways through Essex). ISBN: 1852811498. 1997\A5\16pp\£2.50.

Robin Hood Way 373

Notts	169 km / 105 miles

The Way features areas of Nottingham associated with the legendary figure of Robin Hood and his exploits, crossing lowland farmland and heathland, and visiting the great houses and parks of the Dukeries and forests, including Sherwood Forest.

Start	Nottingham, Notts	SK569392
Finish	Edwinstowe, Notts	SK626669
On OS maps	120, 129	
Waymark	Bow and arrow, green on white	

Publication(s)
Paperback: *The Robin Hood Walks* by Nottingham Wayfarers (Nottinghamshire County Council). ISBN:1871890020. 1994\192 x 133\156pp\£4.95(+35p).

Rosedale Circuit 374

N Yorks	59 km / 37 miles

A route through Rosedale, Farndale, Bransdale, Westerdale, Danby Dale, Great Fryup Dale and Glaisdale, which includes many points of natural and historical interest, with moorland tracks and grassy dales. This is a strenuous route with 4,000ft of ascent.

Start and finish	Rosedale Abbey, N Yorks	SE723959
OS maps	94, 100	
Waymark	Letters RC for most of the way	

Publication(s)
Leaflet: *Rosedale Circuit* (Kim Peacock). A4\Free(+9" x 6" SAE).

Badge and certificate (£1.30/ 9" x 6" SAE) available from Kim Peacock.

Roses Walk 375

Lancs, N Yorks	161 km / 100 miles

Derived from the historic emblems of the houses of Lancaster and York, the walk starts at Lancaster Castle, the site of the Roman fort, travels along the Lune Valley, through the Yorkshire Dales National Park, the eastern Pennines, along the banks of the River Nidd, skirting Harrogate and through Knaresborough, to follow the River Ouse to York Minster.

Start	Lancaster, Lancs	SD474618
Finish	York, N Yorks	SE602522
OS maps	97, 98, 99, 100, 104, 105	

Publication(s)
Paperback: *The Roses Walk* by Stan Jones (Camelot Books). 1995 \ A5 \ 108pp \ £6.95.

Rossendale Way 376

Lancs	72 km / 45 miles

A high-level route around Bacup, Rawtenstall, Haslingden and Whitworth in the Rossendale Valley, crossing the open moors and farmland of the South Pennines which roughly follows the Rossendale Borough boundary. Although easy to follow, it does need care in poor conditions. See Irwell Valley Way.

Start and finish	Sharneyford, Lancs	SD889246
On OS maps	103, 109	
Waymark	Letters RW	

Publication(s)
Folder: *Rossendale Way* (Rossendale Borough Council). 1982 \ A4/3 \ 9pp \ £0.76(incl p+p).

Rotherham Round Walk 377

S Yorks	40 km / 25 miles

This route takes in parkland, woods, lakes and the architectural monuments of Wentworth, followed by the steelworks of Parkgate, Wickersley and back into the town centre. The route can be completed as an anytime challenge - details from John Wadsworth (with SAE).

Start and finish	Rotherham, S Yorks	SK428928

OS maps	111
Waymark	Named discs with Chantry Bridge logo

Publication(s)
Leaflet: *Rotherham Roundwalk* (Rotherham Metropolitan Borough Council). A4/3 \ Free.
Badge and certificate available - details from John Wadsworth.

Round Fetlar Walk 378

Shetland	50 km / 31 miles

A coast walk around one of the islands of Shetland, with its crofting communities and bird sanctuaries, Pictish brochs and ponies. Starting where the ferry from Gutcher lands at Oddsta, the route follows the coastline as near as possible via Gruting, The Snap and Tresta.

Start and finish	Oddsta, Shetland	HU582943
OS maps	1	

Publication(s)
Paperback: *Walking the Coastline of Shetland: 3 - Island of Fetlar* by Peter Guy (Shetland Times Ltd). ISBN:0951584510. 1991 \ A5 \ 70pp \ £5.99(incl p+p).

Round Northmavine Trek 379

Shetland	201 km / 125 miles

This walk around the largest parish in Shetland excels in wild rock scenery. Although part of Mainland, Shetland's largest island, Northmavine is almost an island itself as the neck of land connecting it is only 100 yards across. The route includes Shetland's highest hill, Ronas Hill (1,486ft), and visits Urafirth, Hillswick, Stenness, Hamnavoe, Swinister, Lang Clodie Wick, Sandvoe, North Roe and Ollaberry.

Start and finish	Mavis Grind, Shetland	HU340683
OS maps	1, 2, 3	

Publication(s)
Paperback: *Walking the Coastline of Shetland: 4 - Northmavine* by Peter Guy (Shetland Times Ltd). ISBN:0952002604. 1993 \ A5 \ 112pp \ £5.00(incl p+p).

Round Preston Walk 380

Lancs	37 km / 23 miles

Created by the RA, this route around the town takes in the River Ribble (partly coincident with the Ribble Way), Grimsargh, Broughton, Woodplumpton and Lea.

Start and finish	Penwortham Bridge, Lancs	SD527288
OS maps	102	
Waymark	Preston Guild logo (cross-bearing lamb)	

Publication(s)
Booklet: *The Round Preston Walk* (RA Preston Group). 1991\ 32pp\£1.80.

Round Unst Trek 381

Shetland	101 km / 63 miles

A coastline walk around the northernmost island of Shetland, taking in many historical sites, bird and other wildlife and cliff scenery. It visits Westing, Woodwick, Burrafirth, Norwick, Harold-swick, Baltasound, Muness and Uyeasound.

Start and finish	Belmont, Shetland	HP566004
OS maps	1	

Publication(s)
Paperback: *Walking the Coastline of Shetland: 2 - Unst* by Peter Guy (Shetland Times Ltd). ISBN:0951584502. 1994\A5\80pp\ £5.99(incl p+p).

Round Yell Trek 382

Shetland	162 km / 101 miles

Another route around one of the islands of Shetland, taking in bird and other wildlife, cliff scenery and historical remains and visiting West Sandwick, Windhouse, Gloup, Cullivoe, Gutcher, Sellafirth, Mid Yell, Otterswick, Burravoe and Bridge of Arisdale.

Start and finish	Ulsta, Shetland	HU463795
OS maps	1, 2	

Publication(s)
Paperback: *Walking the Coastline of Shetland: 1 - Yell* by Peter Guy (Shetland Times Ltd). ISBN:1898852189. 1996\A5\96pp\£8.34 (incl p+p).

Royal Military Canal Path 383

E Sussex, Kent	43 km / 27 miles

The Royal Military Canal Path mainly follows a canal-side path, which fringes the northern edge of Romney Marsh and which was built in the early 19th century as a defence against a possible invasion by Napoleon. The Canal is a Scheduled Ancient Monument and a SSSI. In addition to its historical and archaeological interest it is a valuable wetland habitat for a variety of species of flora and fauna. Links are made with the Saxon Shore Way at various points.

Start	Pett Level, E Sussex	TQ888134
Finish	Seabrook, Kent	TR188349
On OS maps	189, 199	
Waymark	Reeds and canal	

Publication(s)
Leaflet: *Royal Military Canal: Walk Through History* (Kent County Council). 1996\A4/6\Free.
Booklet: *Along and Around the Royal Military Canal Path* edited by Philip Rutt (Kent County Council). ISBN:1873010974. 1998\details TBA.

Rutland Water Challenge Walk 384

Leics	38 km / 24 miles

A route around the largest man-made reservoir in Europe.

Start and finish	Rutland Water, Leics	SK935083
OS maps	141	

Publication(s)
Paperback: *The Rutland Water Challenge Walk* by John Merrill (Happy Walking International Ltd). ISBN: 0907496881. 36pp\ £3.00.
Badge and certificate (£3.00/post free) available from Happy Walking International Ltd.

Rydal Round 385

Cumbria	45 km / 28 miles

A demanding route with 9000ft of ascent, visiting Fairfield, Patterdale, Thornthwaite Crag and Kirkstone Pass. Navigational skills are appropriate in poor weather conditions.

Start and finish	Pelter Bridge, Cumbria	NY365059
OS maps	90	

Publication(s)
Looseleaf: *Rydal Round* (Jim Strother). Free(+9" x 4" SAE).
Certificate (£1.00/post free) available from Jim Strother (cheques
payable to Oxfam).

Saddleworth Five Trig Points Walk 386

Gtr Man	32 km / 20 miles

A tough high level circuit over open moorland and across peat
groughs, with parts of the Walk being coincident with the Pennine
Way and other routes in this area. As its name suggests, the route
links five trig points on the Saddleworth Moors, namely Alphin
Pike, Featherbed Moss, Black Hill, West Nab and Broadstone Hill.
See New Five Trig Points Walk.

Start and finish	Greenfield, Gtr Man	SE002040
OS maps	109, 110	

Publication(s)
Looseleaf: *Saddleworth Five Trig Points Walk* (Bob Tait). A4 \
Free(+SAE).
Badge and certificate (£1.00/£0.20/9" x 5" SAE) available from Bob
Tait.

Saddleworth Skyline 387

Gtr Man	45 km / 28 miles

A mainly high-level route linking the tops of Saddleworth over
moorland, hills and valleys.

Start and finish	Dovestones Reservoir, Gtr Man	SE013034
OS maps	109, 110	

Publication(s)
Looseleaf: *The Saddleworth Skyline* (Sam R Taylor). Free(+SAE).
Badge and certificate (£1.80/SAE/£0.20/SAE) available from Sam
R Taylor.

St Cuthbert's Way 388

Borders, Northumb	100 km / 62 miles

The Way was inspired by the life of St Cuthbert, who began his
ministry at Melrose in 650AD, eventually becoming the Bishop of
Lindisfarne. The route provides a link over the Cheviot Hills,
between the Southern Upland Way (at Melrose) and the Pennine
Way (at Kirk Yetholm), with the Northumbrian Coastline.

Start	Melrose Abbey, Borders	NT548341

Finish	Lindisfarne, Northumb	NU126418
OS maps	73, 74, 75	
Waymark	Celtic Cross	

Publication(s)

Paperback: *St Cuthbert's Way - The Official Guide* by Roger Smith & Ron Shaw (Stationery Office). ISBN:0114957622. 1997\220 x 135\96pp\£12.99.
Booklet: *St Cuthbert's Way - Melrose to Lindisfarne* by Roger Smith & Ron Shaw (Harestanes Countryside Visitor Centre). 1996\A5\ 18pp\£1.50(+SAE).
Stripmap: *St Cuthbert's Way (Harvey Maps)*. ISBN:1851372474. 1997\£6.95(+80p).
Leaflet: *St Cuthbert's Way - Accommodation List* (Scottish Borders Enterprise). 1996\A4/3\Free(+SAE).
Leaflet: *St Cuthbert's Way - Melrose to Lindisfarne* (Harestanes Countryside Visitor Centre). 1996\A4/4\Free(+SAE).
Certificate (£1.00) available from Berwick-upon-Tweed Borough Council.

St Edmund Way   389

Essex, Suffolk	142 km / 88 miles

A route across Suffolk, the Way uses the Stour Valley Path (East Anglia) to Sudbury and Long Melford, then via Lavenham and Little Welnetham to Bury St Edmunds, along the Lark Valley Path (13 miles) to the Icknield Way at West Stow before striking over the Brecks to Thetford and the Hereward Way.

Start	Manningtree, Essex	TM094322
Finish	Brandon, Suffolk	TL784866
OS maps	143, 144, 155, 168	

Publication(s)

Paperback: *The St Edmund Way - A Walk across Suffolk* (J & J Andrews) . 1994\208 x 146\66pp\£3.75(+£0.50 p&p).
Leaflet: *Lark Valley Path* (Suffolk County Council). A4/3\ £0.20 (+SAE).

St Illtyd's Walk   390

Carmarthen, Neath	103 km / 64 miles

From the sands, a walk across varied terrain, canals, woodlands and gentle hills crossing the rivers Loughor, Tawe, Neath and Afan. The Walk links with the Coed Morannwg Way at Margam, giving access to the Rhymney Valley Ridgeway Walk and Taff Trail.

Start	Pembrey, Carmarthen	SN405008
Finish	Margam, Neath	SS814852

| OS maps | 159, 160, 170 |
| Waymark | Black turreted tower |

Publication(s)
Booklet: *St Illtyd's Walk* by G Colin Davies (Carmarthenshire County Council). ISBN:0953002706. A5\30pp\£2.20(+£0.30 p&p).

St Peter's Way 391

| Essex | 72 km / 45 miles |

The Way is across the open agricultural land of Essex passing Hanningfield Reservoir and inlets of the Blackwater Estuary and reaches the coast to the east of Tillingham, then following the sea wall from where there are extensive views across the Essex marshes.

Start	Chipping Ongar, Essex	TL551036
Finish	St Peter's Flat, Essex	TM032082
On OS maps	167, 168, 177	

Publication(s)
Booklet: *The St Peter's Way* by Fred Matthews and Harry Bitten (Ways through Essex). 1985\A5\25pp\£1.20.

Saints Way/Forth an Syns 392

| Cornwall | 42 km / 26 miles |

The Way follows the route thought to have been taken by the ancient Cornish and Welsh Saints. It comprises a series of linking parish walks through the attractive but little-known area of mid-Cornwall. From the north coast, it crosses St Breock Downs to reach Lanivet, continues on to Helman Tor and then goes via either St Samsons or St Blazey to the south coast.

Start	Padstow, Cornwall	SW920754
Finish	Fowey, Cornwall	SX127522
On OS maps	200, 204	
Waymark	Celtic cross	

Publication(s)
Paperback: *The Saints Way: Forth an Syns* (Cornwall County Council). 1991\A5\32pp\£2.50.

Salt & Sails Trail 393

| Cheshire | 32 km / 20 miles |

A route following the Weaver Navigation from the River Mersey and passing a number of locks and the Anderton Lift.

Start	Weston Point, Cheshire	SJ813804
Finish	Winsford, Cheshire	SJ655663
OS maps	117, 118	

Publication(s)
Booklet: *The Salt & Sails Trail* by David Burkhill-Howarth (Happy Walking International Ltd). ISBN:1874754586. A5\£3.25.
Badge and certificate (£3.00/incl p+p) available from Happy Walking International Ltd.

Salter's Way 394

Cheshire	38 km / 24 miles

The Way follows an old salt track across lowland Cheshire from the salt area around Northwich to the moors above Macclesfield. It passes still-working brine pumps, as well as such varied features as Jodrell Bank and the raised lowland bog of Danes Moss.

Start	Broken Cross, Cheshire	SJ682732
Finish	Salterford, Cheshire	SJ983763
OS maps	118	

Publication(s)
Softback: *The Salter's Way* by John N Merrill (Happy Walking International Ltd). ISBN:0907496970. 132 x 210\32pp\£3.00.
Badge and certificate (£3.00/post free) available from Happy Walking International Ltd.

Samaritan Way 395

Cleveland, N Yorks	64 km / 40 miles

A strenuous high-level route across the North York Moors National Park, crossing Commondale, Great Fryup Dale, Glaisdale and Farndale Moors to return via Westerdale, Baysdale and part of the Cleveland Way.

Start and finish	Guisborough, Cleveland	NZ615160
OS maps	93, 94, 100	

Publication(s)
Looseleaf: *Samaritan Way* (R T Pinkney). Free(+SAE).
Badge and certificate (£2.25/SAE/£0.25/SAE) available from R T Pinkney.

Sandstone Trail 396

Cheshire, Shrops	51 km / 32 miles

The Trail, follows the dissected central Cheshire sandstone ridge rising to heights of over 700ft and taking in Delamere Plain, Beeston Gap, the wooded Peckforton Hills and Bickerton Hills, to the Shropshire Union Canal where it links with the South Cheshire Way. See also Maelor Way and Lancashire Trail.

Start	Frodsham (Beacon Hill), Cheshire	SJ517767
Finish	Grindley Brook, Shrops	SJ522433
On OS maps	117	
Waymark	Black bootmark and yellow letter S	

Publication(s)
Booklet: *Sandstone Trail* by Ruth Rogers (Mara Publications). ISBN:0952240920. 1995\A5\68pp\£3.95.
Booklet: *Longer Trails in Vale Royal* by Carl Rogers (Vale Royal Borough Council). 1993\A5\76pp\£1.95.
Booklet: *Sandstone Trail* (Cheshire County Council). 212 x 200\16pp\£1.95(+31p).

Sarn Helen 397

Aberconwy, Caernarfon, Cardigan, Carmarthen, Powys	258 km / 160 miles

Sarn Helen generally refers to Roman roads. This route traces the line of Roman roads through West Wales, connecting various Roman remains. In places the old road is clearly visible, but in others it is a matter of conjecture. From the Roman fort at Caerhun, the route heads along the edge of Snowdonia to the Swallow Falls, Dolwyddelan, skirts Ffestiniog to Trawsfynydd, continuing to Dolgellau and Machynlleth. After crossing the Rheidol valley, the route becomes less wild and more agricultural, to Bronant, Lampeter, and Carmarthen. Navigational skills would be appropriate on the northern part of the route.

Start	Caerhun, Aberconwy	SH775704
Finish	Carmarthen	SN400210
OS maps	115, 124, 135, 146, 159	

Publication(s)
Paperback: *Sarn Helen: Walking a Roman Road through Wales* by Arthur Rylance and John Cantrell (Cicerone Press). ISBN: 185284101X. 1992\116 x 176\248pp\£8.99 .

Saxon Shore Way   398

E Sussex, Kent	262 km / 163 miles

The Way around the ancient coastline offers a diversity of scenery, following the wide expanses of marshland bordering the Thames and Medway estuaries and the White Cliffs of Dover. There are views over Romney Marsh from the escarpment that marks the ancient coastline between Folkestone and Rye, and from the cliffs of the High Weald at Hastings. Here the Romans invaded Britain and, later, built the Saxon Shore forts to defend the island against a new wave of invaders, and St Augustine landed to bring the Gospel to the Anglo-Saxon Kingdom which would later fall to the Normans who, in their turn, erected great fortresses like Dover Castle to defend their conquests. The Swale Heritage Trail - from Murston to Goodnestone (11 miles), caters for circular walks of up to 20 miles when incorporated with the Saxon Shore route between Murston and Faversham. Likewise, the shorter Wantsum Walks can be incorporated with the Way to provide extended circular routes. At Rye the route connects with the 1066 Country Walk. See Greensand Way/Royal Military Canal Path and Thanet Coastal Path.

Start	Gravesend, Kent	TQ647745
Finish	Hastings, E Sussex	TQ825094
On OS maps	177, 178, 179, 189, 199	
Waymark	Red Viking helmet	

Publication(s)
Paperback: *The Saxon Shore Way* by Bea Cowan (Aurum Press). ISBN:185410392X. 1996\210 x 130\£10.99.
Booklet: *Swale Heritage Trail* (Kent County Council). ISBN: 1873010508. 1995\210 x 148\36pp\£2.95.
Folder: *Wantsum Walks* (Kent County Council). ISBN:1873010001. 1995\A4/3\4 leaflets\£2.45.

Scarborough Rock Challenge   399

N Yorks	42 km / 26 miles

A route supported by the East Yorkshire Group of the LDWA taking in the coast, Oliver's Mount, Hackness, Burniston and Scalby.

Start and finish	Peasholm Park, Scarborough, N Yorks	TA035897
OS maps	101	

Publication(s)
Looseleaf: *Scarborough Rock Challenge Walk* (Mike Ellis). A4\ Free(+9" x 4" SAE).
Badge (£1.00/SAE) available from Mike Ellis.

Seahorse Saunter 400

N Yorks	69 km / 43 miles

The route crosses the North York Moors to the old Nordic settlement of Whitby on the east coast. Following a mixture of field paths, bridleways and paved packhorse ways, the Saunter passes through farmland, open moors and wooded valleys, in an ever changing facet of this popular National Park. Most of the route is easy to follow, but in poor weather conditions navigational skills are required.

Start	Kilburn White Horse, N Yorks	SE515814
Finish	Whitby, N Yorks	NZ901113
OS maps	94, 100	

Publication(s)
Leaflet: *Seahorse Saunter* (Simon Townson). A4 \ Free(+SAE).
Badge and certificate (£2.00/10" x 8" SAE) available from Simon Townson.

Sefton Coastal Footpath 401

Merseyside	34 km / 21 miles

From the northern outskirts of Liverpool, the route, through dunes, marshes and the towns of Southport and Crosby, passes the Ainsdale Nature and Formby National Trust Reserves. There are plans to link the path with the Lancashire Coastal Way at the Ribble Estuary.

Start	Waterloo Station, Merseyside	SJ321981
Finish	Crossens, Merseyside	SD374205
On OS maps	102, 108	
Waymark	Natterjack toad logo	

Publication(s)
Booklet: *Walks on the Sefton Coast* by John Houston (Sefton Metropolitan Borough Council). 1994 \ 250 x 225 \ 26pp \ £2.50.

Settle Scramble 402

N Yorks	40 km / 25 miles

A route taking in Fountain's Fell, Helwith Bridge and Feizor.

Start and finish	Settle, N Yorks	SD821632
OS maps	98	

Publication(s)
Looseleaf: *Settle Scramble* (Ian Parker). A4 \ Free(+SAE).

Badge and certificate (£2.00/£0.50/SAE) available from Ian Parker.

Severn Way   403

Avon, Glos, Heref & Worc, Shrops, Somerset, Powys	338 km / 210 miles

A route along the entire Severn Valley from the source to the sea. Starting on the wild Plynlimon plateau in Mid-Wales, the route takes in Hafren Forest, Llanidloes, Newtown, Welshpool, Shrewsbury and Ironbridge before heading south through Worcester, Tewkesbury and Gloucester to the finish. A link into Bristol is being created. A comprehensive guide book is to be available from early summer, 1998 - details from the Conservation and Recreation Officer, Environment Agency.

Start	Plynlimon, Powys	SN822899
Finish	Severn Beach, Avon	ST540847
On OS maps	136, 137, 138, 150, 162, 172	
Waymark	Severn Trow logo and named posts	

Publication(s)
Leaflet: *The Severn Way* (Environment Agency). 1997\A5\ Free(+SAE).

Sheffield Country Walk   404

Derbys, S Yorks	85 km / 53 miles

This varied route around the outskirts of the city passes many sites and buildings of archaeological, historical and industrial interest. It follows woodland and riverside paths, crossing undulating farmland and the open gritstone moorlands.

Start and finish	Eckington, Derbys	SK434798
OS maps	110, 111, 120	
Waymark	Yellow arrows and sheaf symbols	

Publication(s)
Booklet: *Sheffield Country Walk* by John Harker (RA Sheffield). 1996\£2.50.

Sheffield Way   405

Derbys, S Yorks	72 km / 45 miles

A similar route to the Sheffield Country Way but is shorter by deliberately keeping to a tighter circuit mostly within the City boundary. Starting near the M1 it follows a route soon into woodlands and moors bordering the Peak District followed by Stanage, Totley and Coal Aston.

Start and finish	Tinsley, S Yorks	SK399912
OS maps	110, 111, 119, 120	

Publication(s)
Looseleaf: *Sheffield Way* by Peter Price (RA Sheffield). A4\52pp\ £4.00.

Shieldsman Walk 406

Tyne & Wear	53 km / 33 miles

A route along the coast and through the countryside of Tyneside with an historic theme, crossing the Tyne by pedestrian tunnel and ferry.

Start and finish	South Shields, Tyne & Wear	NZ370676
OS maps	88	

Publication(s)
Leaflet: *Shieldsman Walk* (David Kidd). A4\Free(+SAE).
Certificate (Free/A4 SAE) available from David Kidd.

Shropshire Challenge Walk 407

Shrops	122 km / 76 miles

A route linking the youth hostels at Ludlow, Wheathill, Wilderhope Manor, Bridges and Clun, taking in climbs of the Long Mynd, the Clees, Caer Caradoc and Wenlock Edge. It is partly coincident with the Shropshire Way.

Start and finish	Ludlow, Shrops	SO510745
OS maps	137, 138	

Publication(s)
Booklet: *Shropshire Challenge Walk* (YHA Northern Region). 147 x 210\£0.50(+SAE).

Shropshire Peaks Walk 408

Shrops	160 km / 99 miles

A walk taking in the main peaks of South Shropshire, including Hopesay Hill, Bury Ditches, Hergan, Linley Hill, Stiperstones, Long Mynd, Caer Caradoc, the Lawley, Wenlock Edge, Brown Clee and Titterstone Clee and passing through the villages of Craven Arms, Clun, Bishop's Castle, Bridges, Church Stretton and Much Wenlock. The route utilizes some parts of the Shropshire Way.

Start and finish	Ludlow, Shrops	SO510746
OS maps	127, 137, 138	

Publication(s)
Booklet: *The Shropshire Peaks Walk* (Ian R Jones). 1996\A5\
42pp\£1.80(+£0.30).

Shropshire Union Canal 409

Cheshire, Staffs, W Midlands	60 km / 37 miles

The Birmingham and Liverpool Junction Canal, opened in 1835
and later forming part of the Shropshire Union, was Thomas
Telford's last great engineering challenge. From the edge of the
Black Country, it passes through rural Shropshire via Gnosall,
Norbury, Market Drayton and Audlem to Nantwich. The canal
itself continues via Chester to Ellesmere Port. See Sandstone Trail.

Start	Autherley Junction, W Midlands	SJ902020
Finish	Nantwich, Cheshire	SJ640530
OS maps	118, 127	

Publication(s)
Leaflet: *The Shropshire Union Canal* (British Waterways - Chester). 1996\A5\Free(+SAE).
Stripmap: *Shropshire Union Canal* (GEOprojects). ISBN:
0863510329. 1996\945 x 428\£3.75.

Shropshire Way 410

Shrops	224 km / 139 miles

A varied route crossing lowland farmland and many of the notable
hills of Shropshire. It passes through Shrewsbury, Clun and Ludlow (the most southerly point), and on the return takes in the Clee
Hills, Wenlock Edge, Ironbridge and the Wrekin. An 11 mile spur
runs north from Wem to meet the Sandstone Trail, the Marches,
Maelor and South Cheshire Ways at Grindley Brook.

Start and finish	Wem, Shrops	SJ513289
On OS maps	117, 126, 127, 137, 138, 148	
Waymark	Buzzard	

Publication(s)
Paperback: *Rambler's Guide to the Shropshire Way* by R.W. Moore
(Management Update Ltd). ISBN:0946679444.
1995\A5\70pp\£5.99(+£0.95).

Sidmouth Saunter 411

Devon	40 km / 25 miles

A circuit combining coastal footpath and picturesque East Devon
scenery. There is also a shorter 13-mile route.

Start and finish	The Ham, Sidmouth, Devon	ST128872
OS maps	192	

Publication(s)
Looseleaf: *Sidmouth Saunter* (Terry Bound). Free(+SAE).
Badge and certificate (£1.00/ - /A4 SAE) available from Terry Bound.

Silkin Way 412

Shrops	23 km / 14 miles

A route following dry canal beds and former railway lines close to the many natural and historical features within Telford. The Ironbridge Way - Ironbridge to Leegomery (10 miles) connects with the route at Leegomery.

Start	Coalport, Shrops	SJ703023
Finish	Bratton, Shrops	SJ634141
On OS maps	127	
Waymark	Wheeled logo	

Publication(s)
Leaflet: *The Silkin Way* (Wrekin Countryside Service). A4/3\ Free(+SAE).
Leaflet: *The Ironbridge Way* (Wrekin Countryside Service). A3/6\ Free(+SAE).

Sirhowy Valley Walk 413

Blaenau, Caerphilly, Newport	42 km / 26 miles

A challenging route from the built-up fringes of Newport to the mountain ridges of Mynyddd Machen and Mynydd Manmoel. It passes lowland and upland farms, woodlands and riverside parks, many sites of historical interest, including an Iron Age hill fort, an old mill and a canal centre, before finishing near Tredegar. The Walk links with the Ebbw Valley Walk near to Wattsville (Full Moon Visitor Centre).

Start	Newport	ST310879
Finish	Tredegar, Blaenau	SO151105
On OS maps	161, 171	
Waymark	Letter S on standard waymarks	

Publication(s)
Folder: *The Sirhowy Valley Walk* (Caerphilly County Borough Council). 175 x 240\14pp\£2.75.

Six Shires Circuit 414

Beds, Bucks, Cambs, Leics, Lincs, Northants	331 km / 206 miles

A route linking the Nene, Three Shires, Grafton, Knightley, Roman, Spaldwick, Ermine Street and Torpel Ways. The publications comprise details of 15 linear routes (ranging from 10 miles to 20 miles) and the price includes certificates.

Start and finish	Wellingborough, Northants	SP888683
OS maps	141, 142, 152, 153	

Publication(s)
Booklet: *Six Shires Circuit* (Waendel Walkers Club). £10.00.,
Looseleaf: *Six Shires Circuit - information sheet* (Waendel Walkers Club). Free(+A6 SAE).
Badge (£2.50/A5 SAE) available from Waendel Walkers Club.

Six Shropshire Summits 415

Powys, Shrops	56 km / 35 miles

A route over Shropshire's six hills exceeding 1500ft namely Corndon, Brown Clee, Long Mynd, Stiperstones, Titterstone Lee and Caer Caradoc.

Start	Corndon Hill, Shrops	SO301971
Finish	Clee Hill, Shrops	SO594771
OS maps	137	

Publication(s)
Looseleaf: *Six Shropshire Summits* (Vivian Bird OBE). A4\1pp\ Free(+SAE).
Badge and certificate (£0.60/Free/SAE) available from Vivian Bird OBE.

Skipton-Settle Link 416

N Yorks	32 km / 20 miles

A walk linking two North Craven market towns and visiting the trig points on Sharp Haw and Weets, through moorland, field and fells.

Start	Aireville Park,Skipton, N Yorks	SD979518
Finish	Settle, N Yorks	SD821632
OS maps	98, 103	

Publication(s)
Looseleaf: *Skipton-Settle Link* (Ian Parker). A4\Free(+SAE).
Badge and certificate (£2.00/£0.50/SAE) available from Ian Parker.

Sky to Sea 417

Bridgend, Rhondda, Vale of Glamorgan	56 km / 35 miles

A route taking in the spectacular countryside of the West Glamorgan Heritage Coast. There are links with the many other long distance routes in South Wales.

Start	Dare Valley Country Park, Rhondda	SN983026
Finish	Gileston, Vale of Glamorgan	SS956675
OS maps	170	
Waymark	Blue cloud & waves logo	

Publication(s)
Leaflet: *Sky to Sea - over the Bwlch* (Groundwork Bridgend). A4/3 \
Free(+SAE).
Leaflet: *Sky to Sea - Through the Vale* (Groundwork Bridgend).
A4/3 \ Free(+SAE).

Snowdon Challenge Walk 418

Caernarfon	48 km / 30 miles

5,000ft of ascent to the top of Snowdon and back, this is a tough walk. From Caernarfon Bay, it climbs via Penygroes and the Ranger Path, and then descends again via the Rhyd-ddu path.

Start and finish	Pontllyfni, Caernarfon	SH435526
OS maps	115	

Publication(s)
Paperback: *John Merrill's Snowdon Challenge Walk* by John Merrill (Happy Walking International Ltd). ISBN: 0907496792. 210 x 130 \ 40pp \ £3.00.
Badge and certificate (£3.00/post free) available from Happy Walking International Ltd

Snowdonia 24hr Circuit 419

Aberconwy, Caernarfon	72 km / 45 miles

A tough rollercoaster-type circuit of approximately 16,500ft of ascent, which includes the Snowdon Horseshoe, Glyders, Carneddau and Moel Siabod massifs.

Start and finish	Capel Curig, Aberconwy	SH721583
OS maps	115	

Publication(s)
Looseleaf: *Snowdonia 24hr Circuit* (Ed Dalton). Free(+9" x 4" SAE).

Certificate (Free/9" x 6" SAE) available from Ed Dalton.

Snowdonia Challenges   420

Caernarfon	Various km

These comprise the *Heart of Snowdonia Circuit* (50 miles) which traverses the 24 traditionally accepted 2000ft summits (20,000ft of ascent), the *Snowdonia Five Ranges Round* (40 miles) which visits the highest summit in each of the principal mountain ranges of Central Snowdonia (12,500ft of ascent) and the *Welsh 1000m Peaks Marathon* (26 miles) which takes in Snowdon, Carnedd Ugain, Carnedd Llewelyn and Carnedd Dafydd (9050ft of ascent).

Start	Various	Various
Finish	Various	Various
OS maps	115	

Publication(s)
Looseleaf: *Three Snowdonia Challenge Walks* (Dave Irons). 1994 \
A4 \ 14pp \ £2.00(post free).

Socratic Trail   421

Surrey, W Sussex	76 km / 47 miles

The Trail, follows paths and country lanes with little traffic, across rolling Surrey hills and the Sussex Weald making use of short stretches of the North Downs Way, Greensand Way, Sussex Border Path and the South Downs Way, with panoramic views along the journey to the sea.

Start	Old Coulsdon, Surrey	TQ312582
Finish	Brighton, W Sussex	TQ333034
OS maps	177, 187, 198	

Publication(s)
Booklet: *The Socratic Trail Guide* (Maurice Hencke). 1995 \ A5 \
30pp \ £1.00(+£0.31 SAE).

Solent Way   422

Hants	96 km / 60 miles

The route crosses coastal marshes to Lymington before going inland past the heaths, woods and villages of the New Forest, Bucklers Hard and Beaulieu to reach Hythe on the Test Estuary. The ferry is taken to Southampton, from where it follows the Solent shoreline, crossing the River Hamble to reach Portsmouth via the Gosport ferry. It continues along the historic waterfront of

Portsmouth and Southsea and passes the coastal marshes and quays around Langstone Harbour. See Staunton Way.

Start	Milford-on-Sea, Hants	SZ292918
Finish	Emsworth, Hants	SU753055
On OS maps	196, 197	
Waymark	Dark blue bird on light blue ground	

Publication(s)
Paperback: *Exploring the Solent Way* by Anne-Marie Edwards (Countryside Books). ISBN:1853062723. 210 x 150 \ 128pp \ £5.95. Leaflet: *The Solent Way* (Hampshire County Council). A4/3 \ Free(+SAE).

South Bucks Way 423

Bucks	37 km / 23 miles

From the Ridgeway, the route descends through woodland to the source of the River Misbourne which it follows through Amersham to Denham at the confluence of the river with the River Colne and where the walk concludes on the towpath of the Grand Union Canal.

Start	Coombe Hill, Bucks	SP849067
Finish	Denham, Bucks	TQ053862
On OS maps	165, 175, 176	
Waymark	Standard waymark with name	

Publication(s)
Leaflet: *South Bucks Way* (Buckinghamshire County Council). A4/3 \ Free(+SAE).

South Cheshire Way 424

Cheshire, Shrops	50 km / 31 miles

A route linking the Sandstone Trail with the Staffordshire Way running through lowland farmland, passing Crewe and Alsager, before climbing to the finish. See also the Maelor Way.

Start	Grindley Brook, Shrops	SJ522433
Finish	Mow Cop, Cheshire	SJ856573
On OS maps	117, 118	
Waymark	Letters SCW on standard waymarks	

Publication(s)
Booklet: *Guide to the South Cheshire Way* by Justin McCarthy (Mid-Cheshire Footpath Society). 1988 \ 145 x 203 \ 20pp \ £0.75(+Large SAE).

South Downs Way 425

E Sussex, Hants, W Sussex	162 km / 101 miles

This National Trail follows the northern escarpment of the chalk Downs from where there are extensive views across the Weald to the north and over the rounded hills and dry valleys to the sea to the south. There are several steep ascents when crossing the valleys of the Rivers Cuckmere at Alfriston, Ouse at Southease, Adur south of Bramber and Arun at Amberley. It visits Jevington and passes iron age hillforts and barrows. There is an alternative path running along the cliff tops to Beachy Head and the Seven Sisters turning inland at Cuckmere Haven along the Cuckmere Valley to rejoin the Way at Alfriston where there is a connection to the 1066 Country Walk. See Downs Link and Staunton Way.

Start	Eastbourne (Holywell), E Sussex	TV600972
Finish	Winchester, Hants	SU483293
On OS maps	185, 197, 198, 199	
Waymark	National Trail Acorn	

Publication(s)
Softback: *South Downs Way* (Official Guide) by Paul Millmore (Aurum Press). ISBN:1854104071. 1995\210 x 130\168pp\ £10.99.
Hardback: *Guide to the South Downs Way* by Miles Jebb (Constable and Co Ltd). ISBN:0094711704. 171 x 114\336pp\£10.95.
Paperback: *The South Downs Way and Downs Link* by Kev Reynolds (Cicerone Press). ISBN:1852840234. 116 x 176\136pp\ £5.99.
Paperback: *Along the South Downs Way to Winchester* (Society of Sussex Downsmen). £5.00.
Stripmap: *South Downs Way* (Harvey Maps). 1997\£6.95(+80p).
Leaflet: *Accommodation Guide to the South Downs Way* (South Downs Way Officer). £1.50.
Leaflet: *South Downs Way* (Countryside Commission Postal Sales). 1997\A4/3\Free.

South of the Landsker Trail 426

Pembroke	97 km / 60 miles

The walk uses footpaths, bridleways and quiet roads, passing through farmland, woodland and small villages of the inland area of South Pembrokeshire, taking in a 20 mile section of the Pembrokeshire Coast Path along spectacular cliffs. The Trail also links with the Landsker Borderlands Trail.

Start and finish	Narberth, Pembroke	SN121147
OS maps	158	
Waymark	Green Celtic knot symbol and name	

Publication(s)
Folder: *South of the Landsker* (SPARC). 1996\A5\6pp\£2.80(incl p&p).
Certificate (Free/SAE) available from SPARC.

South West Coast Path   427

Cornwall, Devon, Dorset, Somerset	966 km / 600 miles

Often referred to simply as the South West Way, this, the longest of the National Trails, forms a route around the south-west peninsular. For the most part, the route keeps to the immediate coastline with just short sections diverted away. To avoid inland walking around some estuaries, ferry services are generally available. At Lulworth, because of military activity, there are access restrictions on certain days. The St Michael's Way (12 miles) links Lelant (north coast of Cornwall) with Penzance/Marazion/St Michael's Mount on the south and can be extended into a much longer circular route when combined with the coast path.

Start	Minehead, Somerset	SS972467
Finish	South Haven Point, Dorset	SZ036866
On OS maps	180, 181, 190, 192, 193, 194, 195, 200, 201, 202, 203, 204	
Waymark	National Trail Acorn	
User group	South West Way Association	

Publication(s)
Softback: *South West Coast Path: Minehead to Padstow* (Official Guide) by Roland Tarr (Aurum Press). ISBN:1854104152. 1995\210 x 130\168pp\£10.99.
Softback: *South West Coast Path: Padstow to Falmouth* (Official Guide) by John Macadam (Aurum Press). ISBN:1854103873. 1995\210 x 130\£10.99.
Softback: *South West Coast Path: Falmouth to Exmouth* (Official Guide) by Brian le Messurier (Aurum Press). ISBN:1854103881. 1995\210 x 130\168pp\£10.99.
Softback: *South West Coast Path: Exmouth to Poole* (Official Guide) by Roland Tarr (Aurum Press). ISBN:185410389X. 1995\210 x 130\168pp\£10.99.
Paperback: *The South West Way Vol 1: Minehead to Penzance* by Martin Collins (Cicerone Press). ISBN:1852840250. 1989\116 x 176\184pp\£8.99.
Paperback: *The South West Way Vol 2: Penzance to Poole* by Martin Collins (Cicerone Press). ISBN:1852840269. 1989\116 x 176\198pp\£8.99.
Paperback: *Exploring the Dorset Coast Path* by Leigh Hatts (Countryside Books). ISBN:1853062243. 1993\210 x 150\128pp\£4.95.
Paperback: *Footpath Touring: Land's End and the Lizard* by Ken Ward (Footpath Touring). ISBN:0711701938. 1985\224 x 114\64pp\£3.50.

Softback: *The South West Way 1997: the Complete Guide to the South West Coast Path* (South West Way Association). ISBN: 1872640400. 1997\£4.99.
Softback: *Walk the Cornish Coastal Path* by John H N Mason (Collins). ISBN:000448701X. 210 x 148\£5.99.
Paperback: *Explore the Coast of Devon* by Paul Wreyford (Sigma Leisure). ISBN:1850584400. 1995\136pp\ £6.95.
Leaflet: *The South West Coast Path* (Countryside Commission Postal Sales). 1992\A4/3\Free.
Booklet: *St Michael's Way* (Cornwall County Council). 1994\A5\ 20pp\£2.25.
Leaflet: *St Michael's Way* (Cornwall County Council). 1994\A4/3\ Free(+SAE).

Southam Circular Way   428

Warks	34 km / 21 miles

A route around the town of Southam initially along the River Stowe to Ufton, passing Stoney Thorpe Hall, Harbury, Bishop's Itchington, Ladbroke and Napton-on-the-Hill. The Way then joins the Oxford Canal and Grand Union Canal, finally passing through Bascote.

Start and finish	Southam, Warks	SP419619
OS maps	151	

Publication(s)
Booklet: *Southam Circular Way* by Harry Green (RA Southam & District). 1988\A5\32pp\£1.20(incl p+p).

Southern Upland Way   429

Borders, Dumfries & Gall, S Lanark	343 km / 213 miles

This National long distance path provides a varied route through sparsely populated terrain, avoiding the high tops. Across the Rhinns of Galloway and Glen Trool Forest Park to Sanquhar, the open, heather-clad Lowther Hills, it reaches St Mary's Loch near Broad Law. From here the Way passes through Melrose, where it can be linked with the St Cuthbert's Way, Lauder and over the foothills of the Lammermuir Hills to reach the east coast. See Central Scottish Way.

Start	Portpatrick, Dum & Gall	NW998542
Finish	Cockburnspath, Borders	NT774709
On OS maps	67, 73, 74, 77, 78, 79, 82	
Waymark	Spannered thistle	

Publication(s)
Paperback: *The Southern Upland Way* by Anthony Burton (Aurum Press). ISBN:1854104551. 1997\210 x 130\168pp\£12.99.
Folder: *The Southern Upland Way* by Roger Smith (Stationery Office). ISBN:0114951705. 1994\220 x 135\208pp\£17.50.
Softback: *Guide to the Southern Upland Way* by David Williams (Constable and Co Ltd). ISBN:009467910X. 1989\171 x 114\333pp\£9.95.
Leaflet: *Southern Upland Way* (Scottish Natural Heritage). 1994\A4/3\Free(+SAE).
Leaflet: *The Southern Upland Way* (Dumfries and Galloway Regional Council). 1994\A4/3\Free(+SAE).
Leaflet: *The Southern Upland Way - Accommodation List* (Dumfries and Galloway Regional Council). Annual\A4/3\Free(+SAE).
Leaflets: *The Southern Upland Way - various wildlife/history etc* (Dumfries and Galloway Regional Council). 1997\A4/3\Free(+SAE).
Freesheet: *Southern Upland Wayfarer* (Famedram Publishers Ltd). Annual\Free(+A5 SAE).

Spanners Round 430

Gtr Man, Lancs	32 km / 20 miles

A circuit across open moorland and along riverside and farmland paths, linking three reservoirs of the old Bolton Water Authority with three reservoirs of the former Irwell Valley Water Board (now all controlled by North West Water).

Start and finish	Jumbles Reservoir, Gtr Man	SD736139
OS maps	103, 109	

Publication(s)
Booklet: *Ramsbottom Round / Spanners Round* (Derek Magnall). 1992\A5\36pp\£1.85.
Badge and certificate (£1.50/SAE) available from Derek Magnall.

Spen Way Heritage Trail 431

W Yorks	34 km / 21 miles

A circuit of the former borough of Spenborough and the Spen, a tributary of the River Calder, the Way concentrates on the history of this old textile manufacturing area, visiting Scholes, East Bierley and Gomersal through a varied mixture of urban areas, parkland and farmland.

Start and finish	Cleckheaton, W Yorks	SE246199
On OS maps	104	
Waymark	Letters HT on standard waymarks	

Publication(s)
Leaflet: *Spen Heritage Trail Walk* (Rotary Club of Cleckheaton). A4\5pp\£2.00.
Badge details available from Rotary Club of Cleckheaton.

Speyside Way 432

Moray 72 km / 45 miles

One of the National long distance routes in Scotland, it is hoped to extend the existing Way from Spey Bay to Buckie in the north with a spur created from Ballindalloch to Aviemore in the south, making a total distance of approximately 81 miles. The existing route passes numerous whisky distilleries, with a spur provided at Craigellachie to the Glenfiddich distillery.

Start	Spey Bay, Moray	NJ350653
Finish	Tomintoul, Moray	NJ165195
On OS maps	28, 36	
Waymark	Spannered thistle	

Publication(s)
Leaflet: *Speyside Way* (Moray District Council). A4/3\£0.50.
Leaflet: *Speyside Way Accommodation Guide* (Moray District Council). Annual\A4/3\Free(+SAE).

Staffordshire Moorlands Challenge Walk 433

Staffs 38 km / 24 miles

A walk from the Churnet Valley, involving 2,000ft of ascent, the route takes in Froghall Wharf, the Weaver Hills, Ordley Dale, Alton and Ousal Dale.

Start and finish	Oakamoor, Staffs	SK053448
OS maps	128	

Publication(s)
Paperback: *John Merrill's Staffordshire Moorlands Challenge Walk* by John Merrill (Happy Walking International Ltd). ISBN: 0907496679. 1988\137 x 210\32pp\£3.00.
Badge and certificate (£3.00/post free) available from Happy Walking International Ltd.

Staffordshire Way 434

Cheshire, Derbys, Staffs 153 km / 95 miles

The route initially is along Congleton Edge to The Cloud, where it links with the southern end of the Gritstone Trail, and continues along the towpath of the Caldon Canal, through the Churnet Valley and follows the River Dove to Uttoxeter. The Trent and Mersey Canal is then followed to Shugborough Hall with Cannock Chase and Highgate Common visited before reaching Kinver Edge where it connects with the Worcester Way and North Worcestershire Path. The early part of the walk is coincident with the Mow Cop Trail. See Limestone Way/South Cheshire Way.

Start	Mow Cop, Cheshire	SJ856573
Finish	Kinver Edge, Staffs	SO829822
On OS maps	118, 119, 127, 128, 138, 139	
Waymark	Staffordshire knot	

Publication(s)
Softback: *The Staffordshire Way* by Les Lumsdon and Chris Rushton (Sigma Leisure). ISBN:1850583153. 1993\A5\120pp\ £6.95.
Softback: *Walking on & around The Staffordshire Way* by Geoff Loadwick (Sigma Leisure). ISBN:1850585946. 1997\A5\116pp\ £5.95.
Leaflet: *The Staffordshire Way* (Staffordshire County Council). 1997\A5/4\Free.
Leaflet: *Where to Stay along the Staffordshire Way* (RA Staffordshire). 1995\A4/3\Free(+SAE).
Booklet: *Mow Cop Trail* (Cheshire County Council). ISBN: 0906759048. 200 x 210\12pp\£1.50(+31p).

Staunton Way 435

Hants	21 km / 13 miles

The Way connects with the Hangers Way and South Downs Way at Queen Elizabeth Country Park and roughly follows the Hampshire/Sussex border through Chalton and Finchdean, then following a stream through Havant to Langstone Harbour, it connects with the Solent Way. See Wayfarer's Walk.

Start	QE Country Park, Hants	SU718182
Finish	Broadmarsh, Hants	SZ700057
On OS maps	197	
Waymark	Brown deer's head on standard arrows	

Publication(s)
Leaflet: *Staunton Way* (Hampshire County Council). 1993\A4/3\ Free(+SAE).

Stort Valley Way 436

Essex, Herts	45 km / 28 miles

A route around Harlow, the River Stort Navigation is followed to Sawbridgeworth and from where the villages of Sheering, Matching, Magdalen Laver and Epping Green are visited.

Start and finish	Roydon, Essex	TL406105
OS maps	167	
Waymark	Green and yellow Dragonfly	

Publication(s)
Leaflet: *Stort Valley Way* (Epping Forest Countrycare). 1996 \
A4/3 \ Free(+SAE).

Stour Valley Path (East Anglia) 437

Cambs, Essex, Suffolk	96 km / 60 miles

The Path follows the river valley downstream and links the Icknield Way Path, which it crosses at Stetchworth, with Sudbury and the Essex Way at Manningtree passing through some of the most attractive country in East Anglia, including Constable country towards the end around East Bergholt.

Start	Newmarket, Suffolk	TL646636
Finish	Cattawade, Suffolk	TM101332
OS maps	154, 155, 168, 169	
Waymark	Named discs and posts with stylised river and dragonfly logo	

Publication(s)
Folder: *Stour Valley Path* (Suffolk County Council). 1994 \ A5 \
10pp \ £1.80.

Stour Valley Walk (Kent) 438

Kent	82 km / 51 miles

A walk along the valley of the River Stour from the source, passing through a varied landscape, and taking in downland, woodland, orchards, hop gardens, lakes, dykes and marshland, unspoilt villages and historic towns. The remainder of the route traces the old Saxon shoreline of the Wantsum Channel to the important Roman site at Richborough, thence to the ancient Cinque Port of Sandwich.

Start	Lenham, Kent	TR899522
Finish	Pegwell Bay, Kent	TR347625
On OS maps	179, 189	

Waymark	Head of grey heron

Publication(s)
Booklet: *Along and Around the Stour Valley Walk* by Veronica Litten (Kent County Council). ISBN:1873010516. 1995\210 x 210\118pp\£5.45.

Stour Valley Way (Dorset)   439

Dorset	50 km / 31 miles

Currently under development, this route follows the course of the River Stour as it winds through the south-east Dorset countryside. The path is way-marked from Christchurch Priory to Sturminster Marshall. It is hoped to extend the route through the villages of Spetisbury and Charlton Marshall to Blandford Forum, and beyond. The Green Fields publication describes a 97km un-way-marked route, beyond Sturminster to the source of the river in Wiltshire. The way-marked Wareham Forest Way connects at Sturminster Marshall and provides a 12 miles long route to Wareham. See the Castleman Trailway.

Start	Christchurch, Dorset	SZ160925
Finish	Blandford Forum, Dorset	ST888067
On OS maps	195	
Waymark	Name & kingfisher logo	

Publication(s)
Paperback: *The Stour Valley Path* by Edward R Griffiths (Green Fields Books). ISBN:0951937677. 1997\A5\168pp\£5.95(+80p). Folder: *The Stour Valley Way* (Greenlink). 1994\A5/4 cards\£1.00. Leaflet: *Wareham Forest Way* (Avon Heath Country Park). A5\Free(+SAE).

Suffolk Coast and Heaths Path   440

Suffolk	80 km / 50 miles

The Path follows rights of way and permissive paths along the Suffolk Heritage Coast on river and sea walls, and across marsh, heath, foreshore and low cliffs via the foot ferry to Bawdsey. It then follows the river wall along the large shingle spit of Orford Ness to meet the River Alde at Snape Maltings and regain the coast at the festival town of Aldeburgh when it follows the coast to Lowestoft Harbour. It is hoped to extend the Path around the Orwell and Stour estuaries to connect with the Stour Valley Path and Essex Way at Manningtree.

Start	Felixstowe, Suffolk	TM324364
Finish	Lowestoft, Suffolk	TM548926
On OS maps	134, 156, 168, 169	

| Waymark | Small named yellow and purple markers |

Publication(s)
Folder: *The Suffolk Coast and Heaths Path* (Suffolk County Council). 1996\8pp\£4.00(+£1.00).

Suffolk Way 441

| Suffolk | 170 km / 106 miles |

The Suffolk Way is a meandering route across the county taking in Lavenham with its fine half-timbered buildings, Framlingham and Halesworth, where it turns along the river Blyth to the coast at Walberswick which it then follows through to Southwold.

Start	Flatford, Suffolk	TM076332
Finish	Lowestoft, Suffolk	TM548926
OS maps	134, 155, 156, 169	

Publication(s)
Booklet: *Suffolk Way* by Ian St John (Footpath Guides). 1993\A5\36pp\£2.50(+£0.35 p&p).

Sussex Border Path 442

| E Sussex, Hants, Kent, Surrey, W Sussex | 245 km / 152 miles |

The route follows paths approximating to the Sussex border with Hampshire, Surrey and Kent, first following a 9-mile circuit around Thorney Island, and then across the South Downs to South Harting and Liphook, before heading to Gospel Green, Rudgwick, Gatwick and East Grinstead. Here the waymarked Mid Sussex Link (38 miles) branches off along the line of the administrative boundary between East and West Sussex. The main Border Path heads through Ashurst, Wadhurst and Bodiam. Details of Mid Sussex Link included in listed publication

Start	Emsworth, Hants	SU753055
Finish	Rye, E Sussex	TQ918205
On OS maps	186, 187, 188, 189, 197, 198, 199	
Waymark	Martlet on green plaques or wooden signposts	

Publication(s)
Folder: *The Sussex Border Path* by Ben Perkins and Aeneas Mackintosh (Dr Ben Perkins). 1991\A5\9pp\£3.50(+38p).

Swale Way   443

| Cumbria, N Yorks | 124 km / 77 miles |

A route tracing the River Swale from the confluence with the Ure near Boroughbridge, to the source at the head of Swaledale near Keld. Because of a lack of rights of way, the route does not slavishly follow the river, in some places diverging to visit the market towns of Thirsk and Richmond. On route the Pennine Way, Coast to Coast Walk and Yoredale Way are encountered.

Start	Boroughbridge, N Yorks	SE396660
Finish	Kirkby Stephen, Cumbria	NY758988
OS maps	91, 92, 99	

Publication(s)
Booklet: *The Swale Way* (John Brock). 1996\A5\16pp\£1.00 (+30p).

Swan's Way   444

| Bucks, Oxon | 110 km / 68 miles |

From the Northants border, the route crosses the Vale of Aylesbury to meet the Ridgeway near Princes Risborough, then follows the chalk slopes of the Chilterns to the Thames at Goring. There is a link with the Cross Bucks Way at Swanbourne. See Three Shires Way.

Start	Salcey Forest, Bucks	SP811514
Finish	Goring-on-Thames, Oxon	SU601808
On OS maps	152, 164, 165, 174, 175	
Waymark	Swan's head in horseshoe	

Publication(s)
Leaflet: *Swan's Way* (Buckinghamshire County Council). A4/3\ Free(+SAE).

Sweet Pea Challenge Walk   445

| Shrops | 80 km / 50 miles |

A route from the birthplace of the sweet pea through Grinshill and Prees, and along the Llangollen Canal. There are alternative routes of 28 and 22 miles.

Start and finish	Wem, Shrops	SJ514289
OS maps	126	

Publication(s)
Booklet: *Sweet Pea Challenge Walk* by John N Merrill (Happy
Walking International Ltd). ISBN:1874754497. A5\£3.00.
Badge and certificate (£3.00/incl p+p) available from Happy Walking International Ltd.

Taff Trail 446

Cardiff, Merthyr, Neath, Powys, Rhondda	88 km / 55 miles

A route for walkers and cyclists, the Taff Trail is mainly converted railway lines with former canals and forestry tracks. It runs along the Taff valley to Llandaff, Pontypridd and Merthyr Tydfil. From here the main route circles to the east of the Brecon Beacons via Talybont and Pencelli to Brecon. An alternative route via Neuadd reservoir caters for a circular between Merthyr and Brecon. At Gethin Woodland Park near Merthyr the Trail links with the Coed Morgannwg Way.

Start	Cardiff	ST182759
Finish	Brecon, Powys	SO043286
On OS maps	160, 161, 170, 171	
Waymark	Stylised viaduct in yellow arrow on black background	

Publication(s)
Paperback: *The Taff Trail* by Jeff Vinter (Sutton Publishing Ltd).
ISBN:0750903414. 1993\219 x 154\128pp\£6.99.
Leaflet: *The Taff Trail for Walkers and Cyclists* (Merthyr and Rhondda Cynon Taff Groundwork). A4\4/Free(+SAE).

Taff-Ely Ridgeway Walk 447

Caerphilly, Cardiff, Rhondda	34 km / 21 miles

The Walk is a mixture of footpaths, bridleways and lanes, following the line of hills running from Mynydd Maendy in the west, to Caerphilly Common in the east. The route passes through forests taking in ancient hill forts. There are links with the Rhymney Valley Ridgeway Walk at Caerphilly Common, the Taff Trail near to Taffs Well and the Ogwr Ridgeway Walk at the start.

Start	Mynydd Maendy, Rhondda	ST977861
Finish	Caerphilly Common, Caerphilly	ST153856
On OS maps	170, 171	
Waymark	Yellow/black disc with hills motif	

Publication(s)
Leaflet: *Taff Ely Ridgeway Walk/Ffordd y Bryniau* (Caerphilly Mountain Countryside Service). A4/3\Free.

Taith Torfaen 448

| Caerphilly, Powys, Torfaen | 80 km / 50 miles |

The Taith Torfaen consists of two 25 miles loops, both from Ponty-pool forming a figure of eight which can be completed as one or two walks. The northern loop goes through the Brecon Beacons National Park to reach the Blorenge Mountain with extensive views over Abergavenny and returns via Coity Mountain. The southern loop goes via Twmbarlwm and Mynydd Machen with panoramic views across the Bristol Channel. It returns via the Islwyn and Torfaen Hills.

| Start and finish | Pontypool Leisure Centre, Torfaen | SO285006 |
| OS maps | 161, 171 | |

Publication(s)
Looseleaf: *Taith Torfaen* (Gerry Jackson). Free(+9" x 6" SAE).
Badge and certificate (£2.00/£0.50/SAE) available from Gerry Jackson.

Tame Valley Way 449

| Gtr Man | 40 km / 25 miles |

The Way runs from central Stockport to Reddish Vale and Hyde from where canal towpaths are followed through Ashton-under-Lyne, Stalybridge and Mossley. From Uppermill, the route leaves the canal, following riverside paths to Delph and Denshaw. In spite of being through densely populated areas, the route takes in much woodland in addition to the attractions of the waterside route.

Start	Stockport, Gtr Man	SJ893903
Finish	Denshaw, Gtr Man	SD975105
OS maps	109	

Publication(s)
Folder: *The Tame Valley* (Tameside Countryside Wardens Service).
A4/3 \ 10 leaflets \ £2.50.

Tameside Trail 450

| Gtr Man | 64 km / 40 miles |

A walk along the Etherow Valley Way and Tame Valley Way to Stockport, where it turns through Audenshaw and Droylsden and picks up the Medlock Valley Way to Park Bridge. From Mossley it returns via the Swineshaw Valley and Hollingworth.

| Start and finish | Broadbottom, Gtr Man | SJ996936 |
| On OS maps | 109, 110 | |

Waymark	Named discs

Publication(s)
Folder: *The Tameside Trail* (Tameside Countryside Wardens Service). ISBN:1871324114. 1994\A5\27pp\£2.95.

Tarka Trail 451

Devon, Somerset	291 km / 181 miles

The Trail traces the journeys of Tarka the Otter taking in locations featured in the book. The route forms a figure of eight centred around Barnstaple and is set amongst ever changing scenery of rugged coastline, farmland and wild moorland. The northern loop takes in Lynton and the coast path via Ilfracombe to Braunton. The southern loop follows a former railway line through Bideford and Torrington to Meeth, and then continues on footpaths and quiet lanes to Okehampton and Sticklepath where it turns along the Taw valley to Eggesford. The Taw-Teign Link (6 miles) can be used to connect Sticklepath with Chagford Bridge on the Two Moors Way. A second link, by way of the Little Dart Ridge & Valley Walk (11 miles) is available in connecting Eggesford with Witheridge. See West Devon Way & Plymouth Link.

Start and finish	Barnstaple, Devon	SS558331
On OS maps	180, 190, 191	
Waymark	Otter pawmark	

Publication(s)
Paperback: *Tarka Trail - A Walker's Guide* (Devon County Council). ISBN:0861148770. 1995\150 x 230\88pp\£4.95.
Leaflet: *The Tarka Trail* (Devon County Council). A4/3\£0.25.
Leaflet: *Tarka Country Guide & Accommodation List* (Devon County Council). 24pp\Free(+SAE). In Print
Leaflet: *Little Dart Ridge & Valley Walk* (Devon County Council). A4/12pp\£0.25(+SAE).
Leaflet: *The Taw-Teign Link* (Devon County Council). A4/6pp\£0.25(+SAE).

Teesdale Way 452

Cleveland, Cumbria, Durham	161 km / 100 miles

The Way largely follows the banks of the River Tees. From Dufton it connects with the Pennine Way, visiting High Cup Nick, Cauldron Snout and High Force before passing through Barnard Castle, to the south of Darlington and to the North-East coast at Middlesbrough.

Start	Dufton, Cumbria	NY691250
Finish	Middlesbrough, Cleveland	NZ557280

On OS maps	91, 92, 93
Waymark	Named discs with dipper logo in Durham and fish in Cleveland

Publication(s)
Paperback: *The Teesdale Way* by Martin Collins (Cicerone Press). ISBN:1852841982. 1995\115 x 176\112pp\£7.99.

Templer Way   453

Devon	29 km / 18 miles

Named after the Templer family who constructed the Stover Canal and Tramway to bring granite quarried at Haytor to the coast at Teignmouth, the Way provides interest for ecological reasons as well as for the locks and buildings. The terrain ranges from open moor to woodland and estuary foreshore.

Start	Haytor Quarry, Devon	SX750778
Finish	Shaldon, Devon	SX931724
On OS maps	191, 192, 202	
Waymark	White logo on brown	

Publication(s)
Leaflet: *Templer Way* (Devon County Council). A4/6\£0.25(+SAE).

Ten Church Challenge   454

Derbys	34 km / 21 miles

A circuit of ten chapels around the Black Brook, Goyt and Todd Brook valleys of the High Peak. See High Peak 60.

Start and finish	Whaley Bridge, Derbys	SK012811
OS maps	110, 119	

Publication(s)
Paperback: *High Peak Hikes* by David Frith (Sigma Leisure). ISBN:1850584591. 1996\A5\160pp\£6.95.

Ten Reservoirs Walk   455

Derbys, Gtr Man	35 km / 22 miles

A tough circuit over the Saddleworth Moors, linking with the Pennine Way and several walks in this area. It visits Yeoman Hey, Greenfield, Black Moss, Swellands, Blakeley, Wessenden, Wessenden Head, Torside and Chew Reservoirs.

Start and finish	Dovestone Reservoir, Gtr Man	SE014034
OS maps	110	

Publication(s)
Looseleaf: *The Ten Reservoirs Walk* (Bob Tait). A4\Free(+SAE).
Badge and certificate (£1.00/£0.20/SAE) available from Bob Tait.

Tennyson Twenty 456

Lincs	32 km / 20 miles

The route circles the village of Sommersby, birthplace of Alfred, Lord Tennyson, Victorian Poet Laureate, through the Lincolnshire Wolds passing small isolated villages and deserted hamlets as well as nature reserves.

Start and finish	Hagworthingham, Lincs	TF344696
OS maps	122	

Publication(s)
Looseleaf: *Tennyson Twenty* (Martyn Bishop). Free(+SAE).
Badge and certificate (£1.50/post free) available from Martyn Bishop.

Test Way 457

Berks, Hants, Wilts	74 km / 46 miles

The Way follows the Test Valley from the outskirts of Southampton over lowland farmland and woodland paths continuing along a disused railway line past Romsey, Mottisfont Abbey, Stockbridge, Wherwell and St Mary Bourne, before gradually climbing to Inkpen Beacon on the crest of the chalk downs to meet with the Wayfarers' Walk.

Start	Totton, Hants	SU360140
Finish	Inkpen Beacon, Berks	SU365622
On OS maps	174, 185, 196	
Waymark	Green letters TW on white ground	

Publication(s)
Leaflet: *Test & Clarendon Way* (Hampshire County Council). 1986\A4/3\Free(+SAE).

Thame Valley Walk 458

Bucks, Oxon	27 km / 17 miles

A walk following the River Thame which links with the North Bucks Way and Aylesbury Ring at Eythrope and the Oxfordshire Way at Albury.

Start	Hartwell, Bucks	SP794122
Finish	Wheatley, Oxon	SP611052

On OS maps	164, 165
Waymark	Named discs with stylised river logo

Publication(s)
Paperback: *Vale of Aylesbury Walker* by Peter Gulland and Diana Gulland (RA Buckinghamshire). ISBN:090061367X. A5\140pp\ £3.00.
Leaflet: *Thame Valley Walk* (Aylesbury Vale District Council). A4/3\Free(+SAE).

Thames Down Link 459

Gtr London, Surrey	24 km / 15 miles

A route linking the Thames Path (at Kingston) with the North Downs Way and through Maldon Manor, Horton Country Park, Epsom and Ashstead Commons, and Mickleham Downs.

Start	Kingston upon Thames, Gtr London	TQ181673
Finish	Westhumble, Surrey	TQ170520
On OS maps	176, 187	
Waymark	Hills & river logo	

Publication(s)
Leaflet: *The Thames Down Link* (Lower Mole Project). 1997\ A4/3\Free(+SAE).

Thames Path 460

Berks, Bucks, Glos, Gtr London, Oxon, Surrey, Wilts	290 km / 180 miles

This National Trail, unique insofar as it is the only one to mainly follow a river, was officially opened in 1996. From the source, the Path meanders through Cricklade, Lechlade, Oxford, Abingdon, Windsor, passing Windsor Castle and the palaces of Hampton Court and Kew, and Richmond. There is extensive public transport availability along the route by way of rail, bus and river boat. See Beeches Way/Colne Valley - Way & Trail/Thames Down Link/Vanguard Way/Wysis Way.

Start	Thames Source near Kemble, Glos	ST980994
Finish	Thames Barrier, Gtr London	TQ417794
On OS maps	163, 164, 174, 175, 176	
Waymark	National Trail Acorn	

Publication(s)
Paperback: *The Thames Path* (Official Guide) by David Sharp (Aurum Press). ISBN:1854104063. 1996\210 x 130\144/168pp\ £12.99.

Paperback: *The Thames Path - Information & Accommodation Guide* by Andrew McCloy (Benchmark Books). ISBN:095305800X. A5\32pp\£2.99(+£0.50 p+p).
Stripmap: *Thames, the River and the Path* (GEOprojects). ISBN: 0863510043. 1994\1260 x 426\£3.75.
Leaflet: *Thames Path* (Countryside Commission Postal Sales). 1996\A4/3\Free.

Thanet Coastal Path   461

Kent	32 km / 20 miles

A route as close as is possible to the coast passing through Margate, Broadstairs and Ramsgate. The Path links with the Saxon Shore Way (and Wantsum Walks) at the start and there are plans to add a second link to the Saxon Shore Way at the finish.

Start	Near Reculver, Kent	TR243694
Finish	Stonelees Nature Reserve, Kent	TR337625
OS maps	179	
Waymark	Named logo with bird/fish/sandcastle	

Publication(s)
Leaflet: *Thanet Coastal Path* (Thanet District Council). A3/2\Free (+SAE).

Thirlmere Round   462

Cumbria	35 km / 22 miles

A strenuous high level walk around Thirlmere visiting High Seat, Calf Crag, Gibson Knott and Helvellyn.

Start and finish	Grasmere, Cumbria	NY339072
OS maps	96, 97	

Publication(s)
Looseleaf: *The Thirlmere Round* (Brian Richmond). 2pp\Free(+9" x 4"SAE).
Certificate (£0.30/SAE) available from Brian Richmond.

Thirlmere Way   463

Cumbria, Gtr Man, Lancs	209 km / 130 miles

The Way provides a meandering link from the Greater Manchester conurbation through Lancashire to Cumbria visiting Hulton, Abbey Village, Longridge, Dolphinholme, Caton, Kirkby Lonsdale, Kendal, Windermere and Grasmere.

Start	Heaton Park, Gtr Man	SD834044

Finish	Thirlmere, Cumbria	NY310190
OS maps	90, 97, 102, 109	

Publication(s)
Softback: *The Thirlmere Way* by Tim Cappelli (Sigma Leisure).
ISBN:1850582882. 1992\A5\124pp\£6.95.

Three Castles Path   464

Berks, Hants	96 km / 60 miles

This route was inspired by the 13th century journeys of King John
via the Castle built by him near Odiham. The route takes in the
Great Park to Ascot, the Crown Estate south of Bracknell, the
Blackwater valley, the Basingstoke canal and the River Itchen
from Itchen Abbas to the finish.

Start	Windsor, Berks	SU968770
Finish	Winchester, Hants	SU483293
On OS maps	175, 176, 185, 186	

Publication(s)
Booklet: *The Three Castles Path* by David Bounds (RA East Berk-
shire Group). ISBN:1874258082. 1998\128 x 210\48pp\£2.95.
Looseleaf: *Accommodation list* by Dave Ramm (Bracknell Tourist
Information Centre). A4\1pp\Free(9" x 4" SAE).

Three Castles Walk   465

Monmouth	29 km / 18 miles

A route connecting the three Norman fortresses of Skenfrith,
White Castle and Grosmont, the Walk passes through undulating
countryside, with hidden valleys and secluded and historic farm-
houses. The landscape is still that of mixed farming, and most of
the hedgerows have survived, as have the characteristic small
woods, making this area rich in wildlife.

Start and finish	Skenfrith, Monmouth	SO457202
On OS maps	161	
Waymark	Named yellow arrows on white background	

Publication(s)
Booklet: *Three Castles Walk* (Monmouthshire County Council).
1997\172 x 232\16pp\£1.00(+50p).

Three Counties Challenge Walk 466

Cheshire, Derbys, Staffs	45 km / 28 miles

A tough moorland route straggling the borders of Cheshire, Staffordshire and Derbyshire in the Peak District running via The Roaches, Shutlingsloe, Tegg's Nose, Shining Edge and Three Shires Head.

Start and finish	Tittesworth Reservoir, Staffs	SJ994605
OS maps	118, 119	

Publication(s)
Paperback: *Three Counties Challenge Walk* by John Merrill (Happy Walking International Ltd). ISBN:1874754152. 210 x 130\32pp\ £3.25.
Badge and certificate (£3.00/post free) available from Happy Walking International Ltd.

Three Crags Walk 467

N Yorks, W Yorks	25 km / 16 miles

A route passing the crags of Almscliff, Caley and Cow & Calf.

Start	Weeton Station, N Yorks	SE276476
Finish	Cow & Calf, Ilkley, W Yorks	SE130467
OS maps	104	

Publication(s)
Looseleaf: *Three Crags Walk* (Peter Bayer). £0.50(+A5 SAE).
Badge (£2.00/SAE) available from Peter Bayer.

Three Feathers Walks 468

Derbys, N Yorks, S Yorks	Various km

A series of three circular walks, each set in a different National Park and based on; *Kettlewell, Yorkshire Dales* (34 miles); *Kilburn, North York Moors* (30 miles); *Yorkshire Bridge, Peak District* (28 miles). To qualify for a badge, the routes to be completed within a calendar year. All are arduous and should be planned accordingly.

Start and finish	Various	Various
OS maps	98, 100, 110	

Publication(s)
Looseleaf: *Three Feathers Walks* (Keith Bown). A4/Free(+9" x 4" SAE).
Badge (£2.50/SAE) available from Keith Bown.

Three Forests Way 469

Essex, Herts	96 km / 60 miles

A route devised by the West Essex Group of the RA to commemorate Queen Elizabeth's Silver Jubilee, it links three Essex forests,
although only eight miles of the Way are through them. The Way
visits Hatfield Forest and via White Roding, the Roding valley and
Abridge, the Hainault Forest and via Loughton, Epping Forest.
The Stort Valley is followed back to the finish.

Start and finish	Harlow, Essex	TL445113
On OS maps	166, 167, 177	

Publication(s)
Booklet: *Three Forests Way* by Fred Matthews and Harry Bitten
(Ways through Essex). 1986\A5\20pp\£1.00.
Badge (£1.00) available from Ways through Essex.

Three Moors Walk 470

N Yorks, W Yorks	48 km / 30 miles

A walk taking in The Chevin, Rombalds Moor and Round Hill
(Langbar/Middleton Moor), it includes some of the more obscure
paths, hence offering a navigational challenge.

Start and finish	Otley, W Yorks	SE204455
OS maps	104	

Publication(s)
Looseleaf: *Three Moors Walk* (Peter Bayer). £0.50(+A5 SAE).
Badge (£2.00/SAE) available from Peter Bayer.

Three Peaks Circular (Avon) 471

Avon	27 km / 17 miles

Not intended to be in competition with other more well known
like-named routes, it takes in the more gentle tops of Maes Knoll,
Knowle Hill and Blackberry Hill, and connects the main villages
of Pensford, Clutton and Chew Magna.

Start and finish	Pensford, Avon	ST620636
On OS maps	172, 182	

Publication(s)
Leaflet: *Three Peaks Circular Walk* (Bath & North East Somerset
Council). A3/6\Free(+SAE).

Three Peaks of Cheviot Walk   472

Northumb	48 km / 30 miles

This upland walk over rough terrain involving 5,700ft of ascent and requiring good navigational skills, links the Schil, Windy Gyle and Hedgehope. The walk is open April - September with no completions recorded outside this period.

Start and finish	Hawsen Burn, Northumb	NT954225
OS maps	74, 80, 81	

Publication(s)
Looseleaf: *Three Peaks of Cheviot* (LDWA Northumbria Group). A4\Free(+SAE).
Certificate (£0.20/C5 SAE) available from LDWA Northumbria Group.

Three Peaks of Great Britain   473

Caernarfon, Cumbria, Highland	42 km / 26 miles

A challenge which is not truly in keeping with other walks/challenges in this directory and included to draw attention to relevant matters. It is a misnomer that the challenge of climbing the highest peaks of Scotland, England and Wales, Ben Nevis, Scafell and Snowdon respectively, has to be completed within 24 hours. Heed should always be taken of the inconvenience often caused to the residents in the affected areas and of the real dangers for vehicle occupants when travelling between the peak bases. The listed publication provides details of suggested routes to the mountain tops as well as road routes between them and safety advice,
Not included in map section.

Start	Car Park, Glen Nevis Youth Hostel, Highland	NN128718
Finish	Car Park, Pen-y-Pass YH, Caernarfon	SH647556
OS maps	41, 90, 115	

Publication(s)
Paperback: *The National 3 Peaks Walk* by Brian G Smailes (Challenge Publications). ISBN:0952690020. 1996\125 x 185\72pp\ £5.95.
Badge and certificate (£3.25/£0.25/9" x 6" SAE) available from Challenge Publications.

Three Peaks Walk (Yorkshire)   474

N Yorks	39 km / 24 miles

The classic walk, taking in the peaks of Pen-y-ghent (2278ft), Whernside (2416ft) and Ingleborough (2376ft) and involving over

5000ft of ascent. It has suffered from path erosion. The Three Peaks of Yorkshire Club based at the Pen-y-ghent Cafe operates a limited clocking-in service and has accommodation information, full details on application.

Start and finish	Horton in Ribblesdale, N Yorks	SD809725
OS maps	98	

Publication(s)
Paperback: *The Novices Guide to the Yorkshire 3 Peaks Walk* by Brian G Smailes (Challenge Publications). ISBN:0952690004. 1995\A5\34pp\£3.25.
Hardback: *Walks in Limestone Country* by A Wainwright (Michael Joseph). ISBN:0718140117. 1992\178 x 120\£8.99.
Leaflet: *Three Peaks - footpath map & guide* by Arthur Gemmell (Pen-y-ghent Cafe). ISBN:906886627. 1993\A4/8\£1.40(+SAE).
Leaflet: *The Three Peaks Yorkshire Dales - A Hill-Walkers' Map and Guide* by Altos Design Ltd (Pen-y-ghent Cafe). 1997\A4/3\£3.95(+9" x 6" SAE).
Badge - details from Pen-y-ghent cafe.

Three Reservoirs Challenge   475

Derbys, S Yorks	40 km / 25 miles

A strenuous route around the reservoirs of upper Derwent Valley which is flanked by high gritstone edges.

Start and finish	Ladybower, Derbys	SK205865
OS maps	110	

Publication(s)
Paperback: *The Three Reservoirs Challenge* (Mountain Peaks Climbing Club). A5\20pp\£3.00.
Certificate (£0.30/A4 SAE) available from Mountain Peaks Climbing Club.

Three Ridings on Foot   476

Cleveland, E Yorks, S Yorks, W Yorks, N Yorks	706 km / 438 miles

A route tracing the border of Yorkshire on rights of way and permissive paths through the moors of the Pennines, the northern Yorkshire Dales, the North York Moors and the coastline.

Start and finish	Bawtry, S Yorks	SK652932
OS maps	92, 93, 94, 98, 101, 103, 106, 107, 110, 111, 112	

Publication(s)
Paperback: *Three Ridings on Foot* by A & G Birch and others (P3 Publications). 1996\200 x 103\120pp\£7.00.

Three Rivers Walk 477

N Yorks, W Yorks	40 km / 25 miles

A walk from the Aire to the Wharfe at Ilkley and then via Denton to the River Washburn near Swinsty Hall before returning to the Wharfe at the finish.

Start	Shipley, W Yorks	SE149376
Finish	Otley, W Yorks	SE204455
OS maps	104	

Publication(s)
Looseleaf: *Three Rivers Walk* (Peter Bayer). £0.50(+A5 SAE).
Badge (£2.00/SAE) available from Peter Bayer.

Three Shires Way 478

Beds, Bucks, Cambs, Northants	57 km / 35 miles

A bridleway running through quiet rural landscape and remnants of ancient woodland. Linking with the Swans Way at the start, it takes in the county boundaries of Bucks, Beds & Northants at Threeshire Wood. The Grafham Water Circular Ride (13 miles) can be added to the route at the finish.

Start	Tathall End, Bucks	SP821467
Finish	Grafham Water, Cambs	TL116691
OS maps	152, 153	
Waymark	Triple-linked horseshoes	

Publication(s)
Leaflet: *Three Shires Way* (Cambridgeshire County Council). 1990\A4/3\Free(+50p).
Leaflet: *Grafham Water Circular Ride* (Cambridgeshire County Council). 1990\A5\£0.30(+50p).

Three Towers Circuit 479

Gtr Man, Lancs	56 km / 35 miles

Supported by the East Lancashire Group of the LDWA, a route through the West Pennine Moors taking in the towers of Peel, Rivington and Darwen. Navigation skills are appropriate.

Start and finish	Tottington, Gtr Man	SD776129
OS maps	103, 109	

Publication(s)
Looseleaf: *Three Towers Circuit* (Bernard Hushon). Free(+SAE).

Badge and certificate (£0.85/£0.15/9" x 6" SAE) available from
Bernard Hushon.

Tidewater Way 480

Lancs, N Yorks, W Yorks	145 km / 90 miles

A route connecting the tidal waters of the west coast with those of
the east, thus laying the claim to be a coast to coast walk. The Way
follows the Rivers Lune and Wenning, crossing the Pennine Way
near Malham, the Dales Way in Wharfedale and using parts of the
Ebor Way. Part of the proceeds of sales are donated to Christian
Aid.

Start	Skerton Weir, Lancaster, Lancs	SD482632
Finish	Ulleskelf, N Yorks	SE525401
OS maps	97, 98, 104, 105	

Publication(s)
Paperback: *Tidewater Way* by Tony Rablen (Maxiprint).
ISBN:1871125278. 1996\210 x 148\32pp\£4.50(+50p).
Certificate (Free+SAE) available from Tony Rablen.

Tinners Way 481

Cornwall	29 km / 18 miles

The Way traces as closely as possible the ancient paths along which
tin and copper were transported from the mineral-rich area around
St Just to the sheltered anchorage of St Ives Bay. It passes over 20
prehistoric and early Christian sites, from stone circles and cairns
to quoits and menhirs. From Cape Cornwall/St Just, it uses an
inland route parallel to the coast, via Woon Gumpus and Towed-
nack.

Start	Cape Cornwall, Cornwall	SW349318
Finish	St Ives, Cornwall	SW521412
OS maps	203	

Publication(s)
Paperback: *Guide to the Tinners Way and Nearby Ancient Sites* by
Ian Cooke (Men-an-Tol Studio). ISBN:0951237152. 1991\A5\
48pp\£2.95.

Todmorden Centenary Way 482

W Yorks	31 km / 19 miles

A route around Todmorden created to commemorate the centenary
of the granting of Borough status, taking in moors, valleys, woods,
reservoirs, villages and poignant ruins.

Start and finish	Todmorden, W Yorks	SD936242
OS maps	103	
Waymark	Named signs	

Publication(s)
Folder: *Todmorden Centenary Way* (Hebden Bridge Tourist Information Centre). 1996\A5\£2.15.

Traditional Hostels Lakes Walk 483

Cumbria	97 km / 60 miles

This route was devised to connect the smaller traditional style youth hostels namely Thirlmere, Carrock Fell, Skiddaw House, Cockermouth, Ennerdale, Black Sail and Honister House. An additional spur to the south of Honister allows for visits to three other hostels at Grasmere, Elterwater and Coniston, and adds about 20 miles to the walk.

Start and finish	Thirlmere Youth Hostel, Cumbria	NY318191
OS maps	89, 90	

Publication(s)
Folder: *The Traditional Hostels Lakes Walk* by Martyn Hanks (YHA Northern Region). 1996\A4\16\£1.50(+26p).

Trans Pennine Trail 484

Cheshire, Derbys, E Yorks, Gtr Man, Merseyside, N Yorks, S Yorks	322 km / 200 miles

A multi-use trail for cyclists, walkers, and horseriders following disused railway lines, canal towpaths, and other waterside routes, it will eventually link the urban areas of Hull, Doncaster, Barnsley, Greater Manchester and Merseyside. In spite of being in part urban, long stretches of the route in the east are most rural, and other sections pass through attractive country in the Pennines and Greater Manchester. Additional spurs are open or underway from Selby to York, to Wakefield and Leeds, and via Sheffield to Chesterfield. Other paths and converted railway lines that now form part of the Trans Pennine Trail are the Longdendale Trail, the Dove Valley Trail and, from the west of Warrington to Liverpool, the Mersey Way (30 miles). The section from Hull to Merseyside is part of the E8 European long distance path.

Start	Hornsea, E Yorks	TA208479
Finish	Southport, Merseyside	SD338172
OS maps	105, 106, 107, 108, 109, 110, 111	
Waymark	Named discs with trail logo	
User group	Friends of the Trans Pennine Trail	

Publication(s)
Booklet: *Walking The Trans Pennine Trail* (Trans Pennine Trail Officer). 1996\A6\70pp\£1.95.
Looseleaf: *Trans Pennine Trail Accommodation List* (Trans Pennine Trail Officer). 1993\A4\17pp\Free.
Leaflet: *Dove Valley Trail* (Barnsley Metropolitan Borough Council). 1993\A3/6\Free(+SAE).
Leaflet: *The Longdendale Trail* (Barnsley Metropolitan Borough Council). 1996\A4/6\Free(+SAE).
Folder: *Walk the Mersey Way* (Mersey Valley Partnership). A5\Free(+SAE).

Trans-Dales Trail - 1   485

N Yorks	97 km / 60 miles

A route crossing Ribblesdale, Littondale, Wharfedale and Nidderdale, followed by opportunities to visit the rock formations at Brimham Rocks, the historic grandeur of Fountains Abbey, and the valley of the River Skell.

Start	Ingleton, N Yorks	SD695730
Finish	Ripon, N Yorks	SE319705
OS maps	98, 99	

Publication(s)
Paperback: *Trans-Dales Trail 1* by Arnold Underwood and Peter Tomkinson (Dales Trails). ISBN:0952977109. 1997\A5\40pp\£2.50(incl p&p).

Trans-Dales Trail - 2   486

Durham, N Yorks	97 km / 60 miles

A route initially through some of the quieter dales, Arkengarthdale and Swaledale, before visiting the more popular villages of Askrigg, Buckden, Malham and Gargrave, then continuing over wild moors and deep valleys, finishing along a canal tow-path.

Start	Greta Bridge, Durham	NZ086132
Finish	Skipton, N Yorks	SD992521
OS maps	92, 98, 103	

Publication(s)
Paperback: *Trans-Dales Trail 2* by Arnold Underwood and Peter Tomkinson (Dales Trails). ISBN:0952977117. 1997\A5\52pp\£2.50(incl p&p).

Trent Valley Way 487

Derbys, Notts   135 km / 84 miles

Devised to celebrate the Centenary of Nottinghamshire County Council, the Way follows the River Trent to the confluence with the Chesterfield Canal. Though sticking close to the river for the most part, it leaves occasionally, exploring various interesting features in the wider valley. The route passes through Nottingham and Newark, besides numerous smaller places with interesting churches, watermills and windmills.

Start	Long Eaton, Derbys	SK507326
Finish	West Stockwith, Notts	SK791949
On OS maps	112, 120, 121, 129	
Waymark	Wavy blue symbol	

Publication(s)
Paperback: *Trent Valley Way* (Nottinghamshire County Council). 1989\A5\86pp\£2.75(+35p).

Trollers Trot 488

N Yorks   43 km / 27 miles

A varied route in the Yorkshire Dales using footpaths over moorland, alongside riverbanks, through forests and fields. Part of the route passes over access land which on certain days (except Sundays) is closed to the public for grouse-shooting.

Start and finish	Bolton Abbey, N Yorks	SE072539
OS maps	98	

Publication(s)
Leaflet: *Trollers Trot* (John Sparshatt). A4\Free(9" x 4"SAE).
Badge and certificate (£2.00/A4 SAE) available from John Sparshatt (cheques payable to West Yorkshire LDWA).

Two Beacons Challenge 489

N Yorks, W Yorks   58 km / 36 miles

Basically an extension of the Wharfedale Washburn Walk, also visiting Addingham Moor and Beamsley Beacon.

Start and finish	Menston, W Yorks	SE176432
OS maps	104	

Publication(s)
Looselaf: *Two Beacons Challenge* (L. Mallinson). Free(+9" x 4" SAE).

Badge and certificate (£1.50/SAE) available from L. Mallinson.

Two Castles Trail 490

Cornwall, Devon	48 km / 30 miles

The Trail follows river valleys, ridge roads, open downland and woods on the edge of Dartmoor, linking the imposing Norman castles at Oakehampton and Launceston. In part the Trail is coincident with the West Devon Way & Plymouth Link.

Start	Okehampton, Devon	SX589952
Finish	Launceston, Cornwall	SX335845
On OS maps	191, 201	
Waymark	Named logo	

Publication(s)
Leaflet: *Two Castles Trail* (Devon County Council). 1997\A5\ Free(+9" x 6" SAE).

Two Crosses Circuit 491

Gtr Man, Lancs	40 km / 25 miles

Supported by the East Lancashire Group of the LDWA, a route through the West Pennine Moors taking in the Roman Cross at Affetside and the Pilgrim's Cross at Bull Hill passing Turton Tower and the Turton & Entwistle Reservoir. Some navigational skills are appropriate.

Start and finish	Tottington, Gtr Man	SD776129
OS maps	109	

Publication(s)
Looseleaf: *Two Crosses Circuit* (Bernard Hushon). Free(+SAE). Badge and certificate (£0.90/£0.10/9" x 6" SAE) available from Bernard Hushon.

Two Moors Way 492

Devon, Somerset	164 km / 102 miles

A route across Dartmoor over exposed moorland to Teigncombe from where the River Teign is followed to Castle Drogo. The Exmoor National Park is reached at Tarr Steps, the Way then climbing to Exe Head and through Cheriton to the finish. Access to Ivybridge from Plymouth and Wembury on the South Devon coast can be achieved by way of waymarked trails. The Erme Plym Trail (10 miles) provides details of routes from those two locations to Brixton and then a single route to Sequer's Bridge near

Ermington from where the Erme Valley Trail (3 miles) can be taken to Ivybridge. See Tarka Trail for links to that route.

Start	Ivybridge, Devon	SX636563
Finish	Lynmouth, Devon	SS724494
On OS maps	180, 181, 191, 202	
Waymark	Letters MW on standard waymarks	

Publication(s)
Paperback: *The Two Moors Way* by John Macadam (Aurum Press). ISBN:1854104586. 1997\210 x 130\144pp\£12.99.
Paperback: *The Two Moors Way* by James Roberts (Cicerone Press). ISBN:1852841591. 1994\100pp\£5.99.
Paperback: *Two Moors Way* (Two Moors Way Association). £3.00 (+50p).
Looseleaf: *The Two Moors Way - Accommodation List* (Two Moors Way Association). A4/3\£0.50(+9" x 4" SAE).
Leaflet: *Two Moors Way* (Devon County Council). A4/3\£0.25.
Folder: *The Erme Plym Trail* (Devon County Council). A4\£1.00.
Folder: *The Erme Valley Trail* (Devon County Council). A4\£2.00.
Badge and certificate (£1.00/£1.00/SAE) available from Two Moors Way Association.

Two Rivers Way   493

Somerset	32 km / 20 miles

This route from Congresbury on the River Yeo to Keynsham on the River Avon, where the route meets the Avon Walkway, passes through farmland and historic villages, such as Chew Stoke, Chew Magna and Compton Dando.

Start	Congresbury, Somerset	ST438639
Finish	Keynsham, Somerset	ST659690
On OS maps	172, 182	
Waymark	Named discs with wave motif	

Publication(s)
Booklet: *The Two Rivers Way* (Yatton Ramblers). ISBN: 0951134264. 1992\42pp\£1.80(+30p).
Leaflet: *2 Rivers Congresbury to Keynsham* (North Somerset County Council). A4/3\Free.

Tyne and Wear 20   494

Tyne & Wear	34 km / 21 miles

A route following tracks and riverside paths over undulating countryside visiting Blackhall Mill.

Start and finish	Newburn Bridge, Tyne & Wear	NZ165652

OS maps	88

Publication(s)
Looseleaf: *Tyne and Wear 20* (J Tinniswood). A4\Free(+9" x 4" SAE).
Badge and certificate (£1.00/SAE) available from J Tinniswood.

Tyne-Wear Trail 495

Durham, Tyne & Wear	27 km / 17 miles

A link between the Rivers Tyne and Wear passing through high moors and river valleys, and providing access to Beamish Museum. It connects with the Keelman's Trail (13 miles) on the Tyne, and with the Great North Forest Trail at Causey Arch. See Hadrian's Way.

Start	Newcastle, Tyne & Wear	NZ245638
Finish	Chester-le-Street, Tyne & Wear	NZ272513
OS maps	88	
Waymark	Name/fish	

Publication(s)
Leaflet: *Tyne-Wear Trail* (Great North Forest). 1997\A5\ Free(+SAE).

Ullswater Circuit 496

Cumbria	74 km / 46 miles

A strenuous fell walk in the eastern central fells with 8,000ft of ascent.

Start and finish	Pooley Bridge, Cumbria	NY470247
OS maps	90	

Publication(s)
Looseleaf: *Ullswater Circuit* (Paul Miller). Free(+1st class SAE).

Ulster Way 497

Numerous	918 km / 570 miles

The Ulster Way encircles the province and has links with trails in the Republic of Ireland including a 69-mile spur which traverses mountainous country in Co. Donegal. Most AONBs are visited using paths, forest tracks and minor roads together with the North Antrim Coast, the Mourne Mountains and the Fermanagh Lakeland. Within each of the five sections of the Ulster Way, there are individually named trails - including such as the *North Antrim Coast Path*, *Big Dog Trail*, *Mourne Trail* and *St Patrick's Trail*. In upland areas where waymarking is sparse, navigational skills are required.

Start and finish	Belfast Castle, Belfast	IJ290745
OS maps	(OSNI) 4, 5, 7, 8, 9, 12, 13, 15, 17, 18, 19, 21, 26, 27, 29	
Waymark	Walker with rucksack and stick, plus orange-coloured arrows	

Publication(s)
Paperback: *Walking the Ulster Way: A Journal and a Guide* by Alan Warner (Appletree Press Ltd). ISBN:0862812275. 1989\209 x 148\184pp\£5.95.
Booklet: *The Ulster Way* by Paddy Dillon (Northern Ireland Tourist Board). 1994\A5\48pp\Free.
Leaflet: *An Information Guide to Walking* (Northern Ireland Tourist Board). Annual\A5\£0.50(+SAE).
Leaflet: *The Ulster Way: Accommodation for Walkers* (Northern Ireland Tourist Board). Annual\A5\£0.50(+SAE).

Upper Tas Valley Walk 498

Norfolk	30 km / 19 miles

A route along the valley through Swardeston, Mulbarton, Flordon and Aslacton. There are plans to extend the route to Attleborough in the south and Eaton in the north where it will link with the Kett's Country Walk.

Start	Hethersett, Norfolk	TG158048
Finish	New Buckenham, Norfolk	TM090906
On OS maps	134, 144	
Waymark	Named discs	

Publication(s)
Booklet: *Upper Tas Valley Walk* (Norfolk County Council). A5\Free (available 1998).

Usk Valley Walk 499

Monmouth, Newport, Powys	80 km / 50 miles

The Walk follows the Usk valley upstream past the historic market town of Usk, via riverside, field and woodland paths and some minor roads to Abergavenny. Here it takes to the Monmouthshire and Brecon Canal towpath which it follows to Brecon. Mainly an easy waterside walk, there are two climbs, to the Kemeys Ridge north of Caerleon, and to Glanusk Park west of Crickhowell.

Start	Caerleon, Newport	ST342902
Finish	Brecon, Powys	SO043286
On OS maps	161, 171	

Waymark	Named yellow arrows

Publication(s)
Booklet: *Usk Valley Walk* (Monmouthshire County Council).
A5\£1.50(+50p).

Vanguard Way 500

E Sussex, Gtr London, Kent, Surrey	106 km / 66 miles

The Way, from the suburbs of London to the sea, connects with the
Wandle Trail and the London Loop in Greater London and along
the way crosses eight other long distance paths including the North
Downs, Greensand, Eden Valley and South Downs Ways. It passes
the Selsdon Nature Reserve, the woods and heaths of Ashdown
Forest, Alfriston and follows the coast through Seaford to the
finish. The Wandle Trail (11 miles) provides a link to the Thames
Path.

Start	East Croydon, Gtr London	TQ329657
Finish	Newhaven Harbour, E Sussex	TQ449002
On OS maps	176, 177, 187, 188, 198, 199	
Waymark	Named discs	

Publication(s)
Paperback: *Wealdway and the Vanguard Way* by Kev Reynolds
(Cicerone Press). ISBN:0902363859. 1987\116 x 176\160pp\
£4.99.
Paperback: *Vanguard Way* (Vanguards Rambling Club). ISBN:
095300760X. 1997\A5\68pp\£2.95(+45p).
Leaflet: *Wandle Trail* (Wandle Industrial Musuem). A2\
£2.00(+26p).
Badge (£2.00/SAE) available from the Vanguards Rambling Club.

Vectis Trail 501

IOW	120 km / 75 miles

A route taking in the quieter parts of the island. There are seven
other trails on the island, some of which are connecting, they being
- *Bembridge Trail* (15 miles) - Shide to Bembridge; *Nunwell Trail*
(10 miles) - Ryde St Johns to Sandown; *Hamstead Trail* (8 miles) -
Brooke Bay to Hamstead Ledge; *Shepherds Trail* (10 miles) -
Carisbrooke to Atherfield; *Stenbury Trail* (10 miles) - Blackwater
to Week Down; *Tennyson Trail* (15 miles) - Carisbrooke to Alum
Bay; *Worsley Trail* (15 miles) - Shanklin to Brightstone.

Start and finish	Yarmouth, IOW	SZ355897
OS maps	196	

Publication(s)
Paperback: *Vectis Trail* by Iris Evans and Barbara Aze (Barbara Aze). 210 x 149 \ 32pp \ £2.00.
Paperback: *A Walker's Guide to the Isle of Wight* by Martin Collins & Norman Birch (Cicerone Press). ISBN:1852842210 \ 216pp \ £9.99(+75p).
Folder: *Bembridge & other Trails* (Isle of Wight County Council). A4/3 \ 7pp \ £2.00(30p).

Ver-Colne Valley Walk   502

Herts	24 km / 15 miles

A route following the Rivers Ver and Colne with several former watermills and wildlife habitats along the way. The listed publication covers the route along the Ver only from the start to Riverside Way at St Albans, the remainder is waymarked. See the Colne Valley Way & Trail.

Start	Redbourn, Herts	TL103120
Finish	Watford, Herts	TQ116959
On OS maps	166, 176	
Waymark	River symbol within standard waymarks	

Publication(s)
Leaflet: *Ver Valley Walk* (Hertfordshire County Council). 1997 \ A4/3 \ Free.

Vermuyden Way   503

Lincs	32 km / 20 miles

Supported by the Vermuyden Group of the LDWA, the Way follows an elongated circuit along the artificial water courses and low hills of the Isle of Axleholme, much of which was marshland prior to the intervention of Cornelius Vermuyden, a Dutch land drainage engineer of the 17th century.

Start and finish	Belton, Lincs	SE782054
OS maps	112	
Waymark	Stickers with letters VW	

Publication(s)
Looseleaf: *Vermuyden Way* (Frank Lawson). Free(+9" x 4" SAE).
Badge and certificate (£1.00/10" x 7" SAE) available from Frank Lawson.

Viking Way 504

Leics, Lincs	227 km / 141 miles

The Way does not follow a Viking route but is so named because it crosses an area which was occupied by Norse invaders. From the banks of the river Humber it crosses the Lincolnshire Wolds to Caistor, then along the Bain valley to Horncastle from where the Spa Trail is followed along the trackbed of a former railway to Woodhall Spa and along the Witham Valley, crossing flat fenland to Lincoln. Turning along the limestone escarpment of Lincoln Cliff and over Lincoln Heath, the route of the prehistoric Sewstern Lane is traced to reach Woolsthorpe Locks on the Grantham Canal. Another section of Sewstern Lane and other old tracks are followed to Thistleton from where the Way takes fieldpaths and lanes past Greetham, Exton and Rutland Water. At Oakham it links with the Macmillan Way and the Hereward Way.

Start	Barton-upon-Humber, Lincs	TA028227
Finish	Oakham, Leics	SK861088
On OS maps	106, 107, 112, 113, 121, 122, 130, 141	
Waymark	Viking helmet/shield	

Publication(s)
Paperback: *Viking Way* by John Stead (Cicerone Press). ISBN: 1852840579. 1990 \ 116 x 176 \ 172pp \ £5.99.
Paperback: *The Viking Way* (Lincolnshire County Council). ISBN: 1872375251. 1997 \ 125 x 206 \ 64pp \ £4.95(+£1.00).
Looseleaf: *The Viking Way Factsheet - Accommodation, Transport etc.* (Lincolnshire County Council). Annual \ A4 \ 24pp \ Free.
Badge (£1.25/SAE) available from RA Lincs and S Humberside Area.

Wanderlust Way 505

Lincs	32 km / 20 miles

This Way is an elongated circuit passing through attractive small villages and across the woods and farmland of the undulating Lincolnshire Wolds, from where there are views across the mouth of the Humber Estuary.

Start and finish	Bradley Woods, Lincs	TA242059
OS maps	113	
Waymark	Green and yellow letters WW	

Publication(s)
Folder: *Wanderlust Way* (Alec Malkinson. A4 \ Free(+SAE).
Badge and certificate (£2.00/£0.50/9" x 6" SAE) available from Alec Malkinson.

Wardens' Way 506

Glos	22 km / 14 miles

The Way provides a link between the Oxfordshire Way at Bourton-on-the-Water and the Cotswold Way at Winchcombe. Whereas its sister route, the Windrush Way, takes to the hills, the Wardens Way winds through the villages of Lower and Upper Slaughter, Naunton and Guiting Power.

Start	Bourton-on-the-Water, Glos	SP170209
Finish	Winchcombe, Glos	SP025283
On OS maps	163	
Waymark	Letters WW	

Publication(s)
Paperback: *Wardens' Way and Windrush Way* (Cotswold Wardens Service). 1991\A5\32pp\£1.50(+25p).

Waveney Way 507

Suffolk	27 km / 17 miles

It is planned for this route to form a 70 miles circular around the District boundary, but for the present only the Lothingland Loop - to the north of Lowestoft and Oulton Broad - is covered by a publication.

Start and finish	Lowestoft, Suffolk	TM548926
OS maps	134	
Waymark	Green directional arrow in white circle	

Publication(s)
Leaflet: *Waveney Way: No 1 Lothingland Loop* (Waveney District Council). 1986\A4/3\Free.

Wayfarer's Walk 508

Berks, Hants	114 km / 71 miles

Initially coincident with the Solent Way, it crosses the chalk ridge of Portsdown, the Meon Valley and through the villages of Hinton Amper and Drummer before climbing the North Hampshire Ridgeway and over Watership Down and Walbury Hill. See Staunton Way and Test Way.

Start	Emsworth, Hants	SU753055
Finish	Inkpen Beacon, Berks	SU365622
On OS maps	174, 185, 196, 197	
Waymark	Black letters WW on white background	

Publication(s)
Paperback: *Along and Around the Wayfarer's Walk* by Linda Herbst and others (Hampshire County Council). ISBN:0948176040. 1993\210 x 148\96pp\£4.95.
Leaflet: *The Wayfarer's Walk* (Hampshire County Council). A4/3\Free(+SAE).

Wealdway 509

E Sussex, Kent	129 km / 80 miles

The route, linking the English Channel and the Thames Estuary, starts at the foot of Beachy Head and passes through the downland village of Alfriston in the heart of the South Downs. Crossing the Sussex Weald, the highest point on Ashdown Forest is reached at Camp Hill. The route continues over the Kent Weald to Tonbridge where it joins the River Medway and crossing the North Downs, the route passes through Cobham with its Charles Dickens associations. Links with the South Downs Way on Willingdon Hill, near Eastbourne.

Start	Eastbourne, E Sussex	TQ600971
Finish	Gravesend, Kent	TQ647745
On OS maps	177, 188, 198, 199	
Waymark	Letters WW on standard arrows	

Publication(s)
Booklet: *Along and Around the Wealdway* by Helen Livingston (East Sussex County Council or Kent County Councils). ISBN: 1873010931. 1998\Price TBA.
Paperback: *Wealdway and the Vanguard Way* by Kev Reynolds (Cicerone Press). ISBN:0902363859. 1987\116 x 176\160pp\£4.99.
Booklet: *The Wealdway* by Geoffrey King (Dr Ben Perkins). ISBN:951600605. 1990\210 x 152\36pp\£3.50.
Leaflet: *Wealdway Accommodation Guide* (Dr Ben Perkins). 1.00(+SAE).
Badge (£1.40/post free) available from Dr Ben Perkins.

Weardale Way 510

Durham, Tyne & Wear	117 km / 73 miles

A route following the River Wear from the sea to the source keeping as close as is possible and visiting such as Lumley Castle, Durham, Barnard Castle and Stanhope. The River Wear Trail (15 miles) is mainly coincident with the route between Roker and Chartershaugh Bridge.

Start	Roker, Tyne & Wear	NZ408590
Finish	Wearhead, Durham	NY858395

On OS maps	87, 88
Waymark	Named signposts

Publication(s)
Paperback: *Walking the great rivers - The Weardale Way* by Alastair Wallace (Jema Publications). ISBN:1871468639. 1997\A5\85pp\ £5.99.
Booklet: *The Weardale Way Accommodation Guide* (Jema Publications). A5\Free(+9" x 6" SAE).
Leaflet: *River Wear Trail* (Sunderland City Council). To be published Summer, 1998.
Certificate (£1.50/A4 SAE) available from Alastair Wallace.

Weaver Valley Way   511

Cheshire	32 km / 20 miles

The Way follows the lower part of the Weaver Valley, in the main along the Weaver Navigation, and incorporates a detour to the Anderton Boat Lift. From Anderton, use can be made of the Anderton Nature Park and minor roads to re-access the Navigation at Northwich. There would seem to be no immediate plans to provide access to the canal between Anderton and Northwich. The publication includes reference to the Whitegate Way (7 miles) - Winsford to Cuddington.

Start	Frodsham, Cheshire	SJ529784
Finish	Bradford Lane Bridge, Winsford, Cheshire	SJ656662
OS maps	117, 118	

Publication(s)
Booklet: *Longer Trails in Vale Royal* by Carl Rogers (Vale Royal Borough Council). 1993\A5\76pp\£1.95.

Weavers Shuttle   512

Lancs	64 km / 40 miles

The walk extends over open moorland and pastures in the Rossendale, Burnley and Pendle Districts and takes in many historical buildings and areas associated with the Industrial Revolution, Pendle witches and the Bronte Sisters. Items of interest range from an Iron Age clapper bridge to drovers' roads and canal towpaths.

Start and finish	Worsthorne, Lancs	SD876324
OS maps	103	

Publication(s)
Booklet: *Weavers Shuttle* (Max Tattersall). Free(+9" x 6" SAE).

Badge and certificate (£1.00/A4 SAE) available from Max Tatter-sall.

Weavers Way   513

Norfolk	90 km / 56 miles

Use is made of public footpaths, disused railway line and some minor roads in passing through very varied scenery, from the mixed farmland and woodland of the north to the extensive, traditional grazing marshes of the Broadland river valleys. Notable landmarks to be seen along the Way include a number of fine flint churches, several large country houses, and a large number of windpumps. Parts of the Paston Way (18 miles) which visits 16 churches and villages over a meandering and convoluted route in north-east Norfolk can be used in linking Cromer with North Walsham. See Angles Way and Marriott's Way.

Start	Cromer, Norfolk	TG215420
Finish	Great Yarmouth, Norfolk	TG522081
On OS maps	133, 134	
Waymark	Named boards	

Publication(s)
Paperback: *Langton's Guide to the Weavers Way and Angles Way* by Andrew Durham (Langton's Guides). ISBN:1899242015. 1995\210 x 130\144pp\£6.95.
Booklet: *Peddars Way & North Norfolk Coast Path Guide (includes Weavers Way)* by Ian Mitchell (RA Norfolk). 1996\A5\24pp\ £2.10(+26p).
Leaflet: *Weavers Way* (Norfolk County Council). 1997\A5/3\ Free(+SAE).
Booklet: *The Paston Way* (Norfolk County Council). 1996\A5\ 12pp\Free(+A5 SAE).
Badge (Free - with completed Weavers Way Challenge Card) available from Norfolk County Council.

Welsh 3000s   514

· Caernarfon	47 km / 29 miles

The crossing of the 15 Snowdonian summits over 3000ft, taking in the ranges of the Carneddau, the Glyders and the Snowdon Massif itself, involving 12,000ft of ascent, much rough ground and some exposed scrambling. If that challenge is not enough the Welsh 3000s Double Crossing, (28 summits for that by P. Travis) is also available.

Start	Snowdon summit, Caernarfon	SH609544
Finish	Foel Fras summit, Caernarfon	SH697682
OS maps	115	

Publication(s)
Paperback: *The Welsh Three Thousand Foot Challenges* by Ron
Clayton and Ronald Turnbull (Grey Stone Books). ISBN:
0951599666. 1997\175 x 115\128pp\£5.95 (incl p&p).
Looseleaf: *Welsh 3000s Double Crossing* (Ed Dalton). Free(+9" x 4"
SAE).
Looseleaf: *Welsh 3000s Double Crossing* (P Travis). Free(+9" x 4"
SAE).
Certificate for Single Crossing(£1.00/post free) available from P
Travis.
Certificate for Double Crossing (£2.00/post free) available from Ed
Dalton.

Wessex Ridgeway   515

Devon, Dorset, Wilts	221 km / 137 miles

One of the links in a prehistoric route from The Wash to the South
Devon Coast, this route basically extends the Ridgeway. Passed on
the way through Wiltshire are the stone circle at Avebury, the Vale
of Pewsey, the northern edge of Salisbury Plain, the Wylye Valley
and Win Greene Hill. In Dorset, Cranbourne Chase, Cerne Abbas
with the 180ft high Cerne Giant, Pilsden Pen are visited before a
short route through Devon leads to the finish back in Dorset.

Start	Marlborough, Wilts	SU187685
Finish	Lyme Regis, Dorset	SY347922
On OS maps	173, 183, 184, 193, 194, 195	
Waymark	Wessex wyvern (Dorset only)	

Publication(s)
Paperback: *Wessex Ridgeway* by Alan Proctor (Ramblers' Association). 1998\Price TBA.
Paperback: *Walk the Wessex Ridgeway in Dorset* by Priscilla Hous-
toun (Dorset Publishing). ISBN:094869937X. 1994\215 x
160\96pp\£7.00(includes postage).
Leaflet: *Walk the Wessex Ridgeway in Dorset* (Dorset County Council). 1994\A4/3\Free.

West Devon Way & Plymouth Link   516

Devon	57 km / 35 miles

The Way explores the rugged and spectacular countryside on the
western fringe of the Dartmoor National Park, along the 18 miles
between Okehampton, where it links with the Tarka Trail, and
Tavistock. From there the Plymouth Link takes you a further 17
miles to Plymouth.

Start	Okehampton, Devon	SX589953
Finish	Plymouth, Devon	SX497537

On OS maps	191, 202
Waymark	Stylised walker/castle and the word Link where appropriate.

Publication(s)
Folder: *West Devon Way & Plymouth Link* (Devon County Council). 1996\A5\16pp\£1.00(+SAE).

West Highland Way   517

Bute, E Dunbarton, Highland, Stirling	153 km / 95 miles

Scotland's first National long distance path crosses a variety of terrain which becomes more rugged as it moves northwards and between the major mountain groups. The Way follows the eastern side of Loch Lomond, crossing the slopes of the Ben to Crianlarich and the Bridge of Orchy, the western edge of Rannoch Moor and the entrances to Glen Etive and Glen Coe to reach Kinlochleven. The final section follows General Caulfield's military road over the slopes of the Mamores, crossing wild country with extensive views of the Ben Nevis range, to reach Fort William. See Central Scottish Way and Great Glen Way. The book *The Highland High Way* describes an alternative high level route.

Start	Milngavie, E Dunbarton	NS555745
Finish	Fort William, Highland	NN105742
On OS maps	41, 50, 56, 57, 64	
Waymark	Spannered thistle	

Publication(s)
Paperback: *The West Highland Way* by Anthony Burton (Aurum Press). ISBN:1854103911. 1995\210 x 130\144pp\£9.99.
Paperback: *The West Highland Way & OS Map* by Roger Smith (Stationery Office). ISBN:0114952523. 1996\208pp\£15.00.
Softback: *Guide to the West Highland Way* by Tom Hunter (Constable and Co Ltd). ISBN:0094690901. 1988\171 x 114\192pp\£8.95.
Paperback: *The West Highland Way* by Terry Marsh (Cicerone Press). ISBN:1852842350. 1997\122pp\£6.99.
Hardback: *The Highland High Way* by Heather Connon and Paul Roper (Mainstream Publishing Co Ltd). ISBN:1851587918. 1996\220 x 127\223pp\£9.99.
Stripmap: *The West Highland Way* (Footprint). £2.95.
Stripmap: *The West Highland Way* (Harvey Maps). ISBN:1851372237. 1996\£6.95(+80p).
Booklet: *Walk the West Highland Way - Information & Accommodation List* (Scottish Natural Heritage). Annual\A4/3\20pp\Free (+SAE).
Freesheet: *West Highland Wayfarer* (Famedram Publishers Ltd). Free(+A5 SAE).

West Lakes Way   518

Cumbria	112 km / 70 miles

Designed as a tour of western Lakeland, the route climbs to St Bees Head followed by a gentle lowland stretch to Ennerdale Bridge from where it goes up Ennerdale Fell, along Pillar Ridge and down Black Sail Pass to Wasdale Head. Climbing over Scafell Pike, it continues into Eskdale, Hardknott Pass, Harter Fell, the Duddon valley to Seathwaite and Ulpha, and over Thwaites Fell to the Sunkenkirk stone circles before descending to the coast at Haverigg, and ending at Hodbarrow Point in the Duddon Estuary. The booklet provides an alternative route for poor weather conditions.

Start	Whitehaven, Cumbria	NX973182
Finish	Millom, Cumbria	SD182781
OS maps	89, 96	

Publication(s)
Booklet: *The West Lakes Way* by Stuart Burgess (Copeland Borough Council). A5 \ 40pp \ £1.00(+50p).

Westmorland Boundary Way   519

Cumbria	275 km / 171 miles

A meandering circuit over the western Pennines, along river valleys, past lakes and over open fells following a route very roughly approximating to the boundary of the historic county of Westmorland. It crosses Farleton Fell to Kirkby Lonsdale, Sedbergh, Wild Boar Fell, Dufton and Cross Fell, where it turns and meanders across the Lake District via Shap, Patterdale, Helvellyn, Grasmere, Ambleside and Windermere. The book *Westmorland Heritage Walk* describes a 200 miles route which also roughly follows the former county boundary but with diversions made to take in other walking opportunities.

Start and finish	Kendal, Cumbria	SD520931
OS maps	90, 91, 97, 98	

Publication(s)
Paperback: *In Search of Westmorland* by Charlie Emett (Cicerone Press). ISBN:0902363662. 116 x 176 \ 200pp \ £5.50.
Softback: *Westmorland Heritage Walk* by Mark Richards and Christopher John Wright (Cicerone Press). ISBN:0902363948. 1988 \ 116 x 176 \ 256pp \ £7.99.

Westmorland Way   520

| Cumbria | 159 km / 99 miles |

A relatively low-level route across the historic county of Westmorland and the Lake District National Park, it follows footpaths, tracks and country lanes along river valleys and across farmland and the open fells, via Shap, Pooley Bridge, Patterdale, Grasmere, Troutbeck and Kendal to reach Morecambe Bay.

Start	Appleby-in-Westmorland, Cumbria	NY683204
Finish	Arnside, Cumbria	SD461788
OS maps	90, 91, 97	

Publication(s)
Paperback: *Westmorland Way* by Paul Hannon (Hillside Publications). ISBN:187017158X. 1997\175 x 115\£5.99.

Westside Walk (Shetland)   521

| Shetland | 261 km / 162 miles |

A route along the bulwark which bulges into the Atlantic Ocean, meeting the ceaseless challenge of the sea. The walk passes the cliff battlements of Banks Head, Wats Ness and Westerwick.

Start	Mavis Grind, Shetland	HU340683
Finish	Scalloway, Shetland	HU409398
OS maps	3, 4	

Publication(s)
Paperback: *Walking the Coastline of Shetland: 5 - Westside* by Peter Guy (Shetland Times Ltd). ISBN:1898852065. 1995\A5\96pp\ ££6.96(£1.39 p+p).

Wey-South Path   522

| Surrey, W Sussex | 58 km / 36 miles |

From Guildford the Path follows the towpath of the Godalming Navigation along the River Wey to its confluence with the Wey & Arun Junction Canal, crossing the North Downs Way near the start. Wherever possible the path then follows the towpath of the canal, but is supplemented by paths, roads and disused railway, to reach and continue beside the Arun Navigation to the River Arun whence the path continues to meet the South Downs Way above Amberley. Several sections of the canals have been restored. See Arun Way.

| Start | Guildford, Surrey | SU994493 |
| Finish | Amberley, W Sussex | TQ026118 |

On OS maps   186, 187, 197

Publication(s)
Leaflet: *The Wey-South Path* (W & A Enterprises Ltd). 1997\600 x
422\£1.00(+9" x 4" SAE).

Wharfedale Washburn Walk   523

N Yorks, W Yorks	42 km / 26 miles

A route visiting Otley Chevin, Pool, Lindley Wood and Ilkley. A
22-miles alternative is available. Proceeds from sales to Martin
House Hospice.

Start and finish	Menston, W Yorks	SE176432
OS maps	104	

Publication(s)
Looseleaf: *Wharfedale Washburn Walk* (L. Mallinson). Free(+ 9" x
4" SAE).
Badge and certificate (£1.50/SAE) available from L. Mallinson

Whicham Valley Five Trigs Walk   524

Cumbria	32 km / 20 miles

A mountain walk taking in Knott Hill, Blackcombe, Whitfell and
Pike Stickle for which map reading and compass skills are essential.

Start and finish	Duddon Bridge, Cumbria	SD199882
OS maps	96, 97	

Publication(s)
Looseleaf: *The Whicham Valley Five Trigs Walk* (Brian Richmond).
Free(+9" x 4"SAE).
Badge (£0.85/SAE) available from Brian Richmond.

White Peak Challenge Walk   525

Derbys	40 km / 25 miles

A strenuous challenge walk in the Peak National Park following
the most rugged parts of the Peak and passing via Rowsley,
Birchover, Youlgreave, Monyash, Flagg, Taddington and Great
Longstone.

Start and finish	Bakewell, Derbys	SK217685
OS maps	119	

Publication(s)
Paperback: *John Merrill's White Peak Challenge Walk* by John Merrill (Happy Walking International Ltd). ISBN: 0907496776. 134 x 210 \ 32pp \ £3.00.
Badge and certificate (£3.00/post free) available from Happy Walking International Ltd.

White Peak Rollercoaster   526

Derbys, Staffs	38 km / 24 miles

A circular walk set in the southern part of the Peak District National Park based on the Dove, Hamps and Manifold valleys. There is 4500ft of ascent with many villages and varied scenery taken in.

Start and finish	Alstonefield, Staffs	SK131556
OS maps	119	

Publication(s)
Looseleaf: *White Peak Rollercoaster* (Alan S Edwards). A4 \ 4pp \ Free(+SAE).
Badge and certificate (£2.25/post free) available from Alan S Edwards.

White Peak Trails   527

Derbys, Staffs	Various km

Former railway lines providing useful links with many other routes through the White Peak area and which are open for use by walkers and cyclists. They are the *High Peak Trail* (18 miles) Cromford - Dowlow; *Tissington Trail* (13 miles) Ashbourne - Parsley Hay, where it connects with the High Peak Trail; *Monsal Trail* (9 miles) Wye Dale - Coombs Viaduct, Bakewell; *Manifold Trail* (8 miles) Hulme End - Waterhouses. There is no individual publication for the Manifold Way. See Peakland Way.

Start	Various	Various
Finish	Various	Various
On OS maps	119, 128	
Waymark	Named posts	

Publication(s)
Booklet: *Walking the High Peak Trail* by John Merrill (Happy Walking International Ltd). ISBN:187475411X. £3.95.
Booklet: *Walking the Tissington Trail* by John Merrill (Happy Walking International Ltd). ISBN:1874754101. £3.50.
Booklet: *Walking the Monsal Trail & Derby Trails* by John Merrill (Happy Walking International Ltd). ISBN:1874754179. £3.95.

Leaflet: *Peak National Park* (Peak District National Park). 1997\
A4/3\Free(+SAE).
Leaflet: *Monsal Trail* (Peak District National Park). 1996\A4/3\
Free(+SAE).
Leaflet: *Tissington and High Peak Trails* (Peak District National
Park). 1997\A4/3\Free(+SAE).

White Peak Way 528

Derbys	129 km / 80 miles

The walk, based on youth hostels, is a meandering circuit which
visits many of the limestone dales, including Dove Dale, Miller's
Dale and Hay Dale and passes Chatsworth House and Park,
Haddon Hall and the Castleton Show Caves.

Start and finish	Bakewell, Derbys	SK217685
OS maps	110, 119	

Publication(s)
Paperback: *The White Peak Way* by Robert Haslam (Cicerone
Press). ISBN:1852840560. 1997\116 x 176\96pp\£4.99.
Leaflet: *Accommodation Booking Service* (Hathersage YHA).
Free(+SAE).
Badge (£1.25/SAE) available from Hathersage YHA.

Whithorn Pilgrim Way 529

Dumfries & Gall	40 km / 25 miles

The Way was devised to capture the long history of religious
associations centred in and around Whithorn. The route winds
along the west coast of the South Machars mainly following minor
unclassified roads. Reference is included in the book to possible
extensions at either end, to link with the Southern Upland Way.

Start	Glenluce Abbey, Dumfries & Gall	NX182585
Finish	Whithorn, Dumfries & Gall	NX445404
OS maps	82, 83	
Waymark	Celtic cross logo	

Publication(s)
Paperback: *A Way to Whithorn* by Andrew Patterson (Saint Andrew
Press). ISBN:0715206907. 1993\110x210\162pp\£6.95.
Leaflet: *Whithorn Pilgrim Way* (Dumfries & Galloway Regional
Council). A5/4\Free(+SAE).

Wigan Pier Walk 530

Gtr Man, Lancs	43 km / 27 miles

A route around the south-west plains of Lancashire taking in woods, farmlands, Harrock Hill and parts of the Leeds - Liverpool canal. There are alternative 15 and 32 miles routes.

Start and finish	Wigan Pier, Gtr Man	SD577053
OS maps	108	

Publication(s)
Looseleaf: *Wigan Pier Walk* (James and Barbara Rigby). Free(+9" x 4" SAE).
Badge and certificate (£2.00/13" x 9" SAE) available from James and Barbara Rigby.

Wimpole Way 531

Cambs	18 km / 11 miles

The Way, across farmland and through the villages of Caldecote and Kingston to the eighteenth-century Wimpole Hall and Park. See Clopton Way.

Start	Cambridge, Cambs	TL435585
Finish	Wimpole Hall, Cambs	TL343511
On OS maps	154	
Waymark	Wimpole Way logo	

Publication(s)
Leaflet: *Wimpole Way* (Cambridgeshire County Council). 1993\ A4/3\£0.40(+50p).

Windrush Way 532

Glos	22 km / 14 miles

The Way provides a link between the Oxfordshire Way at Bourton-on-the-Water with the Cotswold Way at Winchcombe. Whereas its sister route, the Wardens' Way, winds through villages, the Windrush Way takes to the hills with only remains of lost medieval villages en route.

Start	Bourton-on-the-Water, Glos	SP170209
Finish	Winchcombe, Glos	SP025283
On OS maps	163	
Waymark	Circle, top half white, bottom half black	

Publication(s)
Paperback: *Wardens' Way and Windrush Way* (Cotswold Wardens Service). 1991\A5\32pp\£1.50(+25p).

Wirral Shore Way 533

| Cheshire, Merseyside | 36 km / 22 miles |

From the historic city of Chester to the north western tip of the Wirral Peninsula the route of the Way is dictated by the old coastline of Wirral bordering the Dee Estuary, passing the remains of a Norman fortress used in the Edwardian wars against the Welsh, a line of dried out Elizabethan sea ports, developed as Chester suffered a siltation, and a host of villages and seaside resorts. Along the Dee Estuary, the Way briefly links into the Wirral Way (12 miles) and from Hoylake, the Wirral Coastal Walk provides a 10 miles extension to Seacombe.

Start	Chester Cathedral, Cheshire	SJ406665
Finish	West Kirby, Merseyside	SJ204886
OS maps	108, 117	

Publication(s)
Booklet: *A Walker's Guide to the Wirral Shore Way* by Carl Rogers (Mara Publications). ISBN:0952240904. 135 x 210\48pp\£3.95.
Leaflet: *Wirral Country Park - Wirral Way* (Thurstaston Visitor Centre). A5\£0.40(+9" x 6" SAE).
Leaflet: *North Wirral Coastal Park - Wirral Coastal Walk* (Thurstaston Visitor Centre). A5\£0.20(+9" x 6"SAE).

Witches Way 534

| Lancs | 50 km / 31 miles |

The Way heads from the heart of industrial Lancashire, over the moors between Blackburn and Accrington, and across lowland to Read before climbing to the summit of Pendle Hill, the setting for many of the tales of Lancashire witches. The Way descends to Downham and crosses the Ribble valley before going over Standridge Hill to Slaidburn.

Start	Rawtenstall, Lancs	SD809230
Finish	Slaidburn, Lancs	SD712524
OS maps	103	

Publication(s)
Looseleaf: *The Witches Way* (Jim Ashton). 1997\A4\Free(+SAE).
Badge and certificate (£1.50/SAE/£0.15/SAE) available from Jim Ashton.

Witton Weavers Way   535

Lancs   51 km / 32 miles

The Way is a network of four circular routes (named the *Beamers, Reelers, Tacklers* and *Warpers Trails*), linked together to form a large loop to the west of Blackburn and Darwen. The route runs from Witton Country Park to the west of Blackburn via Abbey Village and Darwen Moor to Jumbles Reservoir on the northern outskirts of Bolton. There is also a link into Darwen itself.

Start and finish	Witton Park, Lancs	SD659273
On OS maps	102, 103, 109	
Waymark	Mill logo on named standard markers	

Publication(s)
Folder: *Witton Weavers Way: Blackburn & Darwen Borough-wide walk* (Blackburn Borough Council). 1993 \ A5 \ 4pp \ £2.00.

Wolds Way   536

E Yorks, N Yorks   127 km / 79 miles

This National Trail goes west along the river Humber, and then north around the western edge of the Yorkshire Wolds, across woods and arable land through Thixendale and along the northern escarpment of the Wolds through dry valleys and sheep pasture to the coast and the Cleveland Way at Filey.

Start	Hessle (Haven), E Yorks	TA035256
Finish	Filey Brigg, N Yorks	TA126817
On OS maps	100, 101, 106, 107	
Waymark	National Trail Acorn	

Publication(s)
Softback: *Wolds Way* (Official Guide) by Roger Ratcliffe (Aurum Press). ISBN:1854101897. 1992 \ 210 x 130 \ £9.99.
Leaflet: *Wolds Way* (Countryside Commission Postal Sales). 1992 \ A4/3 \ Free.
Looseleaf: *Wolds Way Accommodation* (RA East Yorkshire & Derwent Area). A4 \ 1pp \ Free(+SAE).
Badge (£1.00/SAE) available from RA East Yorkshire & Derwent Area.

Worcestershire Way   537

Worc   77 km / 48 miles

Starting on Kinver Edge where it connects with the North Worcestershire Path and Staffordshire Way, the route takes a south-westerly direction to the River Severn passing to the east of Wye Forest to Bewdley. It continues over the hills of Abberley, Penny and Ankerdine before crossing the River Teme. The Suckley Hills on the northern end of the Malvern Hills are also crossed at Cowleigh. See also the Malvern Link and Gloucestershire Way.

Start	Kingsford, Worc	SO836821
Finish	Hollybush, Worc	SO763369
On OS maps	138, 149, 150	
Waymark	Standard waymark with name in arrow	

Publication(s)
Paperback: *The Worcestershire Way Walker's Guide* (Worcestershire County Council). ISBN:1853010197. 1996\A5\70pp\ £4.50(incl p+p).

Wychavon Way   538

Glos, Heref & Worc	66 km / 41 miles

A link from the River Severn to the Cotswolds, the Way, opened to commemorate the Silver Jubilee in 1977, takes in Ombersley, Hampton Lovell, the north of Droitwich, Church Lench and Fladbury. Just after Netherton there is an optional detour up Bredon Hill, then on to Ashton under Hill, Gretton and the finish at Winchcombe on the Cotswold Way.

Start	Holt Fleet, Heref & Worc	SO824633
Finish	Winchcombe, Glos	SP025283
On OS maps	138, 150, 163	
Waymark	Crown symbol with letter W	

Publication(s)
Paperback: *The Wychavon Way* (Wychavon District Council). ISBN: 095080990X. 1993\A5\80pp\£2.95(+50p).

Wye to the Thames   539

Heref & Worc, Oxon	192 km / 119 miles

A route devised to encourage walkers in using the train when planning walks between Hereford and Oxford, it takes in Ledbury, Great Malvern, Evesham and Moreton-in-Marsh, and can be linked with several other routes.

Start	Hereford, Heref & Worc	SO515406
Finish	Oxford, Oxon	SP503063
OS maps	149, 150, 151, 163, 164	

Publication(s)
Booklet: *From the Wye to the Thames* (Cotswold Line Promotion Group). ISBN:0952539705. 1996\A5\60pp\£2.50(incl p+p).

Wye Valley Walk 540

Glos, Heref & Worc, Monmouth, Powys	178 km / 111 miles

A walk following the banks of the river for most of its length but including some hill climbing, it passes Lovers Leap and Tintern Abbey. Several vantage points are achieved before crossing over the Wye at Redbrook to continue along the riverside to Monmouth. The route then meanders on to pass English Bicknor, Welsh Bicknor and Goodrich Castle then leaving the Wye to go across country to Ross-on-Wye before reaching Hereford. Passing cider orchards, parkland and farmland, the Way continues to Bredwardine, Merbach Hill, Hay-on-Wye, Builth Wells and Newbridge.

Start	Chepstow, Monmouth	ST529924
Finish	Rhayader, Powys	SN968679
On OS maps	136, 146, 147, 148, 149, 160, 161, 162, 172	
Waymark	Named arrows with yellow spot, & leaping salmon	

Publication(s)
Paperback: *Wye Valley Walk - Official Route Guide* (Herefordshire County Council). ISBN:1853010200. 1997\A5\44pp\£3.95(incl p+p).
Paperback: *Walking Down the Wye* by David Hunter (Cicerone Press). ISBN:1852841052. 1992\116 x 176\192pp\£6.99.
Folder: *Wye Valley Walk: Hay-on-Wye to Rhayader* (Powys County Council). 1997\8 cards\£1.50(+30p).
Leaflet: *Wye Valley Walk - Accommodation & Transport Guide* (Powys County Council). Annual\A5\Free(+30p).

Wyre Forest Alpine Walk 541

Worc	32 km / 20 miles

A demanding walk in the Wyre Forest area encircling the Severn Valley and always within sound of the Severn Valley Railway.

Start and finish	Bewdley, Worc	SO788754
OS maps	138	

Publication(s)
Looseleaf: *Wyre Forest Alpine Walk* (Eric Perks). Free(+9" x 6" SAE).
Badge and certificate (£2.00/£0.75/9" x 6" SAE) available from Eric Perks.

Wyre Way   542

Lancs   26 km / 16 miles

A walk exploring the history and wildlife of the Wyre estuary from its mouth inland as far as the Shard Bridge and making use of the ferry between Fleetwood and Knott End. The ferry is subject to tide times and the route is also subject to flooding on Spring tides.

Start	Fleetwood, Lancs	SD340480
Finish	Knott End, Lancs	SD346485
On OS maps	102	
Waymark	Named posts	

Publication(s)
Leaflet: *The Wyre Way* (Wyre Estuary Country Park). 1995\A5/8\ £0.40(+A5 SAE).
Badge and certificate available, details from Wyre Estuary Country Park.

Wysis Way   543

Glos, Monmouth   88 km / 55 miles

The Way links the Offa's Dyke Path with the Thames Path taking in the northern part of the Forest of Dean, with the River Severn crossed at Gloucester.

Start	Monmouth, Monmouthshire	SO510130
Finish	Kemble, Glos	ST985975
OS maps	161, 162, 163	

Publication(s)
Paperback: *The Wysis Way* by Gerry Stewart (Countryside Matters). ISBN:0952787016. 1997\A5\80pp\£4.95

Yoredale Way   544

Cumbria, N Yorks   163 km / 101 miles

The Way follows the course of the River Ure from York to its source on Abbotside Common, 2,000ft above sea level near Kirkby Stephen. It passes through Boroughbridge, Ripon, Middleham, Aysgarth and Hardraw Falls before climbing to Ure Head and descending to follow the River Eden to Kirkby Stephen.

Start	York, N Yorks	SE603522
Finish	Kirkby Stephen, Cumbria	NY775087
OS maps	91, 98, 99, 105	

Publication(s)
Folder: *The Yoredale Way - a 100 mile walk from York to Kirkby Stephen* by J.K.E. Piggin (Yorkshire Footpath Trust). ISBN: 1898978018. £3.45.
Badge and certificate (£1.50/SAE) available from Yorkshire Footpath Trust.

Yorkshire Dales Challenge Walk 545

N Yorks	40 km / 25 miles

A challenge walk through the National Park including much high moorland.

Start and finish	Kettlewell, N Yorks	SD971724
OS maps	98	

Publication(s)
Paperback: *John Merrill's Yorkshire Dales Challenge Walk* by John Merrill (Happy Walking International Ltd). ISBN: 0907496865. 32pp \ £3.00.
Badge and certificate (£3.00/post free) available from Happy Walking International Ltd.

ROUTES BY DISTANCE

Path	Miles	Km	Page(s)
Land's End to John O'Groats	850	1,368	111
Monarch's Way	609	981	129-130
Great English Walk	602	969	80
South West Coast Path	600	966	180-181
Ulster Way	570	918	208-209
Three Ridings on Foot	438	706	200
Land's End Trail	298	480	111-112
Macmillan Way	290	467	121-122
Southern Coast-to-Coast Walk	283	456	43
Cambrian Way	274	441	27
Alternative Pennine Way	268	432	150-152
Cambrian & Lleyn Coast Path	257	414	26-27
Pennine Way	251	404	150-152
Channel to Channel Walk	242	390	43
Midshires Way	225	362	127-128
Coast to Coast - Wales	222	357	43
Around Norfolk Walk	220	354	11
Hardy Way	213	343	87-88
Southern Upland Way	213	343	181-182
Severn Way	210	338	171
Ravenber	210	338	41-42
Pennine Bridleway	208	335	150
On Foot From Coast to Coast	206	332	41-42
London Countryway	206	331	118-119
Six Shires Circuit	206	331	175
Cape Wrath Trail	205	330	28
Marches Way	204	329	124
Trans Pennine Trail	200	322	203-204
Westmorland Heritage Walk	200	322	219
Alternative Coast to Coast	192	309	41-42
Coast to Coast	190	306	41-42
Fife Walks	190	306	70
Lakeland to Lindisfarne	190	306	41-42
Cumbria Coastal Way	189	305	50
Pembrokeshire Coast Path	186	299	148-149
Tarka Trail	181	291	191
Famous Highland Drove Walk	180	290	69
Thames Path	180	290	194-195
Offa's Dyke Path	178	287	141-142
Northern Coast to Coast	178	287	41-42
Westmorland Boundary Way	171	275	219
Cromer to the M11	165	265	47-48
Saxon Shore Way	163	262	169
Westside Walk (Shetland)	162	261	220

List of Routes by Distance

Path	Miles	Km	Page(s)
Sarn Helen	160	258	168
Central Scottish Way	156	251	32
Durham Round	155	250	61
Sussex Border Path	152	245	187
Lake District Boundary Walk	152	244	105
Reiver's Way	150	242	155-156
Mercian Way	150	241	126
Blackpool to Bridlington	148	238	41-42
Lakeland Fringe	147	237	105
Grand Union Canal Walk	145	234	77-78
Around the Lakes	145	233	13
North Downs Way	142	229	136-137
Harcamlow Way	141	227	87
Viking Way	141	227	212
Shropshire Way	139	224	173
London Loop & Capital Ring	138	222	119
Wessex Ridgeway	137	221	217
Morecambe to Whitby Walk	131	211	41-42
Lancashire Loop	130	209	108
Thirlmere Way	130	209	195-196
Lakeland Round	126	203	106-107
Round Northmavine Trek	125	201	161
Anglesey Coast Path	121	195	11-12
Glyndwr's Way/Ffordd Glyndwr	121	195	76
Lancashire Way	121	195	109
Coast to Coast Trek	120	193	41-42
Wharfedale to Westmorland	120	193	105
Wye to the Thames	119	192	227
Red Rose Walk	117	188	155
Oxbridge Walk	115	185	144
Cestrian Link Walk	113	182	32-33
Wye Valley Walk	111	178	228
Cleveland Way	110	177	39
Nene Way	110	177	132-133
Dyfi Valley Way	109	175	61-62
Greensand Way	107	173	82-83
Abbott's Hike	107	172	9
Peak District Round	107	172	146-147
Suffolk Way	106	170	187
Robin Hood Way	105	169	159
Highland High Way	105	169	218
Abbeys Amble	104	167	8-9
Lakeland Tour	104	167	107
Cotswold Way	103	166	46
Hereward Way	103	166	91
Icknield Way	103	166	97
Two Moors Way	102	164	206-207
Leicestershire Round	101	163	114
Yoredale Way	101	163	229-230
Round Yell Trek	101	162	162
South Downs Way	101	162	179

Path	Miles	Km	Page(s)
Chilterns Hundred	100	161	37
Exmoor & Lorna Doone	100	161	68-69
Gloucestershire Way	100	161	76
Heart of England Way	100	161	90
High Pennine Trail	100	161	93
Lady Anne's Way	100	161	105
Lindsey Loop	100	161	117
Navigation Way	100	161	132
Roses Walk	100	161	160
Teesdale Way	100	161	191-192
Waterwitch 100	100	161	109-110
Shropshire Peaks Walk	99	160	172-173
Westmorland Way	99	159	220
Centenary Way (Warwickshire)	98	158	31
Cheshire Ring Canal Walk	98	158	34-35
North York Moors Walk	98	158	139-140
Peakland Way	97	156	147
Bowland-Dales Traverse	95	153	22
Staffordshire Way	95	153	183-184
West Highland Way	95	153	218
Peddars Way & Norfolk Coast Path	94	151	147-148
Green London Way	93	150	82
Peak District High Level Route	91	147	146
Dorset Jubilee Trail	90	145	58
Isle of Man Coast Path	90	145	98-99
Tidewater Way	90	145	202
High Weald Landscape Trail	89	144	94
Jurassic Way	88	142	101
St Edmund Way	88	142	165
Hertfordshire Chain Walk	87	140	91-92
Ridgeway	85	137	157
East Riding Heritage Way	84	136	62-63
Kennet and Avon Walk	84	135	101-102
Trent Valley Way	84	135	205
Eskdale Way	83	134	67
Centenary Way (North Yorkshire)	83	133	31
Cotswolds Walk	83	133	46-47
Oxford Canal Walk	83	133	144-145
Fife Coast Path	82	132	70
Dark Peak Boundary Walk	81	131	55
Dales Way	81	130	53
Essex Way	81	130	68
Hadrian's Wall Path	81	130	84-85
Apostles Walk	80	129	12-13
Cumberland Way	80	129	50
Wealdway	80	129	214
White Peak Way	80	129	223
Bowland Round	79	128	21
Lune Valley Walk	79	127	120-121
Wolds Way	79	127	226
Angles Way	78	126	11

List of Routes by Distance

Path	Miles	Km	Page(s)
Eden Way	78	126	65
Swale Way	77	124	188
Cranborne Chase Path	76	122	47
Inn Way	76	122	98
Shropshire Challenge Walk	76	122	172
Bunyan Trail	75	121	24
Furness Way	75	121	74
Vectis Trail	75	120	210-211
Barnsley Boundary Walk	74	119	15
Red Kite Trail	74	119	155
Kirklees Way	73	118	104
Ribble Way	73	118	156
Weardale Way	73	117	214-215
Jack Mytton Way	72	116	100
Capital Ring	72	116	119
Blackmore Vale Path	71	114	19
Lancashire-Lakeland Link	71	114	109
Wayfarer's Walk	71	114	213-214
Danum Trail	70	113	54
Lancashire Trail	70	113	108-109
Cumbria Way	70	112	51
Dales Walk	70	112	52-53
Ebor Way	70	112	64
West Lakes Way	70	112	219
Swan's Way	68	110	188
Lancashire Coastal Way	66	106	108
Vanguard Way	66	106	210
Great North Forest Trail	65	105	81
d'Arcy Dalton Way	65	104	51-52
Isle of Wight Coast Path	65	104	99
Jorvic Way	65	104	100
Oxfordshire Way	65	104	145
Oxfordshire Trek	64	103	145
St Illtyd's Walk	64	103	165-166
Great Glen Way	63	101	80
Round Unst Trek	63	101	162
St Cuthbert's Way	62	100	164-165
Black and White Village Trail	61	99	18
Donnington Way	61	99	58
South of the Landsker Trail	60	97	179-180
Traditional Hostels Lakes Walk	60	97	203
Trans-Dales Trail - 1	60	97	204
Trans-Dales Trail - 2	60	97	204
High Peak 60	60	96	92-93
Landsker Borderlands Trail	60	96	110
Leeds Country Way	60	96	113
North Cotswold Diamond Way	60	96	136
North Wales Path	60	96	137-138
Northumbrian Coastline	60	96	140-141
Solent Way	60	96	177-178
Stour Valley Path (East Anglia)	60	96	185

Path	Miles	Km	Page(s)
Three Castles Path	60	96	196
Three Forests Way	60	96	198
Nev Cole Way	58	93	133
Durham Railway Paths	57	92	61
Lakeland Top Ten	57	91	107
Lancaster Canal	57	91	109-110
Weavers Way	56	90	216
Cotswold Ring	55	89	45
Herriot Way	55	88	91
Taff Trail	55	88	189
Wysis Way	55	88	229
Allerdale Ramble	54	87	10
Formartine and Buchan Way	54	87	72
Nidderdale Way	53	85	135
Sheffield Country Walk	53	85	171
Northern Fells	52	84	140
Stour Valley Walk (Kent)	51	82	185-186
Heart of Snowdonia Circuit	50	81	177
Lyke Wake Way	50	81	121
Airedale Way	50	80	9-10
Calderdale Way	50	80	26
Carpet Baggers 50	50	80	29
Chesterfield Round	50	80	36
Dartmoor Perambulation	50	80	56
Denby Way	50	80	56
Gallo Way Round	50	80	74-76
Land's End Round	50	80	110
Lea Valley Walk	50	80	112
Limestone Way	50	80	116-117
Lost Lancs Way	50	80	120
Minster Way	50	80	129
North Western Fells	50	80	138
Ripon Rowel	50	80	157-158
River Parrett Trail	50	80	158
Suffolk Coast and Heaths Path	50	80	186-187
Sweet Pea Challenge Walk	50	80	188-189
Taith Torfaen	50	80	190
Usk Valley Walk	50	80	209-210
Mendip Ways	49	79	125-126
Worcestershire Way	48	77	226-227
Tabular Hills Link Walk	48	77	39
Socratic Trail	47	76	177
Cuckoo Way	46	74	49-50
Test Way	46	74	193
Ullswater Circuit	46	74	208
Exe Valley Way	45	72	68
Four Pikes Hike	45	72	73
King's Way	45	72	103
Pendle Way	45	72	149-150
Plogsland Round	45	72	153
Rossendale Way	45	72	160

Path	Miles	Km	Page(s)
Sheffield Way	45	72	171-172
Snowdonia 24hr Circuit	45	72	176-177
Speyside Way	45	72	183
St Peter's Way	45	72	166
Ainsty Bounds Walk	44	71	9
Community Forest Path	44	71	45
Bromley Circular Walks	43	69	22-23
Middlesex Greenway	43	69	127
Rivers Way	43	69	158
Seahorse Saunter	43	69	170
North to South Surrey Walk	41	66	137
Wychavon Way	41	66	227
Around the Carneddau	40	64	13
Bronte Way	40	64	23
Cat Walk	40	64	29-30
Chalkland Way	40	64	33
East Devon Way	40	64	62
Greensand Ridge Walk	40	64	82
Limey Way	40	64	117
Malvern Link	40	64	123
Oldham Way	40	64	143
Samaritan Way	40	64	167
Tameside Trail	40	64	190-191
Weavers Shuttle	40	64	215-216
Shepherd's Round	40	64	121
Snowdonia Five Ranges Round	40	64	177
Lyke Wake Walk	39	63	121
Green Chain Walk	39	62	81
Boudica's Way	38	61	21
Compo's Way	38	61	45
Langbaurgh Loop	38	61	112
Mid Sussex Link	38	61	187
Basingstoke Canal Walk	37	60	15-16
Clitheroe 60K	37	60	40
Derbyshire Twenty Dales Challenge	37	60	57
Shropshire Union Canal	37	60	173
Capital Walk - Cardiff	37	59	28
Downs Link	37	59	59
Rosedale Circuit	37	59	159-160
Bell Walk Major	36	58	17
Coed Morgannwg Way	36	58	44
Douglas Way	36	58	58-59
Limestone Link Path	36	58	116
Two Beacons Challenge	36	58	205-206
Wey-South Path	36	58	220-221
Three Shires Way	35	57	201
West Devon Way & Plymouth Link	35	57	217-218
Esk Valley Walk	35	56	66-67
Ivanhoe Way	35	56	99-100
Limestone Lion	35	56	116
Montgomery Canal	35	56	130

Path	Miles	Km	Page(s)
North Bucks Way	35	56	135-136
Six Shropshire Summits	35	56	175
Sky to Sea	35	56	176
Three Towers Circuit	35	56	201-202
Avon Valley Path	34	55	14
Three Feathers Walk (Kettlewell)	34	55	197
Nar Valley Way	34	54	131-132
Charnwood Round	33	53	34
Cistercian Way	33	53	38
Cloud 7 Circuit	33	53	40-41
Doncastrian Way	33	53	57
Grantham Canal	33	53	79
Shieldsman Walk	33	53	172
Tesrod Elddod	33	53	154
Glen Feshie	32	52	24-25
Lairig an Laoich	32	52	24-25
Bradford Ring	32	51	22
Ducal Nottinghamshire	32	51	59-60
Greenway Challenge Walk	32	51	83
Lower Dales Three Hostels Walk	32	51	120
North York Moors Wobble	32	51	140
Sandstone Trail	32	51	168
Witton Weavers Way	32	51	226
1066 Country Walk	31	50	8
Aylesbury Ring	31	50	14
Hambleton Hobble	31	50	86
Hyndburn Clog	31	50	96
North Bowland Traverse	31	50	135
Round Fetlar Walk	31	50	161
South Cheshire Way	31	50	178
Stour Valley Way (Dorset)	31	50	186
Witches Way	31	50	225
Offa's Dyke Path Castles Alternative	31	50	141-142
Almscliff Amble	30	48	10
Belmont 30	30	48	17
Bilsdale Circuit	30	48	18
Cal-Der-Went Walk	30	48	25-26
East Thriding Treble Ten	30	48	63
High Street Stroll	30	48	93-94
Imber Range Perimeter Path	30	48	97
Irwell Valley Way	30	48	98
Longshaw Limber	30	48	119
Mortimer Trail	30	48	130-131
Pride of the Peak Walk	30	48	153
Snowdon Challenge Walk	30	48	176
Three Moors Walk	30	48	198
Three Peaks of Cheviot Walk	30	48	199
Two Castles Trail	30	48	206
Mersey Way	30	48	203-204
Three Feathers Walk (Kilburn)	30	48	197
West Mendip Way	30	48	125-126

List of Routes by Distance

Path	Miles	Km	Page(s)
Welsh 3000s	29	47	216-217
Cross Wight Traverse	29	47	154
Back o' Skidda	28	45	15
Derby Canal Ring	28	45	57
Essex Country to the Coast	28	45	67
Foss Walk	28	45	73
High Peak Way	28	45	93
High Weald Walk	28	45	94
Leland Trail	28	45	114
Liberty Trail	28	45	114-115
Little John Challenge Walk	28	45	118
Medway Valley Walk	28	45	125
Millennium Way	28	45	128
Nidd Valley Link	28	45	134
Painters Way	28	45	146
Rhymney Valley Ridgeway Walk	28	45	156
Rydal Round	28	45	163-164
Saddleworth Skyline	28	45	164
Stort Valley Way	28	45	185
Three Counties Challenge Walk	28	45	197
Lairig Ghru	28	45	24-25
Three Feathers Walk (Yorkshire Bridge)	28	45	197
Hardy Hobble	27	44	154
Cavendish 27 Circuit	27	43	30
Crowthorn Crawl	27	43	49
Gritstone Edge Walk	27	43	83
North Worcestershire Path	27	43	139
Pendle Marathon	27	43	149
Royal Military Canal Path	27	43	163
Trollers Trot	27	43	205
Wigan Pier Walk	27	43	224
Caistor Challenge Alternative	26	42	25
Daffodil Dawdle	26	42	52
Flower of Suffolk	26	42	71
Forest of Bowland Challenge Walk	26	42	71
Glevum Way	26	42	75
Heart of Arden Walk	26	42	89
Kesteven 25	26	42	102
Kielder Water Circuit Challenge Walk	26	42	103
Lipchis Way	26	42	117-118
Nidd Vale Circuit	26	42	134
North Worcestershire Hills Marathon	26	42	138
Ouse Valley Way	26	42	143
Poppyline Marathon	26	42	153
Ramblers Route	26	42	154
Saints Way/Forth an Syns	26	42	166
Scarborough Rock Challenge	26	42	169
Sirhowy Valley Walk	26	42	174
Three Peaks of Great Britain	26	42	199
Wharfedale Washburn Walk	26	42	221
Locus Classicus	26	42	154

Path	Miles	Km	Page(s)
Welsh 1000m Peaks Marathon	26	42	177
Belvoir Witches Challenge Walk	25	40	17-18
Caistor Challenge	25	40	25
Charnwood Forest Challenge Walk	25	40	33-34
Cheltenham Circular Footpath	25	40	34
Cheviot Hills 2,000ft Summits	25	40	36-37
Dales Traverse	25	40	52
Forest Way	25	40	71-72
Founders Footpaths	25	40	73
Harden Hike	25	40	87
Myrtle Meander	25	40	131
North York Moors Challenge Walk	25	40	139
Old Sarum Challenge	25	40	142-143
Ox Drove Way	25	40	144
Pennington Round	25	40	152
Rotherham Round Walk	25	40	160-161
Settle Scramble	25	40	170-171
Sidmouth Saunter	25	40	173-174
Tame Valley Way	25	40	190
Three Reservoirs Challenge	25	40	200
Three Rivers Walk	25	40	201
Two Crosses Circuit	25	40	206
White Peak Challenge Walk	25	40	221-222
Whithorn Pilgrim Way	25	40	223
Yorkshire Dales Challenge Walk	25	40	230
Churnet Valley Challenge Walk	24	39	37-38
Clarendon Way	24	39	38
High Hunsley Circuit	24	39	92
Holme Valley Circular Walk	24	39	95
Limestone Dale Walk	24	39	115
Three Peaks Walk (Yorkshire)	24	39	199-200
Purbeck Steam Package	24	39	154
Centenary Way (Derbyshire)	24	38	30-31
Cross Bucks Way	24	38	48-49
Dark Peak Challenge Walk	24	38	55
Grand Western Canal	24	38	78-79
Holme Valley Circular Challenge Walk	24	38	95
Lead Mining Trail	24	38	113
Maelor Way	24	38	122
Rutland Water Challenge Walk	24	38	163
Salter's Way	24	38	167
Staffordshire Moorlands Challenge Walk	24	38	183
White Peak Rollercoaster	24	38	222
Black Mountains Traverse Challenge	23	37	18-19
Bronte Round	23	37	23
Centenary Circle	23	37	30
Dunford Round	23	37	60
Elham Valley Way	23	37	65
Roach Valley Way	23	37	159
Round Preston Walk	23	37	162
South Bucks Way	23	37	178

List of Routes by Distance

Path	Miles	Km	Page(s)
Hutton Hike	23	37	62-63
Bollin Valley Way	22	36	20
Haslemere Circular Walk	22	36	88
Wirral Shore Way	22	36	225
Arun Way	22	35	13-14
Chaddesley Chase	22	35	33
Crooked Spire Walk	22	35	48
Edale Skyline	22	35	64
Hidden Valley Walk	22	35	92
Lambourn Valley Way	22	35	107-108
Maldon Millennium	22	35	122-123
Middlewich Challenge Walk	22	35	127
Ten Reservoirs Walk	22	35	192-193
Thirlmere Round	22	35	195
Bealach Dearg	22	35	24-25
Delamere Way	22	35	35
Ridge Too Far	22	35	154
Anglezarke Amble	21	34	12
Burley Bridge Hike	21	34	24
Chorley Botany Bay Round	21	34	37
Gordon Way	21	34	77
Hangers Way	21	34	86
Harrogate Ringway	21	34	88
Marriott's Way	21	34	124
Sefton Coastal Footpath	21	34	170
Southam Circular Way	21	34	181
Spen Way Heritage Trail	21	34	182-183
Taff-Ely Ridgeway Walk	21	34	189
Ten Church Challenge	21	34	192
Tyne and Wear 20	21	34	207-208
Rudston Roam	21	34	62-63
Abberley Amble	20	32	8
Anglezarke Anguish	20	32	12
Bourne Blunder	20	32	21
Carneddau Challenge Walk	20	32	28-29
Dambusters Challenge Walk	20	32	54
Duddon Horseshoe	20	32	60
Duddon Triangle Walk	20	32	60
Epperstone Park to Southwell Minster	20	32	66
Grasmere Skyline Classic Walk	20	32	79
Hanslope Circular Ride	20	32	86
Helm Wind Walk	20	32	90
Hillingdon Trail	20	32	95
Howden 20	20	32	96
Kett's Country Walk	20	32	103
Kinver Clamber	20	32	104
Knaresborough Round	20	32	104-105
Malvern Hills Challenge Walk	20	32	123
Mansell Way	20	32	123-124
Mid Suffolk Footpath	20	32	126
Mini-Alps	20	32	129

Path	Miles	Km	Page(s)
Newtondale Trail	20	32	134
North Wolds Walk	20	32	138
Offa's Hyke	20	32	142
Pendle and Ribble Round	20	32	149
Pioneers Round	20	32	152
Ramsbottom Round	20	32	154-155
Saddleworth Five Trig Points Walk	20	32	164
Salt & Sails Trail	20	32	166-167
Skipton-Settle Link	20	32	175
Spanners Round	20	32	182
Tennyson Twenty	20	32	193
Thanet Coastal Path	20	32	195
Two Rivers Way	20	32	207
Vermuyden Way	20	32	211
Wanderlust Way	20	32	212
Weaver Valley Way	20	32	215
Whicham Valley Five Trigs Walk	20	32	221
Wyre Forest Alpine Walk	20	32	228
Beverley Twenty	20	32	62-63
Headland Walk	20	32	62-63
Inter-City Challenge	20	32	154
Darent Valley Path	19	31	54-55
Todmorden Centenary Way	19	31	202-203
West Dorset Enigma	19	31	154
Blackwater Valley Footpath	19	30	19
Camel Trail	19	30	27-28
Cown Edge Way	19	30	47
Haworth-Hebden Bridge Walk	19	30	88-89
Upper Tas Valley Walk	19	30	209
East Mendip Way	19	30	125-126
Chess Valley Walk and Chiltern Link	18	29	36
Cuckoo Walk	18	29	49
Gritstone Trail	18	29	84
Haematite Trail	18	29	85
Heart of Bowland Walk	18	29	89
Lakeland Challenge Walk	18	29	106
Moyle Way	18	29	131
New Five Trig Points Walk	18	29	133
Templer Way	18	29	192
Three Castles Walk	18	29	196
Tinners Way	18	29	202
Day Return to Charmouth	18	29	154
Eddisbury Way	18	29	35
High Peak Trail	18	29	222-223
Majesty of the Wiltshire Downs	18	29	154
Paston Way	18	29	216
Bonnie Prince Charlie Walk	17	28	20
Altrincham Circular	17	27	10-11
Beacon Way	17	27	16
Colne Valley - Way & Trail	17	27	44
Dart Valley Trail	17	27	55-56

List of Routes by Distance

Path	Miles	Km	Page(s)
Fen Rivers Way	17	27	69
Forest & Worth Ways (Sussex)	17	27	72
Gipping Valley River Path	17	27	75
Lakeland Heritage Trail	17	27	106
Thame Valley Walk	17	27	193-194
Three Peaks Circular (Avon)	17	27	198
Tyne-Wear Trail	17	27	208
Waveney Way	17	27	213
Beating the Bounds	16	26	16
Blue Man Walk	16	26	19-20
Castleman Trailway	16	26	29
Ebbw Valley Walk	16	26	63-64
Howdenshire Way	16	26	96
Jubilee Way (South Gloucestershire)	16	26	101
Wyre Way	16	26	229
Beeches Way	16	25	16-17
Kerry Ridgeway	16	25	102
Leicestershire Jubilee Way	16	25	113
Three Crags Walk	16	25	197
Eden Valley Walk	15	24	64-65
Epping Forest Centenary Walk	15	24	66
Flitch Way	15	24	70-71
Thames Down Link	15	24	194
Ver-Colne Valley Walk	15	24	211
Bembridge Trail	15	24	210-211
River Wear Trail	15	24	214-215
Tennyson Trail	15	24	210-211
Worsley Trail	15	24	210-211
Silkin Way	14	23	174
Beane Valley Walk	14	23	112
Brampton Valley Way	14	23	127-128
Herring Road/Bayr ny Skiddan	14	23	128
Frome Valley Walkway	14	22	74
Glamorgan Heritage Coast	14	22	75
Wardens' Way	14	22	213
Windrush Way	14	22	224-225
Grafton Way	13	21	77
Limestone Link	13	21	115
Ogwr Ridgeway Walk	13	21	142
Staunton Way	13	21	184
Grafham Water Circular Ride	13	21	201
Keelman's Way	13	21	85
Lark Valley Path	13	21	165
Ridley Round	13	21	68
Tissington Trail	13	21	222-223
Hadrian's Way	12	20	85
Medlock Valley Way	12	20	125
Etherow-Goyt Valley Way	12	19	127-128
Lanchester Valley Walk	12	19	61
Lon Eifion	12	19	26-27
Northern Rhymney Valley Ridgeway Walk	12	19	156

242

LIST OF ADDRESSES

A G Publications, Attorney Garth, Motherby, Penrith, Cumbria, CA11 0RJ

Abbott, Peter, 5 Hillstone Close, Greenmount, Bury, Lancashire, BL8 4EZ

Aberdeenshire County Council, Woodhill House, Westburn Road, Aberdeen, AB51 5NL

Alexius Press, 114 Sandhurst Road, Kingsbury, London, NW9 9LN

Allen, JJ., 5 Moorgate Cottages, Astley Bank, Darwen, Lancashire, BB3 2QB

Amadorn, 18 Brewery Lane, Keswick, Cumbria, CA12 5LJ

Andrews, J & J., 6 Priory Close, Ingham, Bury St Edmunds, IP31 1NN

Appletree Press Ltd, 19-21, Alfred Street, Belfast, BT2 8DL

Archard, Richard, 57 Countess Road, Amesbury, Wiltshire, SP4 7AS

Ashridge Press, PO Box 5975, Birmingham, B29 7EZ

Ashton, Jim, 19 Leslie Avenue, Bury, Lancashire, BL9 8DL

Ashworth, AT., 22 Laneside, Haworth Road, Wilsden, Bradford, West Yorkshire, BD15 0LH

Atkinson, Frank, 5 Edge Hall Road, Orrell, Wigan, Lancashire, WN5 8TL

Aurum Press, 25 Bedford Avenue, London, WC1B 3AT

Avon Heath Country Park, Dorset County Council, Birch Road, St Ives, Ringwood, Dorset, BH24 2DA

Aylesbury Vale District Council, Countryside Management Project, Haydon Mill, Rabans Lane, Aylesbury, Buckinghamshire, HP19 3ST

Aze, Barbara, Shalinion, Upper Hyde Farm Lane, Shanklin, IOW, PO37 7PS

Barnsley Metropolitan Borough Council, Department of Planning, Central Offices, Kendray Street, Barnsley, South Yorkshire, S70 2TN

Barrow Tourist Information Centre, Forum 28, Duke Street, Barrow in Furness, Cumbria, LA14 1HH

Bashforth, Peter, 23 Effeningham Road, Harden, Bingley, W Yorks, BD16 1LQ

Basildon Greenways, Pitsea Hall Country Park, Pitsea, Basildon, Essex, SS16 4UW

Bath & North East Somerset Council, Development & Environmental Services, Trimbridge House, Trim Street, Bath, BA1 2DP

Bayer, Peter, 12 Brooklands Lane, Menston, Ilkley, West Yorkshire, LS29 6PJ

Bedfordshire County Council, Dept of Environment & Economic Development, County Hall, Cauldwell Street, Bedford, MK42 9AP

Benchmark Books, Greystones Cottage, Bankside, Youlgreave, Derbys, DE45 1WD

Bennachie Project, Aberdeenshire County Council, Gordon House, Blackhall Road, Inverurie, AB51 9WA

Berkshire County Council, Babtie Public Services Division, Shinfield Park, Reading, RG2 9XG

Berwick-upon-Tweed Borough Council, Tourism Department, Wallace Green, Berwick-upon-Tweed, TD15 1ED

Bird, Vivian, OBE., 486 Shirley Road, Hall Green, Birmingham, B28 8QN

Bishop, Martyn, 79 Sydney Street, Boston, Lincolnshire, PE21 8NZ

Blackburn Borough Council, Tourist Information, King George's Hall, Northgate, Blackburn, Lancashire, BB2 1AA

Blackwater Valley Team, Ash Lock Cottage, Government Road, Aldershot, Hampshire, GU11 2PS

Bollin Valley Project, County Offices, Chapel Lane, Wilmslow, Cheshire, SK9 1PU

Bound, Terry, 3 Alpha Street, Heavitree, Exeter, Devon, EX1 2SP

Bown, Keith, Dale House, 35 Bawtry Road, Listerdale, Rotherham, South Yorkshire, S66 0AR

Bracknell Forest Borough Council, Recreational Paths Officer, Easthampstead House, Town Centre, Bracknell, Berks, RG12 3AQ

Bracknell Tourist Information Centre, The Look Out, Nine Mile Ride, Bracknell, Berks, RG12 7QW

Braintree & District Outdoor Pursuits, c/o 3 Beaufort Gardens, Braintree, Essex, CM7 6JY

Bridgend County Borough Council, Planning Department, Civic Offices, Angel Street, Bridgend, CF31 1LX

Bristol City Council, Rights of Way Section, 4th Floor, Wilder House, Wilder Street, Bristol, BS2 8BH

British Aerospace Ltd, c/o Harry Cadman, Engineering Skill Centre, Greengate, Middleton, Manchester, M24 1SA

British Waterways - Braunston, Stop House, Braunston, Northants, NN11 7JQ

British Waterways - Chester, Tower Wharf, Raymond Street, Chester, CH1 4EZ

British Waterways - Kennet & Avon, The Locks, Bath Road, Devizes, Wiltshire, SN10 1HB

Brock, John, 15 Sycamore Avenue, Richmond, N Yorks, DL10 4BN

Buckinghamshire County Council, Technical Clerk, Environmental Services, County Hall, Aylesbury, Buckinghamshire, HP20 1UY

Caerphilly County Borough Council, Countryside & Landscape Services, Council Offices, Pontllanfraith, Blackwood, NP2 2YW

Caerphilly Mountain Countryside Service, Taff Gorge Countryisde Centre, Heol-y-Fforest, Tongwynlais, Cardiff, CF4 7JR

Cambridgeshire County Council, Environment & Transport, Shire Hall, Castle Hill, Cambridge, CB3 0AP

Camel Trail Ranger, Cornwall County Council, Eddystone Road, Wadebridge, PL27 7AL

Camelot Books, Pointer House, Lancaster Road, Preesall, Poulton-le-Fylde, FY6 0HN

Carmarthenshire County Council, Leisure Services, Ty-Elwyn, Llanelli, SA15 3AH

Carnegie Press, 18 Maynard Street, Preston, Lancashire, PR2 2AL

Carr, Geoffrey, Fern Cottage, Cardigan Lane, Manor Road, Ossett, West Yorks, WF5 0LT

Carrivick, Dave and Anne, Elm View, Trispen, Truro, Cornwall, TR4 9AZ

Castlemead Publications, 12 Little Mundells, Welwyn Garden City, Hertfordshire, AL7 1EW

Challenge Publications, PO Box 132, Barnsley, S71 5YX

Chelmsford Borough Council, Technical Services Department, Civic Centre, Chelmsford, Essex, CM1 1JE

Cheshire County Council, Heritage and Recreation, Floor 2, Goldsmith House, Hamilton Place, Chester, CH1 1SE

Chesterton, Keith, Firle, Chestnut Avenue, Guildford, Surrey, GU2 5HD

Chiltern Society, c/o Mrs Susan Slocombe, 18 Hillfield Road, Chalfont St Peter, Bucks, SL9 0DX

Cicerone Press, 2 Police Square, Milnthorpe, Cumbria, LA7 7PY

Collier, Major Brett (retd), Chloris House, 208 Nettleham Road, Lincoln, LN2 4DH

Collins, PO Box, Glasgow, G4 0NB

Collins, Stephen J., 51 Russell Gardens, Sipson, Middlesex, UB7 0LR

Constable and Co Ltd, 3 The Lanchesters, 162 Fulham Palace Road, London, W6 9ER

Conwy Borough Council, Civic Offices, Colwyn Bay, LL29 8AR

Copeland Borough Council, Tourist Information Office, The Market Hall, Market Place, Whitehaven, Cumbria, CA28 7JG

Cordee Ltd, 3a De Montfort Street, Leicester, LE1 7HD

Cornwall County Council, Transportation & Estates, Highways Central Group Centre, Castle Canyke Road, Bodmin, Cornwall, PL31 1DZ

Coronet, c/o Hodder & Stoughton, 238 Euston Road, London, NW1 3BH

Corporation of London, City Secretary's Department, PO Box 270, Guildhall, London, EC2P 2EJ

Cotswold Line Promotion Group, c/o Derek J Potter, Homerswood, Boon Street Eckington, Pershore, Worcs, WR10 3BL

Cotswold Wardens Service, Environment Department, Shire Hall, Gloucester, GL1 2TH

Countryside Books, 2 Highfield Avenue, Newbury, Berkshire, RG14 5DS

Countryside Commission Postal Sales, PO Box 124, Walgrave, Northampton, NN6 9TL

Countryside Council for Wales, Plas Penrhos, Penrhos Road, Bangor, Gwynedd, LL57 2LQ

Countryside Matters, 15 Orchard Road, Alderton, Tewkesbury, Gloucestershire, GL20 8NS

Cox, Vic, 36 Elwood Road, Bradway, Sheffield, S17 4RH

Crowood Press, The Stable Block, Crowood Lane, Ramsbury, Marlborough, Wiltshire, SN8 2HR

Cumbria County Council, Rights of Way Section, Construction Services, Viaduct Estate, Carlisle, CA2 5BN

Dalby Forest Visitor Centre, Low Dalby, Pickering, North Yorkshire, YO18 7LT

Dales Trails, 41 The Orchards, Leven, East Yorkshire, HU17 5QA

Dales Way Association, c/o David Smith, Dalegarth, Moorfield Road, Ilkley, W Yorkshire, LS29 8BL

Dalesman Publishing Ltd, Stable Courtyard, Broughton Hall, Skipton, N Yorks, BD23 3AE

Dalton, Ed, Mountain View, Fachell, Hermon, Bodorgan, Gwynedd, LL62 5LL

Davies, George, 33 Fir Tree Road, Fernhill Heath, Worcester, WR3 8RE

Derbyshire County Council, Middleton Top Visitor Centre, Wirksworth, Matlock, Derbyshire, DE4 4LS

Derbyshire Dales District Council, c/o Tourist Information Centre, The Pavillion, Matlock Bath, Derbyshire, DE4 3NR

Derbyshire Footpaths Preservation Society, c/o E.W. Hodgkinson, 3 Crabtree Close, Allestree, Derby, DE22 2SW

Devon County Council, Tourist Information Centre, Exeter Motorway Services Area (M5), Sidmouth Road, Exeter, EX2 7HF

Diadem/Baton Wickes, Clough House, Cochall Lane, Langley, Macclesfield, Cheshire, SK11 0DE

Doncaster Tourist Information Centre, Central Library, Waterdale, Doncaster, DN1 3JE

Dorset County Council, Rights of Way Section, County Hall, Dorchester, Dorset, DT1 1XJ

Dorset Publishing Co, National School, North Street, Wincanton, Somerset, BA9 9AT

Dumfries and Galloway Regional Council, Countryside Ranger Service, English Street, Dumfries, DG1 2DD

Dunderdale Press, PO Box 94, Ilkley, W Yorks, LS29 0YA

Durham County Council, Countryside Group, Environment & Technical Services Department, County Hall, Durham, DH1 5UQ

East Sussex County Council, Transport and Environment, Sackville House, Brooks Close, Lewes, E Sussex, BN7 1UE

Eckersley, John, 30 Howard Drive, Shipton Road, York, YO3 6XB

Edwards, Alan S., 6 Brittain Road, Cheddleton, Leek, Staffordshire, ST13 7EH

Edwards, G.J., 10 Howard Close, Haynes, Bedford, MK45 3QH

Ellenbank Press, The Lathes, Selby Terrace, Maryport, Cumbria, CA15 6LX

Ellis, C Dexter, 4 Prospect Place, Holmfirth, W Yorks, HD7 1RH

Ellis, Mike, 74 Nelson Road, Hull, East Yorkshire, HU5 5HN

Emery, Gordon, 27 Gladstone Road, Chester, CH1 4BZ

Environment Agency, Hafren House, Welshpool Road, Shelton, Shrewsbury, SY3 8BB

Epping Forest Countrycare, c/o Planning & Technical Services, Civic Offices, High Street, Epping, Essex, CM16 4BZ

Epping Forest Information Centre, High Beach, Loughton, Essex, IG10 4AF

Essex Ranger Service, Essex County Council, County Planning Dept, County Hall, Chelmsford, Essex, CM1-1LF

Famedram Publishing Ltd, PO Box 3, Ellon, AB41 9EA

Foot, A.G., Coombe House, Brithem Bottom, Cullompton, Devon, EX15 1ND

Footpath Guides, Old Hall, East Bergholt, Colchester, CO7 6TG

Footpath Touring, Sea Chimneys, Southdown, Beer, Devon, EX12 3AE

Footprint, c/o Cordee Ltd, 3a De Montfort Street, Leicester, LE1 7HD

Forest Enterprise N Scotland, 21 Church Street, Inverness, IV1 1EL

Forest of Avon, Ashton Court Visitors Centre, Ashton Court Estate, Long Ashton, Bristol, BS41 9JN

French, Richard, Wilkinstile, Sedbergh, Cumbria, LA10 5LS

Friends of Ridgeway, c/o Peter Gould, 18 Hampton Park, Bristol, BS6 6LH

Friends of the Trans Pennine Trail, c/o 164 High Street, Hook, Goole, DN14 5PL

GEOprojects, 9-10 Southern Court, South Street, Reading, Berkshire, RG1 4QS

Gateshead Metropolitan Borough Council, Director of Planning, Civic Centre, Regent Street, Gateshead, NE8 1HH

Glamorgan Heritage Coast Centre, Dunraven Park, Southerndown, Bridgend, CF32 0RP

Glasgow City Council, Roads & Transportation, Richmond Exchange, 20 Cadogan Street, Glasgow, G2 7AD

Gomer Press, Wind Street, Llandysul, Dyfed, SA44 4BQ

Goole Rambling Club, c/o Wendy Wales, 29 Mount Pleasant Road, Goole, East Yorkshire, DN14 6LH

Gordon, Sheila, 12 Barff Lane, Brayton, Selby, North Yorkshire, YO8 9ER

Great North Forest, Whickham Thorns, Market Lane, Dunston, NE11 9NX

Green Chain Working Party, John Humphries House, Stockwell Street, Greenwich, London, SE10 9JN

Green Fields Books, 13 Dalewood Avenue, Bear Cross, Bournemouth, Dorset, BH11 9NR

Greenlink, Dorset County Council, First Floor, Dorset House, 20-22, Christchurch Road, Bournemouth, BH1 3NL

Grey Stone Books, c/o Cordee Ltd, 3a DeMontfort Street, Leicester, LE1 7HD

Griffiths, Margaret, 288 Turton Road, Bradshaw, Bolton, BL2 3EF

Groundwork Bridgend, The Environment Centre, Maesteg Road, Tondu, Bridgend, CF32 9BT

Groundwork Thames Valley, Colne Valley Park Centre, Denham Court Drive, Denham, Uxbridge, Middlesex, UB9 5PG

Guest, Michael, 76 Priorwood Gardens, Ingleby, Barwick, Stockton-on-Tees, TS17 0XH

Gunn, Garth H., Mam Tor, Scarf Road, Cranford Heath, Poole, Dorset, BH17 8QH

Gwynedd County Council, Economic Development & Planning Dept, County Offices, Caernarfon, Gwynedd, LL55 1SH

Hall, J. & Yeates, J., 2 Barnards Road, Exeter, EX2 4NE

Hallamshire Press, c/o Interleaf Productions Ltd, Exchange Works, Sidney Street, Sheffield, S1 3QF

Halsgrove Press, Halsgrove House, Lower Moor Way, Tiverton, Devon, EX16 6SS

Hampshire County Council, Countryside & Community Dept, Mottisfont Court, High Street, Winchester, Hants, SO23 8ZF

Happy Walking International Ltd, Unit 1, Molyneux Business Park, Whitworth Road, Darley Dale, Matlock, DE4 2HJ

Harestanes Countryside Visitor Centre, by Ancrum, Jedburgh, TD8 6UQ, (Open April - October)

Harrogate Borough Council, Tourist Information, Royal Baths Assembly Rooms, Crescent Road, Harrogate, North Yorkshire, HG1 2RR

Harvey Maps, 12-16 Main Street, Doune, Perthshire, FK16 6BJ

Hathersage YHA, Castleton Road, Hathersage, Sheffield, S32 1EH

Haworth Tourist Information Centre, West Lane, Haworth, West Yorks, BD22 8EF

Heart of England Way Association, 20 Throckmorton Road, Alcester, Warwickshire, B49 6QA

Hebden Bridge Tourist Information Centre, 1, Bridgegate, Hebden Bridge, HX7 8EX

Hencke, Maurice, 25 Placehouse Lane, Old Coulsdon, Surrey, CR5 1LA

Hendon Publishing Co, Hendon Mill, Nelson, Lancashire, BB9 8AD

Herefordshire County Council, Queenswood Country Park, Dinmore Hill, Leominster, Herefordshire, HR6 0PY

Hertfordshire County Council, Countryside Management Service, Environment Department, County Hall, Peggs Lane, Hertford, SG13 8DN

Hill, Richard, Cuckoo Cottage, Railwayside, South Clydach, Abergavenny, Gwent, NP7 0RD

Hillingdon Borough Council, Central Library, 14/15 High Street, Uxbridge, UB8 1HD

Hillside Publications, 11 Nessfield Grove, Keighley, West Yorkshire, BD22 6NU

Hodson, Frank, Toll Bar Cottage, Underbarrow, Kendal, Cumbria, LA8 8HB

Holme Valley Civic Society, c/o Tourist Information Centre, 49-51 Huddersfield Road, Holmfirth, West Yorkshire, HD7 1JP

Hood, Glen, 329 Kingston Road, Willerby, Hull, HU10 6PY

Hopkin, W., 9 Arklow Road, Intake, Doncaster, DN2 5LG

Huddersfield Examiner, Market Street, Huddersfield, HD1 2EH

List of Addresses

Huntingdon District Council, Tourist Information Centre, Princess Street, Huntingdon, PE18 6PH

Hushon, Bernard, 83 Nottingham Drive, Bolton, BL1 3RH

Ibbotson, Peter, 135 Bradbury Road, Olton, Solihull, West Midlands, B92 8AL

Icknield Way Association, c/o Ken Payne, 19 The Ridgeway, Hitchin, Herts, SG5 2BT

Irons, Dave, 57 Reservoir Road, Selly Oak, Birmingham, B29 6ST

Island Tourist Products, 27 Wilton Park Road, Shanklin, Isle of Wight, PO37 7BU

Isle of Man Department of Tourism & Leisure, Tourist Information Centre, Sea Terminal Building, Douglas, Isle of Man, IM1 2RG

Isle of Wight County Council, Tourist Information Centre, 67 High Street, Shanklin, Isle of Wight, PO37 6JJ

Jackson, Gerry, 15 Edgehill, Llanfrechfa, Cwmbran, Gwent, NP44 8UA

Jema Publications, 40 Ashley Lane, Moulton, Northampton, NN3 7TJ

John Edwards Footpath Guides, 91 Colchester Road, White Colne, Colchester, Essex, CO6 2PP

Johnson, David, The Hollies, Stainforth, Settle, North Yorkshire, BD24 9PQ

Jolly, F., 15 Lawrence Road, Chorley, Lancashire, PR7 2DP

Jones, Glyn, Bing, Kirkinner, Wigtownshire, DG8 9BZ

Jones, Ian R., 11 Alison Road, Church Stretton, Shropshire, SY6 7AT

Jones, Richard, Mariners, Chapel Lane, Osmington, Weymouth, DT3 6ET

Kent County Council, Planning Department, Springfield, Maidstone, Kent, ME14 2LX

Kidd, David, 14 Froude Avenue, South Shields, Tyne and Wear, NE34 9TB

Kimberley Publishing, 68 Kings Avenue, Christchurch, Dorset, BH23 1NB

Kingdom of Fife, Forth Bridge Tourist Information Centre, c/o Queensferry Lodge Hotel, St Margaret's Head, North Queensferry, KY11 1HP

Kirkpatrick, Ian & Caroline, 6 Tor View, Horrabridge, Yelverton, Devon, PL20 7RE

LDWA Cumbria Group, c/o David Hammond, 13 Broomy Hill, Aglionby, Carlisle, CA4 8AF

LDWA Northumbria Group, c/o Mike Rayner, 1 Corriedale Close, Pity Me, Durham, DH1 5GY

Lancashire County Council, Countryside Section, P O Box 160, East Cliff County Offices, Preston, Lancashire, PR1 3EX

Lancaster City Council, Lancaster Tourism, 29 Castle Hill, Lancaster, LA1 1YN

Land's End to John O'Groats Association, PO Box 2243, Caversham Road, Reading, RG1 8YF

Langbaurgh Loop, Bywood, Victoria Terrace, Saltburn-by-the-Sea, Cleveland, TS12 1JE

Langton's Guides (LDWAH), Freepost (NG6236), Newark, Nottinghamshire, NG22 8YT

Lawrence and Wishart Ltd, 99a Wallis Road, London, E9 5LN

Lawson, Frank, 74 Tatenhill Gardens, Cantley, Doncaster, South Yorkshire, DN4 6TL

Lee Valley Regional Park Authority, Myddleton House, Bulls Cross, Enfield, Middlesex, EN2 9HG

Leeds City Council, Leisure Services, The Town Hall, The Headrow, Leeds, LS1 3AD

Leicestershire County Council, Countryside Section, County Hall, Glenfield, Leicester, LE3 8RJ

Leicestershire Footpath Association, Gamekeepers Lodge, 11 London Road, Great Glen, Leics, LE8 0DJ

Lincolnshire County Council, Environmental Services, County Offices, Newland, Lincoln, LN1 1DN

Liphook Ramblers, c/o David & Margaret Clark, 21 Chestnut Close, Liphook, Hants, GU30 7JA

Local Studies Section, Central Library, High Street, Bromley, Kent, BR1 1EX

London Walking Forum, Lea Valley Regional Park Authority, Middleton House, Bulls Close, Enfield, Middlesex, EN2 9HG

Lowe, William J., 3, Roman Court, Kimberworth, Rotherham, S Yorks, S61 2HN

Lower Mole Project, Highway House, 21 Chessington Road, West Ewell, Surrey, KT17 1TT

Lungmuss, Clive, 36 Bracken Close, Lichfield, Staffordshire, WS14 9RU

Lyke Wake Club, PO Box 24, Northallerton, North Yorkshire, DL6 3HZ

Macmillan Way Association, St Mary's Barn, Pillerton Priors, Warwick, CV35 0PG

Magnall, Derek, Spanners Retreat, 5 Caldy Drive, Holcombe Brook, Ramsbottom, BL0 9TY

Mainstream Publishing Co Ltd, 7 Albany Street, Edinburgh, EH1 3UG

Malkinson, Alec, 2 Southern Walk, Scartho, Grimsby, DN33 2PG

Mallinson, Mrs L., 17 Prod Lane, Baildon, West Yorks, BD17 5BN

Management Update Ltd, c/o Powney's Bookshop, 4-5 St Alkmund's Place, Shrewsbury, Shropshire, SY1 1UJ

Mara Publications, 22 Crosland Terrace, Helsby, Warrington, CheshireWA6 9LY

Maxiprint, Kettlestring Lane, Clifton Moor, York, YO3 4XF

Men-an-Tol Studio, Bosullow, Newbridge, Penzance, Cornwall, TR20 8NR

Meridian Books, 40 Hadzor Road, Oldbury, Warley, West Midlands, B68 9LA

Mersey Valley Partnership, The Coach House, Norton Priory, Tudor Road, Manor Park, Runcorn, WA7 1SX

Merthyr and Rhondda Cynon Taff Groundwork, Fedw Hir, Llwydcoed, Aberdare, CF44 0DX

Michael Joseph, 27 Wright's Lane, London, W8 5TZ

Mid-Cheshire Footpath Society, c/o Mrs Pauline Stott (Hon Sec), 17 Oakways, Appleton, Warrington, WA4 5HD

Mid Devon District Council, Tourism Office, 1 Westexe South, Tiverton, Devon, EX16 5DQ

Mid Suffolk District Council, Countryside Section, 131 High Street, Needham Market, Suffolk, IP6 8DL

Miller, Paul, 25 St Hugh's Close, Birkenhead, Merseyside, L43 4YS

Minerva Press, 195 Knightsbridge, London, SW7 1RE

Missing Link Recorder, 80 Howe Road, Norton, Malton, North Yorkshire, YO17 9BL

Miway Publishing, PO Box 2, Keswick, Cumbria, CA12 4GA

Monarch's Way Association, 15 Alison Road, Lapal, Halesowen, B62 0AT

Monmouthshire County Council, County Hall, Cwmbran, NP44 2XH

Montgomery Waterway Restoration Trust, c/o Mrs M. Awcock, Oakhaven, Longdon-upon-Tern, Shropshire, TF6 6LJ

Moray District Council, Dept of Technical and Leisure Services, High Street, Elgin, IV30 1BX

Mountain Peaks Climbing Club, 2 Chapel Cottages, Main Road, Hathersage, Derbyshire, S30 1BB

Moyle District Council, Sheskburn House, 7 Mary Street, Ballycastle, County Antrim, BT54 6QH

Nash, Derek, White Lodge, Birmingham Road, Shenstone, Lichfield, Staffordshire, WS14 0LB

Neath & Port Talbot County Borough Council, Leisure Services Department, Afan Argoed Countryside Centre, Port Talbot, SA13 3HG

Neuadd Arms Hotel, c/o,Gordon Green, Llanwrtyd Wells, Powys

Newcastle City Council, Planning Department, Civic Centre, Newcastle upon Tyne, NE1 8PW

Nightingale Publications, 23 Grange Road, Biddulph, Staffordshire Moorlands, ST8 7SB

Norfolk County Council, Planning & Transportation, County Hall, Martineau Lane, Norwich, NR1 2SG

North Somerset County Council, PO Box 141,. Town Hall, Weston-Super-Mare, BS23 1AE

North York Moors Adventure Centre, Park House, Ingleby Cross, Northallerton, North Yorkshire, DL6 3PE

North York Moors National Park, Information Service, The Old Vicarage, Bondgate, Helmsley, North Yorkshire, YO6 5BP

North Yorkshire County Council, Highways & Transportation Dept, County Hall, Northallerton, North Yorkshire, DL7 8AH

Northamptonshire County Council, Countryside Services, 9 Guildhall Road, Northampton, NN1 1DP

Northern Ireland Tourist Board, 59 North Street, Belfast, BT1 1NB

Northumberland County Council, Countryside Section, Technical Services, County Hall, Morpeth, Northumberland, NE61 2EF

Northumbrian Water, Leaplish Waterside Park, Kielder Water, Falstone, Hexham, Northumberland, NE48 1BT

Nottinghamshire County Council, Rights of Way Section, Trent Bridge House, Fox Road, West Bridgford, Nottingham, NG2 6BJ
Noyes, Trevor, Cherry Plum Cottage, Compton Dundon, Somerton, Somerset, TA11 6NZ

Offa's Dyke Association, Old Primary School, West Street, Knighton, Powys, LD7 1EW
Oldham Countryside Ranger Service, The Stables, Park Bridge, Ashton under Lyne, OL6 8AQ
Oldham Metropolitan Borough Council, 3rd Floor Metropolitan House, Hobson Street, Oldham, OL1 1QD
Ordnance Survey, Romsey Road, Maybush, Southampton, SO9 4DH
Owl Books, 58 Queens Walk, Cleveleys, Lancashire, FY5 1JW
Oxfordshire County Council, Countryside Service, Dept of Leisure and Arts, Holton, Oxford, OX33 1QQ

P3 Publications, 13 Beaver Road, Carlisle, Cumbria, CA2 7PS
Pamplin, Elizabeth, Little Critchmere, Manor Crescent, Haslemere, Surrey, GU27 1PB
Parker, Ian, 4, Raikeswood Drive, Skipton, North Yorkshire, BD23 1LY
Pathway Publishing, 16 Parkhill, Middleton, King's Lynn, Norfolk, PE32 1RJ
Peacock, Kim, 26 Fulford Crescent, Ganton Way, Kingston Road, Willerby, Hull, HU10 6NR
Peak District National Park, Baslow Road, Bakewell, Derbyshire, DE45 1AE
Peak Publishing Ltd, 88 Cavendish Road, London, SW12 0DF
Pembrokeshire Coast National Park, Winch Lane, Haverfordwest, Dyfed, SA61 1PY
Pendle Borough Council, Bank House, Albert Road, Colne, Lancashire, BB8 0AG
Penguin Books Ltd, Bath Road, Harmondsworth, Middlesex, UB7 0DA
Pennine Way Association, c/o Chris Sainty, 29 Springfield Park Avenue, Chelmsford, Essex, CM2 6EL
Pennine Way Coordination Project, Clegg Nook, Cragg Road, Mytholmroyd, West Yorkshire, HX7 5EB
Pentland Press Ltd, 3 Regal Lane, Soham, Ely, Cambridgeshire, CB7 5BA
Pen-y-ghent Cafe, Horton-in-Ribblesdale, North Yorkshire, BD24 0HE
Pepperdine, J., 15 Ascot Drive, Hucknall, Nottinghamshire, NG15 6JA
Perkins, Dr Ben, 11 Old London Road, Brighton, Sussex, BN1 8XR
Perks, Eric, Selbhome, 10 Cordle Marsh Road, Bewdley, Worcestershire, DY12 1EW
Pestell, Allen, 8 Sledbrook Crescent, Crowedge, Sheffield, S30 5HD
Peterborough City Council, Planning Dept, Town Bridge, Bridge St, Peterborough, PE1 1HB
Pinkney, RT., 11 Pine Road, Ormesby, Middlesbrough, TS7 9DH

Powys County Council, Planning and Economic Development, County Hall, Llandrindod Wells, Powys, LD1 5LG
Preston, R., The Chantry, Wilkes Walk, Truro, Cornwall, TR1 2UF
Printability Publishing Ltd, 10/11, Lower Church Street, Hartlepool, TS24 7DJ
Pritchard-Jones, John, 2 Sycamore Close, Etwall, Derby, DE65 6JS
Pugh, Paul, 190 Cobden View Road, Sheffield, S10 1HT

Ramblers' Association, 1-5 Wandsworth Road, London, SW8 2XX
RA Beverley Group, c/o Dennis Parker, 11 Elmsall Drive, Beverley, East Yorkshire, HU17 7HL
RA Bolton Group, c/o Lawrence Hubbard, 2 Coniston Road, Blackrod, Bolton, BL6 5DN
RA Buckinghamshire, c/o Mr P Gulland, 14 Wykeham Way, Haddenham, Buckinghamshire, HP17 8BL
RA Cardiff, c/o Jim Hargreaves, 92 St Fagans Road, Fairwater, Cardiff, CF5 3AN
RA Chesterfield & NE Derbyshire, c/o Mr A W Hunt, 108 Peveril Road, Newbold, Chesterfield, Derbyshire, S41 8SG
RA Doncaster, c/o Mrs M Thompson, 31 Broomhill Drive, Cantley, Doncaster, DN4 6QZ
RA Dorset, c/o Mrs Susan Blake, 19 Shaston Crescent, Dorchester, Dorset, DT1 2EB
RA East Berkshire Group, PO Box 1357, Maidenhead, SL6 7FP
RA East Yorkshire & Derwent Area, c/o Mrs Sheila M Smith, 65 Ormonde Avenue, Beresford Avenue, Beverley High Road, Hull, HU6 7LT
RA Gloucestershire Area, Mail Order Secretary, 1 Sovereign Chase, Staunton, Gloucester, GL19 3NW
RA Hampshire Area, c/o Peter Benham, 72 Kingsway, Chandlers Ford, Eastleigh, Hampshire, SO53 1FJ
RA Harrogate Group, c/o Peter Goldsmith, 20 Pannal Ash Grove, Harrogate, North Yorkshire, HG2 0HZ
RA Lincs and S Humberside Area, c/o Mr S W Parker, 129 Broughton Gardens, Brant Road, Lincoln, LN5 8SR
RA Manchester Area, c/o Terry Perkins, 34 Grangethorpe Drive, Burnage, Manchester, M19 2LG
RA New Forest Group, c/o Mr T Davies, 7 Boundstone, Hythe, Southampton, Hants, SO45 5AZ
RA Norfolk Area, c/o Mr John Harris, 7 Lowther Road, Norwich, NR4 6QN
RA Preston Group, c/o Andrew Manzie, 3 Ruthin Court, Dunbar Road, Ingol, Preston, PR2 3YE
RA Ripon Group, c/o Peter Sleightholm, 9 Melrose Road, Bishop Monkton, Harrogate, HG3 3RH
RA Sheffield, c/o John Harker, 317 Prince of Wales Road, Sheffield, S2 1FJ
RA Southam and District Group, c/o Harry Green, 30 Warwick Road, Southam, Leamington Spa, Warwickshire, CV33 0HN
RA Staffordshire, c/o Colin Brookes, 34 Nethersole Street, Polesworth, Tamworth, B78 1EE
RA West Riding Area, c/o Douglas Cossar, 27 Cookridge Avenue, Leeds, LS16 7NA

Rablen, Tony, 171 Burton Stone Lane, York, YO3 6DG

Reardon Publishing, 56 Upper Norwood Street, Leckhampton, Cheltenham, Gloucestershire, GL53 0DU

Ribble Valley Borough Council, Tourist Information Centre, 14 Market Place, Clitheroe, Lancs, BB7 2DA

Richmond, A., 40 St Mary's Avenue, Birchley, Billinge, Wigan, WN5 7QL

Richmond, Brian, 31 Dartmouth Street, Barrow-in-Furness, Cumbria, LA14 3AS

Richmondshire District Council, Tourism Officer, Swale House, Frenchgate, Richmond, N Yorkshire, DL10 4JE

Ridgeway Trail Officer, Countryside Section, Dept of Leisure & Arts, Holton, Oxford, OX33 1QQ

Rigby, James & Barbara, 36 Park Avenue, Shevington, Near Wigan, WN6 8AQ

Rochdale Pioneers Museum, Toad Lane, Rochdale, OL12 0NU

Rossendale Borough Council, c/o Tourist Information Centre, Kay Street, Rawtenstall, Rossendale, Lancashire, BB4 7LZ

Rotary Club of Cleckheaton, 2 Turnsteads Avenue, Cleckheaton, West Yorks, BD19 3AJ

Rother District Council, Town Hall, Bexhill-on-Sea, East Sussex, TN39 3JX

Rotherham Metropolitan Borough Council, Director of Amenities and Recreation, Recreation Offices, Grove Road, Rotherham, S60 2ER

SPARC, The Old School, Station Road, Narberth, Pembrokeshire, SA67 7DU

Saint Andrew Press, 121 George Street, Edinburgh, EH2 4YN

Sandhill Press Ltd, 17 Castle Street, Warkworth, Morpeth, Northumberland, NE65 0UW

Sauerzapf, Bobbie, 71b Plumstead Road, Thorpe End, Norwich, Norfolk, NR13 5AJ

Sayer, Ann, 29 Twickenham Road, Teddington, Middlesex, TW11 8AQ

Scarthin Books, The Promenade, Cromford, Derbyshire, DE4 3QF

Scholes, Norman F., Danelea, Laburnum Avenue, Robin Hood's Bay, Whitby, North Yorks, YO22 4RR

Scottish Borders Enterprise, Bridge Street, Galashiels, TD1 1SW

Scottish Natural Heritage, Battleby, Redgorton, Perth, PH1 3EW

Scottish Rights of Way Society, John Cotton Business Centre, 10 Sunnyside (Unit 2), Edinburgh, EH7 5RA

Sefton Metropolitan Borough Council, Tourist Information Office, Lord Street, Southport, PR8 1NY

Shetland Times Ltd, 71/79 Commercial Street, Lerwick, Shetland, ZE1 0AJ

Shire Publications, Cromwell House, Church Street, Princes Risborough, Aylesbury, Buckinghamshire, HP27 9AA

Shropshire Books, Column House, 7 London Road, Shrewsbury, SY2 6NW

Shropshire County Council, Countryside Section, Winston Churchill Building, Radbrook Centre, Radbrook Road, Shrewsbury, SY3 9BJ

Sidebottom, Joyce, 8 Mill Lane, Horwich, Bolton, Greater Manchester, BL6 6AT

Sigma Leisure, 1 South Oak Lane, Wilmslow, Cheshire, SK9 6AR

Silver, Owen, 6 Shorehead, St Andrews, Fife, KY16 9RG

Skuse, Michael, Caenant Llangynhafal, Ruthin, Denbighshire, LL15 1RU

Society of Sussex Downsmen, Publications Editor, 254 Victoria Drive, Eastbourne, East Sussex, BN20 8QT

Somerset Tourism, Tourist Information Office, The Round Tower, The Black Swan, 2 Bridge Street, Frome, BA11 1BB

South Downs Way Officer, Sussex Downs Conservation Board, Chanctonbury House, Church Street, Storrington, West Sussex, RH20 4LT

South Gloucestershire County Council, Council Offices, Castle Street, Thornbury, Bristol, BS12 1HF

South Lakeland District Council, Leisure Services Dept, South Lakeland House, Lowther Street, Kendal, Cumbria, LA9 4DL

South Norfolk Council, South Norfolk House, Swan Lane, Long Stratton, Norfolk, NR15 2XE

South Somerset District Council, Tourism & Marketing Unit, Brympton Way, Yeovil, Somerset, BA20 2HT

South West Way Association, Windlestraw, Penquit, Ermington, Nr Ivybridge, Devon, PL21 0LU

Sparshatt, John, 30A Sandholme Drive, Burley in Wharfedale, Ilkley, West Yorkshire, LS29 7RQ

Staffordshire County Council, Cultural & Recreational Services, Shire Hall, Market Street, Stafford, ST16 2LQ

Stationery Office, St Crispins, Duke Street, Norwich, NR3 1PD

Stile Publications, 24 Lisker Drive, Otley, W Yorks, LS21 1DQ

Stockport Metropolitan Borough Council, Countryside Service, 4th Floor, Stopford House, Piccadilly, Stockport, SK1 3XE

Stratford-upon-Avon District Council, Technical and Amenities Department, Elizabeth House, Church Street, Stratford-upon-Avon, Warwickshire, CV37 6HX

Street, John, The Knoll, Crifty Craft Lane, Churchdown, Gloucester, GL3 2LJ

Strother, Jim, Galava Shiel, Borrans Road, Ambleside, Cumbria, LA22 0EN

Suffolk County Council, Environment and Transport Department, St Edmund House, County Hall, Ipswich, Suffolk, IP4 1LZ

Sunderland City Council, c/o Tourist Information Centre, 50 Fawcett Street, Sunderland, SR1 1RF

Surr, Mike, 10 Albany Place, Louth, Lincs, LN11 8EY

Surrey & Hampshire Canal Society, c/o Alec Gosling, 12 Mole Road, Hersham, Walton-on-Thames, Surrey, KT12 4LU

Surrey County Council, Environment Department, County Hall, Kingston Upon Thames, Surrey, KT1 2DY

Sutton Publishing Ltd, Phoenix Mill, Thrupp, Stroud, Gloucestershire, GL5 2BU

Sweeting, Don, The Levels, Portington Road, Eastrington, Goole, DN14 7QE

Tait, Bob, Burnlee House, Burnlee Road, Holmfirth, HD7 1LF

Tameside Countryside Warden Service, Chief Wardens Office, Park Bridge Visitor Centre, The Stables, Park Bridge, Ashton-under-Lyne, OL6 8AQ

Tattersall, Max, 79 Ormerod Road, Burnley, Lancashire, BB11 2RU

Taunton Deane Borough Council, Leisure Dept, The Deane House, Belvedere Road, Taunton, Somerset, TA1 1HE

Taylor, Sam R., 13 Dixon Street, Lees, Oldham, Lancashire, OL4 3NG

Teanby, Mike, The Old School House, Village Street, Adwick-le-Street, Doncaster, DN6 7AA

Thanet District Council, c/o Ramsgate Tourist Information Centre, 19/21, Harbour Street, Ramsgate, Kent, CT11 8HA

Thomas, Norman, The Parsonage, off Ainsworth Avenue, Horwich, Bolton, Lancashire, BL6 6LS

Three Rivers District Council, Development, Plans & Transportation, Three Rivers House, Northway, Rickmansworth, Herts, WD3 1RL

Thursaston Visitor Centre, Wirral Country Park, Station Road, Thursaston, Wirral, Merseyside, L61 OHN

Tinniswood, J., 12 Beaconsfield Terrace, Chopwell, Newcastle-upon-Tyne, NE17 7JG

Townson, Simon, 22 St John's Crescent, Harrogate, North Yorkshire, HG1 3AB

Trans Pennine Trail Officer, c/o Department of Planning, Barnsley Metropolitan Borough Council, Central Offices, Kendray Street, Barnsley, S70 2TN

Travis, P., 23 Kingsway East, Westlands, Newcastle-under-Lyme, Staffordshire, ST5 3PY

Turner, Hugh, Croft End, Bures, Suffolk, CO8 5JN

Turner, L., 3 Ringwood Crescent, Leeds, West Yorkshire, LS14 1AN

Two Moors Way Association, c/o Joe Turner, Coppins, The Poplars, Pinhoe, Exeter, EX4 9HH

Vale Royal Borough Council, Tourism Officer, Wyvern House, The Drumber, Winsford, Cheshire, CW7 1AH

Vanguards Rambling Club, 109 Selsdon Park Road, South Croydon, CR2 8JJ

Viney, Mrs Doreen, 20 George Street, Hindley, Wigan, WN2 3PS

W & A Enterprises Ltd, 24 Griffiths Avenue, Lancing, West Sussex, BN15 0HW

Wadsworth, John, Ratcliffe's Stationers, 31, Corporation Street, Rotherham, S60 1NX

Waendel Walkers Club, c/o Pete Holt, 5 Valley Rise, Desborough, Kettering, NN14 2QR

Walking Routes, 16 Ash Court, Rhyl, Clwyd, LL18 4NZ

Walkways/Quercus, 67 Cliffe Way, Warwick, CV32 5JG

Wallace, Alastair, 10 Gainford, Chester-le-Street, Co Durham, DH2 2EW

Waller, Robert, 33 Hazelmere Road, Fulwood, Preston, Lancashire, PR2 9UL

Wallis, Ray, 75 Ancaster Avenue, Kingston-upon-Hull, HU5 4QR

Walsall Metropolitan Borough Council, Leisure Services, Darwall Street, Walsall, West Midlands, WS1 1TZ

Wanderlust Rambling Club, c/o Mr Don Shaw, 5 Pelham Crescent, Keelby, Nr Grimsby, South Humberside, DN37 8EW

Wandle Industrial Museum, The Vestry Hall Annexe, London Road, Mitcham, Surrey, CR4 3UD

Ward Lock Publishing, Wellington House, 125 Strand, London, WC2R 0BB

Warwickshire County Council, Planning & Transport Dept, PO Box 43, Shire Hall, Warwick, CV34 4SX

Watson, RH., 33 Sutherland Avenue, Endike Lane, Hull, HU6 7UG

Waveney District Council, Chief Executive's Department, Town Hall, High Street, Lowestoft, Suffolk, NR32 1HS

Ways Through Essex, County Planning Department, County Hall, Chelmsford, Essex, CM1 1LF

West Cumbria Tourist Initiative, The Beacon, West Strand, Whitehaven, Cumbria, CA28 7LY

West Sussex County Council, Planning Dept, County Hall, Tower Street, Chichester, W Sussex, PO19 1RL

Western Mail & Echo, Thomson House, Haverlock Street, Cardiff, CF1 1WR

Westmorland Gazette, 22 Stricklandgate, Kendal, Cumbria, LA9 4NE

Weston-super-Mare Civic Society, 3-6 Wadham Street, Weston-super-Mare, Avon, BS23 1JY

Wharncliffe Publishing Ltd, 47 Church Street, Barnsley, S Yorkshire, S70 2AS

Whitehead, Mrs Doreen, Butt House, Keld, Richmond, North Yorkshire, DL11 6LJ

Wilkins, DE., 21 Lane Ings, Marsden, Huddersfield, HD7 6JP

Willow Publishing, Willow Cottage, 36 Moss Lane, Timperley, Altrincham, Cheshire, WA15 6SZ

Wimbush, Tony, 10, Beaufort Grove, Bradford, BD2 4LJ

Wimpole Books, Pip's Peace, Kenton, Stowmarket, Suffolk, IP14 6JS

Worcestershire County Council, Worcester Woods Country Park, Wildwood Drive, Worcester, WR5 2NP

Wrekin Countryside Service, Stirchley Grange, Stirchley Road, Stirchley, Telford, TF3 1DY

Wrexham County Borough Council, Guildhall, Wrexham, Clwyd, LL11 1AY

Wychavon District Council, Civic Centre, Queen Elizabeth Drive, Pershore, Worcestershire, WR10 1PT

Wyre Estuary Country Park, River Road, Stanah, Thornton, Lancashire, FY6 5LR

YHA Northern Region, PO Box 11, Matlock, Derbyshire, DE4 2XA

Yatton Ramblers, c/o Marian Barraclough, 92 Claverham Road, Yatton, Bristol, BS19 4LE

Yorkshire Dales National Park, National Park Centre, Colvend, Hebden Road, Grassington, North Yorkshire, BD23 5LB

Yorkshire Footpath Trust, 37 Hazel Garth, Stockton Lane, York, YO3 0HR

INDEX

MAP SECTION

CONTENTS

MAPPED ROUTES (Waymarked routes plus a small selection of unwaymarked routes)

UNWAYMARKED ROUTES NOT SHOWN IN MAP SECTION

Map section

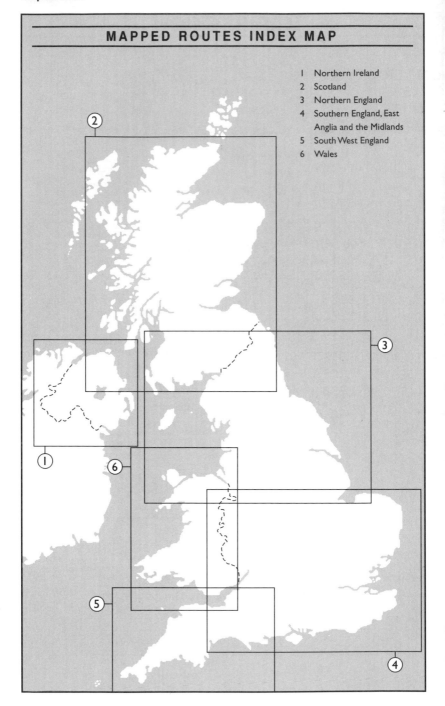

MAPPED ROUTES INDEX MAP

1 Northern Ireland
2 Scotland
3 Northern England
4 Southern England, East Anglia and the Midlands
5 South West England
6 Wales

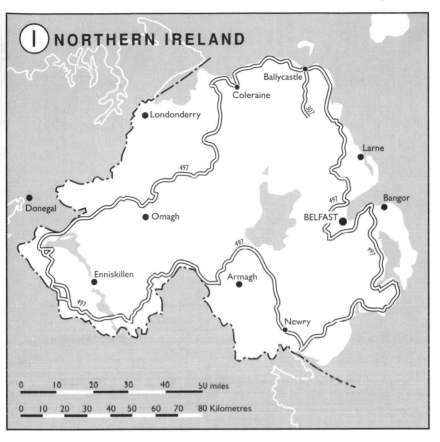

(1) NORTHERN IRELAND

Ballycastle
Coleraine
307
Londonderry
497
Larne
497
Donegal
Bangor
Omagh
497
BELFAST
497
497
Enniskillen
Armagh
497
Newry

| 0 | 10 | 20 | 30 | 40 | 50 miles |

| 0 | 10 | 20 | 30 | 40 | 50 | 60 | 70 | 80 Kilometres |

Key to maps

═══════════	National Trails
▬ ▬ ▬ ▬ ▬ ▬	National Trails planned
═══════════	Waymarked Routes
─ ─ ─ ─ ─ ─ ─ ─	Waymarked Routes planned
─────────────	Selected Unwaymarked Routes (including some named in Ordnance Survey maps)

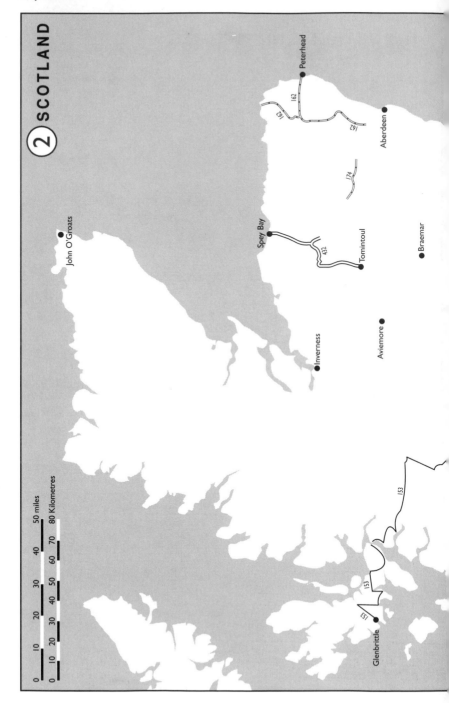

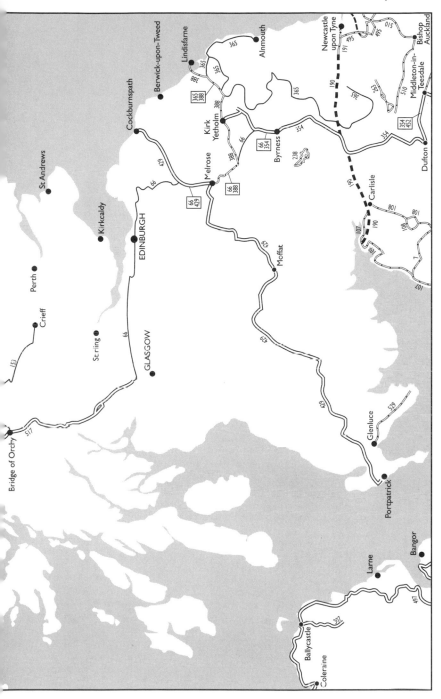

Map section

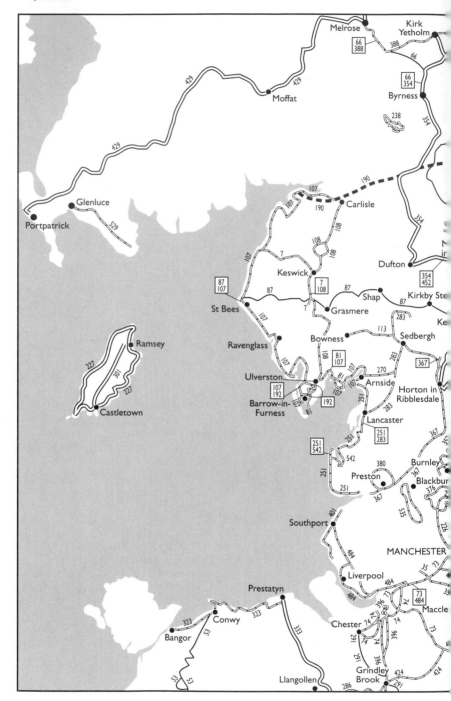

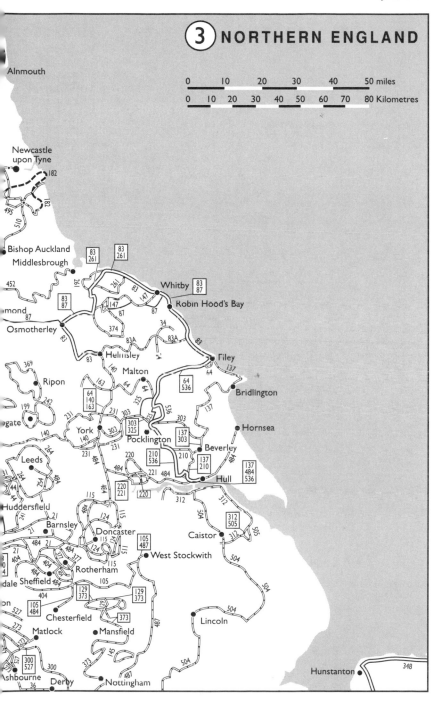

Alnmouth

③ NORTHERN ENGLAND

| 0 | 10 | 20 | 30 | 40 | 50 miles |
| 0 | 10 | 20 | 30 | 40 | 50 | 60 | 70 | 80 Kilometres |

Newcastle upon Tyne

182

495 510

Bishop Auckland

Middlesbrough

452

261

83 261

83 261

Whitby

83 87

261

83

147

83 87

147

Robin Hood's Bay

mond

87

147

87

87

Osmotherley

83

374

34

83A

83A

83

83

Helmsley

Filey

137

369

140

Malton

64

Ripon

163

64

64

64 536

Bridlington

64 140 163

231

303

225

915

303

137

199

231

303

303 325

Hornsea

gate

140

264

York

140

303

231

Pocklington

137 303

Beverley

Leeds

231

484

210 536

210

137 210

484

484

264

254

484

220

221

484

137 484 536

Huddersfield

115

484

220 221

Hull

220

312

241

21

124

115

312

Barnsley

21

Doncaster

115

312

312 505

505

484

21

484

115

Caistor

312

504

377

377

124

105 487

West Stockwith

504

404

115

dale

Sheffield

Rotherham

105

504

404

129 373

129 373

504

on

527

105 484

Chesterfield

373

Lincoln

504

273

121

Matlock

Mansfield

487

527

300

300 527

145

504

shbourne

487

Derby

Nottingham

Hunstanton

348

36

275

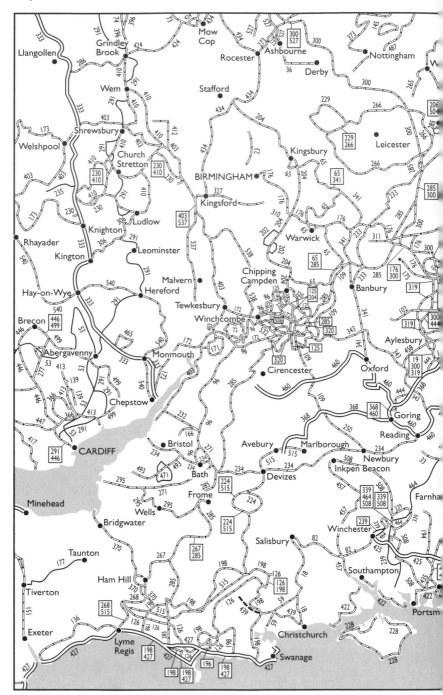

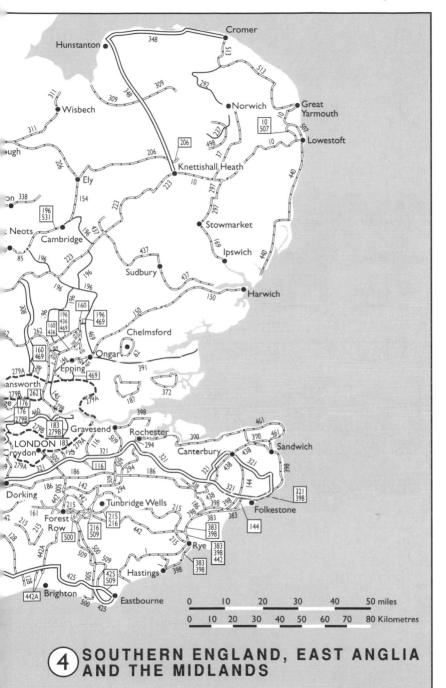

SOUTHERN ENGLAND, EAST ANGLIA AND THE MIDLANDS

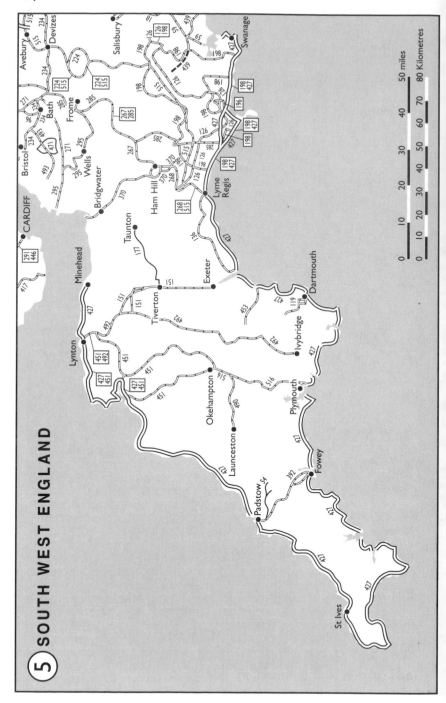

SOUTH WEST ENGLAND

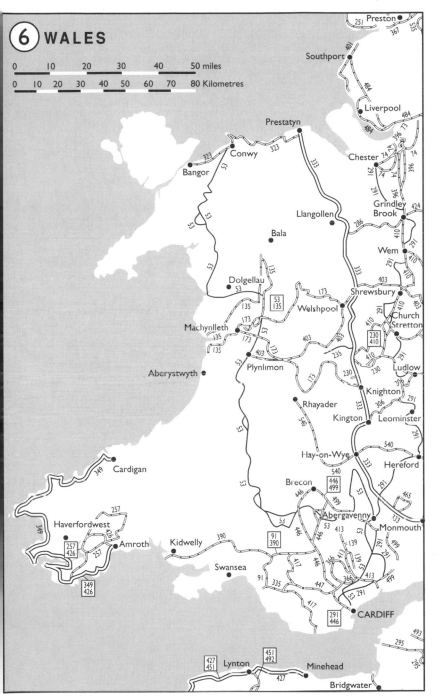

6 WALES

0   10   20   30   40   50 miles

0 10 20 30 40 50 60 70 80 Kilometres

Preston
Southport
Liverpool
Conwy
Prestatyn
Bangor
Chester
Grindley Brook
Llangollen
Bala
Wem
Dolgellau
Welshpool
Shrewsbury
Machynlleth
Church Stretton
Aberystwyth
Plynlimon
Ludlow
Rhayader
Knighton
Kington
Leominster
Hay-on-Wye
Hereford
Cardigan
Brecon
Abergavenny
Monmouth
Haverfordwest
Kidwelly
Amroth
Swansea
CARDIFF
Lynton
Minehead
Bridgwater

279

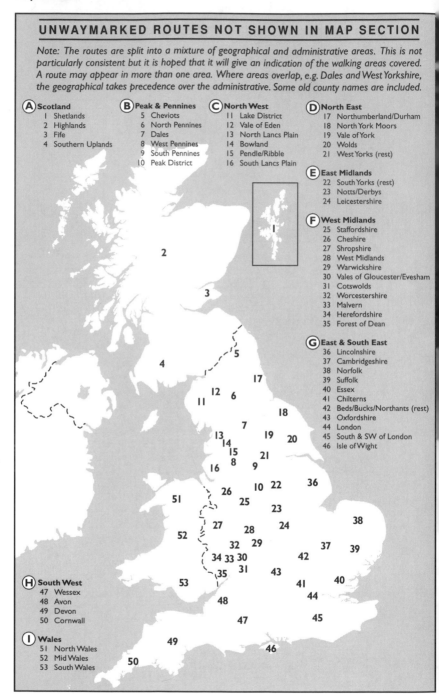

UNWAYMARKED ROUTES NOT SHOWN IN MAP SECTION

Note: The routes are split into a mixture of geographical and administrative areas. This is not particularly consistent but it is hoped that it will give an indication of the walking areas covered. A route may appear in more than one area. Where areas overlap, e.g. Dales and West Yorkshire, the geographical takes precedence over the administrative. Some old county names are included.

(A) Scotland
1. Shetlands
2. Highlands
3. Fife
4. Southern Uplands

(B) Peak & Pennines
5. Cheviots
6. North Pennines
7. Dales
8. West Pennines
9. South Pennines
10. Peak District

(C) North West
11. Lake District
12. Vale of Eden
13. North Lancs Plain
14. Bowland
15. Pendle/Ribble
16. South Lancs Plain

(D) North East
17. Northumberland/Durham
18. North York Moors
19. Vale of York
20. Wolds
21. West Yorks (rest)

(E) East Midlands
22. South Yorks (rest)
23. Notts/Derbys
24. Leicestershire

(F) West Midlands
25. Staffordshire
26. Cheshire
27. Shropshire
28. West Midlands
29. Warwickshire
30. Vales of Gloucester/Evesham
31. Cotswolds
32. Worcestershire
33. Malvern
34. Herefordshire
35. Forest of Dean

(G) East & South East
36. Lincolnshire
37. Cambridgeshire
38. Norfolk
39. Suffolk
40. Essex
41. Chilterns
42. Beds/Bucks/Northants (rest)
43. Oxfordshire
44. London
45. South & SW of London
46. Isle of Wight

(H) South West
47. Wessex
48. Avon
49. Devon
50. Cornwall

(I) Wales
51. North Wales
52. Mid Wales
53. South Wales

UNWAYMARKED ROUTES NOT SHOWN IN MAP SECTION

A **Scotland**

1 Shetlands: *378, 379, 381, 382, 521*
2 Highlands: *47, 55, 181*
3 Fife: *155, 156*
4 Southern Uplands: *168*

B **Peak & Pennines**

5 Cheviots: *77, 472*
6 North Pennines: *205, 213, 519*
7 Dales: *3, 4, 6, 8, 14, 40, 46, 61, 111, 112, 197, 207, 225, 243, 253, 272, 282, 315, 316, 318, 353, 375, 402, 416, 443, 467, 468, 470, 474, 476, 477, 480, 485, 486, 488, 489, 523, 544, 545*
8 West Pennines: *12, 13, 79, 103, 127, 165, 222, 252, 254, 353, 356, 362, 364, 430, 479, 491, 512, 534*
9 South Pennines: *41, 43, 50 ,94, 121, 132, 165, 218, 308, 313, 353, 476*
10 Peak District: *26, 50, 67, 104, 114, 117, 118, 123, 132, 141, 188, 211, 212, 269, 274, 280, 345, 346, 347, 353, 359, 371, 386, 387, 405, 449, 454, 455, 466, 468, 475, 476, 525, 526, 528*

C **North West**

11 Lake District: *4, 16, 20, 60, 106, 130, 131, 167, 179, 214, 244, 245, 246, 247, 248, 249, 255, 256, 281, 324, 331, 355, 385, 462, 463, 483, 496, 518, 519, 520, 524*
12 Vale of Eden: *106, 143, 243, 519, 520*
13 North Lancashire Plain: *60, 254, 255, 256, 364, 375, 463, 480*
14 Bowland: *39, 40, 84, 159, 203, 252, 254, 318, 463, 534*
15 Pendle/Ribble: *84, 209, 252, 253, 254, 350, 351, 361, 512, 531*
16 South Lancashire Plain: *127, 252, 253, 463, 530*

D **North East**

17 Northumberland and Durham: *133, 134, 332, 406, 494*
18 North York Moors: *29, 148, 193, 284, 314, 328, 329, 330, 395, 399, 400, 468, 476*
19 Vale of York: *5, 316, 375, 476, 480, 544*
20 Wolds: *69, 138, 476*
21 West Yorkshire (rest): *6, 14, 41*

E **East Midlands**

22 South Yorkshire: *405, 476*
23 Nottinghamshire and Derbyshire: *26, 63, 76, 122, 178, 277*
24 Leicestershire: *28, 70, 71, 178, 384, 414*

Continued...